©2005 Algrove Publishing Limited
ALL RIGHTS RESERVED.
No part of this book may be reproduced in any form, including photocopying, without permission in writing from the publishers, except by a reviewer who may quote brief passages in a magazine or newspaper or on radio or television.

Algrove Publishing Limited
36 Mill Street, P.O. Box 1238
Almonte, Ontario, Canada K0A 1A0

Telephone: (613) 256-0350
Fax: (613) 256-0360
Email: sales@algrove.com

Library and Archives Canada Cataloguing in Publication

Williams, J. R. (James Robert), 1888-1957.
    The Bull of the Woods, volume 6 / J.R. Williams.

(Classic reprint series)
ISBN 1-897030-28-2

    1. American wit and humor, Pictorial. 2. Machinists--Caricatures and cartoons. 3. Machine shops--Caricatures and cartoons. I. Title. II. Series: Classic reprint series (Almonte, Ont.)

NC1429.W573A4 2005c   741.5'973   C2005-901890-9

Printed in Canada
#1-8-05

Publisher's Note

James Robert Williams was born in Nova Scotia in 1888 and his family moved to Detroit before he started school. At age 15 he quit school to apprentice as a machinist, moving to Arkansas and then Oklahoma where he spent six years drifting around the territory working as a cowboy on different ranches before spending three years in the U.S. Cavalry. After he married, he took a full-time job with a crane company in Ohio. He started cartooning professionally in 1922 with the daily cartoon "Out Our Way", drawing heavily on his experiences in the military, in machine shops and on ranches. At the peak of his career "Out Our Way" was carried by some 700 newspapers. He bought his own ranch in 1930 and continued drawing until his death in 1957. His lifetime production was in excess of 10,000 cartoons.

Leonard G. Lee, Publisher
Almonte, Ontario
August 2005

How We Make Our Books *- You may not have noticed, but this book is quite different from other softcover books you might own. The vast majority of paperbacks, whether mass-market or the more expensive trade paperbacks, have the pages sheared and notched at the spine so that they may be glued together. The paper itself is often of newsprint quality. Over time, the paper will brown and the spine will crack if flexed. Eventually the pages fall out.*

All of our softcover books, like our hardcover books, have sewn bindings. The pages are sewn in signatures of sixteen or thirty-two pages and these signatures are then sewn to each other. They are also glued at the back but the glue is used primarily to hold the cover on, not to hold the pages together.

We also use only acid-free paper in our books. This paper does not yellow over time. A century from now, this book will have paper of its original color and an intact binding, unless it has been exposed to fire, water, or other catastrophe.

There is one more thing you will note about this book as you read it; it opens easily and does not require constant hand pressure to keep it open. In all but the smallest sizes, all our books will also lie open on a table, something that a book bound only with glue will never do unless you have broken its spine.

The cost of these extras is well below their value and while we do not expect a medal for incorporating them, we did want you to notice them.

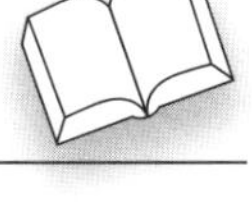

The Bull of the Woods
Volume 6

J.R. Williams

Algrove Publishing
Classic Reprint Series

Foreword

The term "Bull of the Woods" was borrowed from the lumberjacks. I used it to describe a gruff, poker-faced man prowling among hundreds of machine belts in a shop in Alliance, Ohio. Silhouetted against the hazy shop windows, they had a certain resemblance to a dense woods.

The "Bull" was hardboiled, perhaps, but he was kind. He must have been, or I certainly should have been fired. He said to me one day with fine sarcasm, "Pardon my rudeness. You've been turning out two cartoons and one shaft a day on this machine. Couldn't you make it two shafts and one cartoon a day? This is a machine shop."

And now, when I have no shafts to do, I have a terrible time turning out one cartoon a day.

J. R. Williams

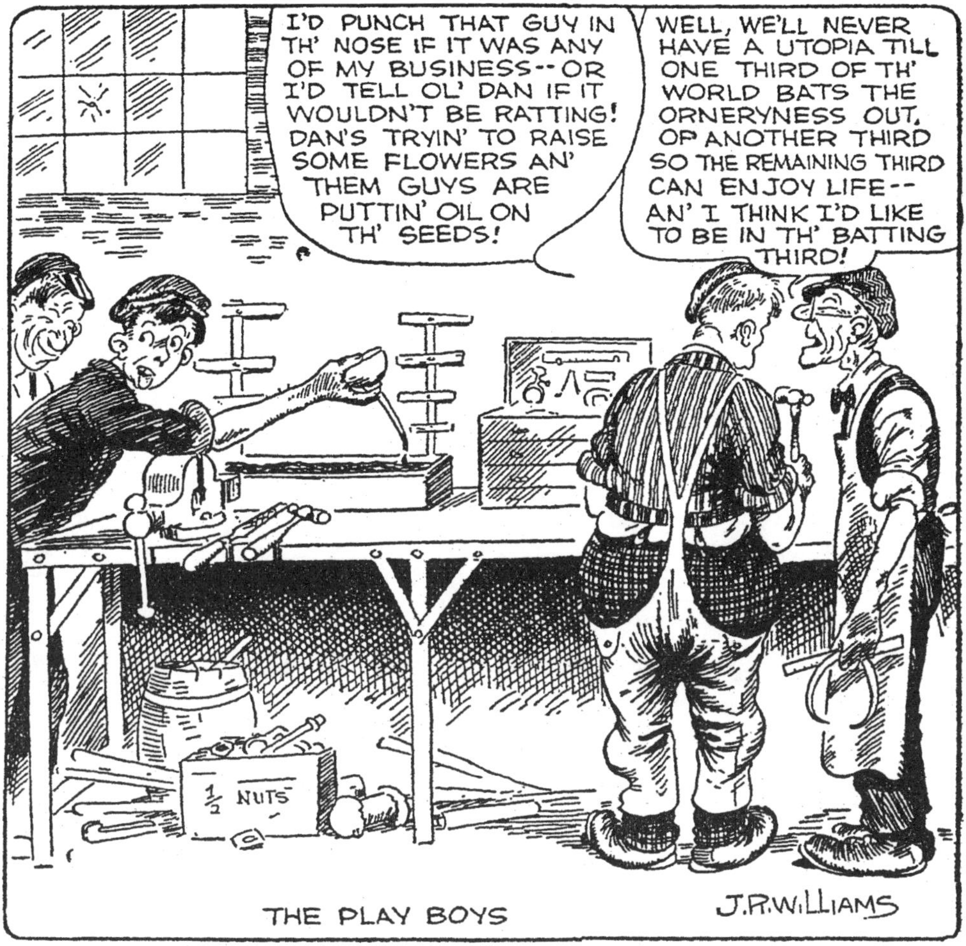
I'D PUNCH THAT GUY IN TH' NOSE IF IT WAS ANY OF MY BUSINESS--OR I'D TELL OL' DAN IF IT WOULDN'T BE RATTING! DAN'S TRYIN' TO RAISE SOME FLOWERS AN' THEM GUYS ARE PUTTIN' OIL ON TH' SEEDS!
WELL, WE'LL NEVER HAVE A UTOPIA TILL ONE THIRD OF TH' WORLD BATS THE ORNERYNESS OUT OF ANOTHER THIRD SO THE REMAINING THIRD CAN ENJOY LIFE-- AN' I THINK I'D LIKE TO BE IN TH' BATTING THIRD!
1/2 NUTS
THE PLAY BOYS
J.R.WILLIAMS

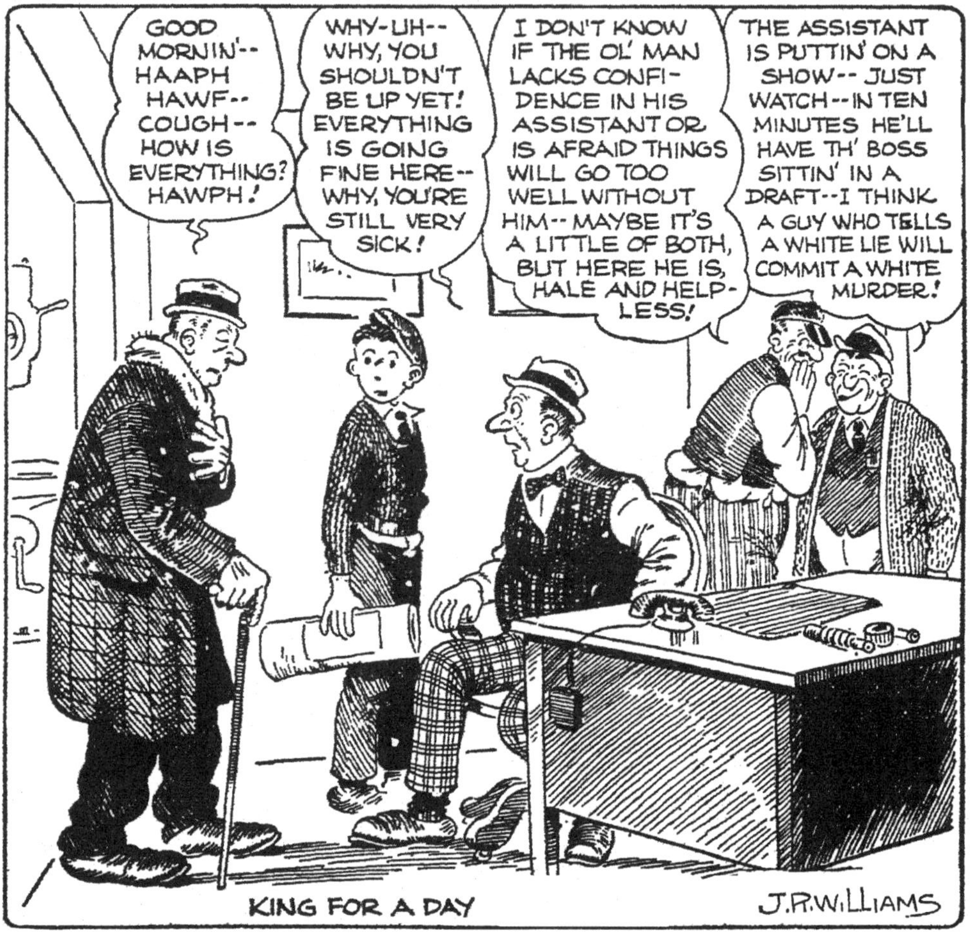
GOOD MORNIN'-- HAAPH HAWF-- COUGH-- HOW IS EVERYTHING? HAWPH!
WHY-UH-- WHY, YOU SHOULDN'T BE UP YET! EVERYTHING IS GOING FINE HERE-- WHY, YOU'RE STILL VERY SICK!
I DON'T KNOW IF THE OL' MAN LACKS CONFI-DENCE IN HIS ASSISTANT OR IS AFRAID THINGS WILL GO TOO WELL WITHOUT HIM-- MAYBE IT'S A LITTLE OF BOTH, BUT HERE HE IS, HALE AND HELP-LESS!
THE ASSISTANT IS PUTTIN' ON A SHOW-- JUST WATCH--IN TEN MINUTES HE'LL HAVE TH' BOSS SITTIN' IN A DRAFT--I THINK A GUY WHO TELLS A WHITE LIE WILL COMMIT A WHITE MURDER!
KING FOR A DAY
J.R.WILLIAMS

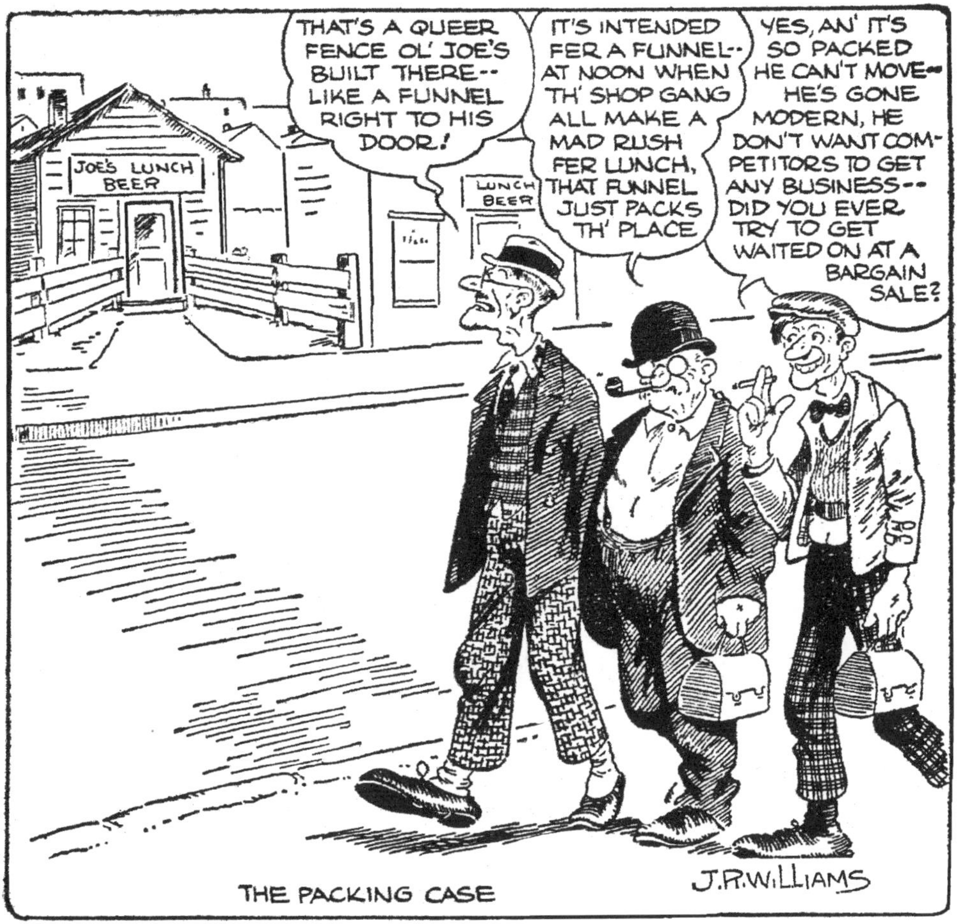
THAT'S A QUEER FENCE OL' JOE'S BUILT THERE-- LIKE A FUNNEL RIGHT TO HIS DOOR!
IT'S INTENDED FER A FUNNEL-- AT NOON WHEN TH' SHOP GANG ALL MAKE A MAD RUSH FER LUNCH, THAT FUNNEL JUST PACKS TH' PLACE
YES, AN' IT'S SO PACKED HE CAN'T MOVE-- HE'S GONE MODERN, HE DON'T WANT COMPETITORS TO GET ANY BUSINESS-- DID YOU EVER TRY TO GET WAITED ON AT A BARGAIN SALE?
JOE'S LUNCH BEER
LUNCH BEER
J.R.WILLIAMS

THE PACKING CASE

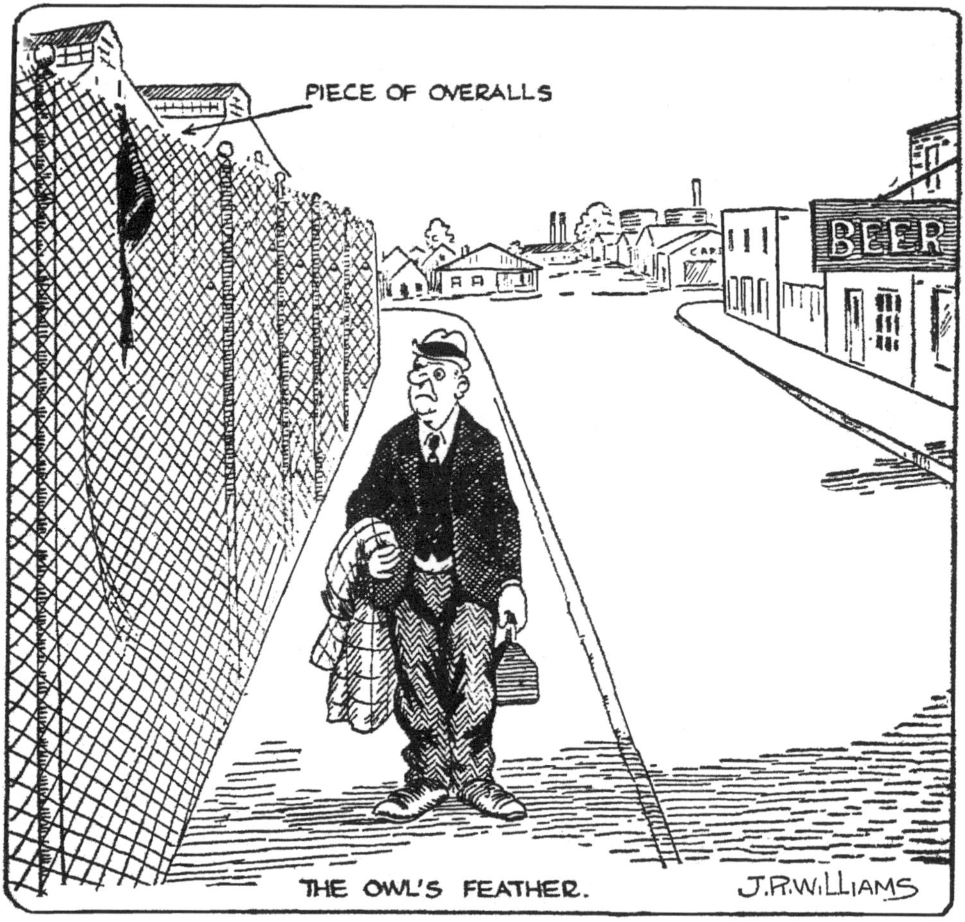
PIECE OF OVERALLS
BEER
J.R.WILLIAMS
THE OWL'S FEATHER.

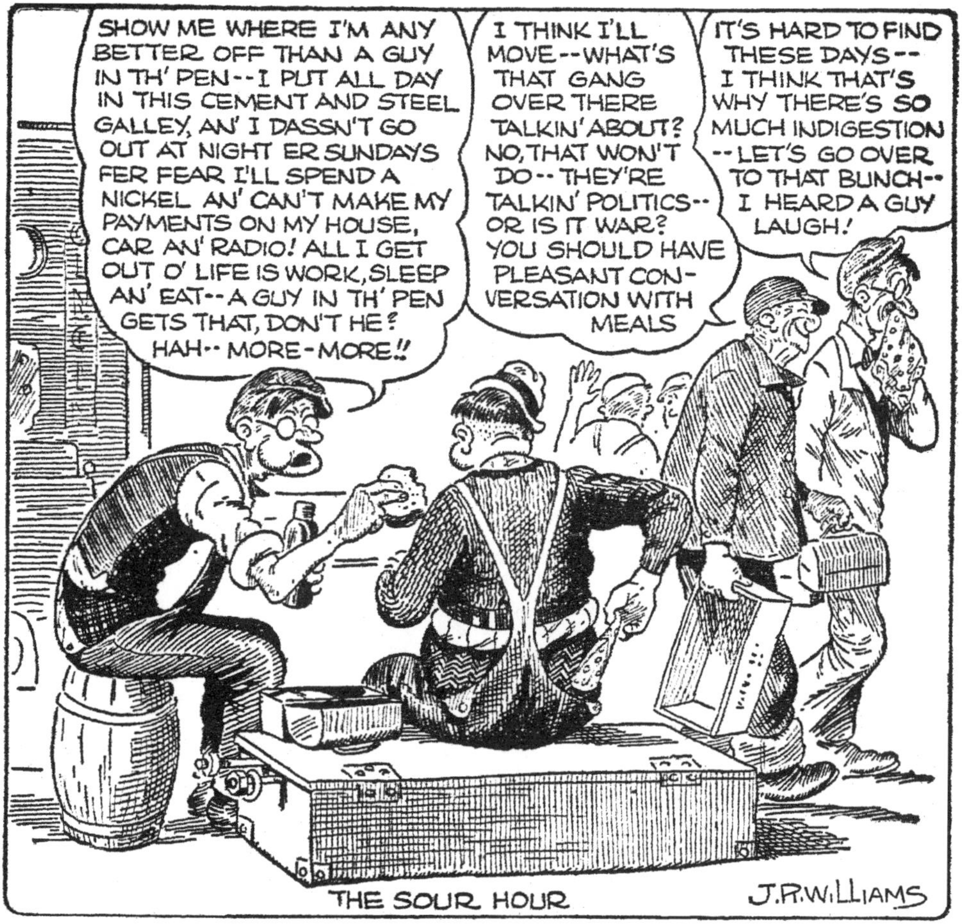
SHOW ME WHERE I'M ANY BETTER OFF THAN A GUY IN TH' PEN--I PUT ALL DAY IN THIS CEMENT AND STEEL GALLEY, AN' I DASSN'T GO OUT AT NIGHT ER SUNDAYS FER FEAR I'LL SPEND A NICKEL AN' CAN'T MAKE MY PAYMENTS ON MY HOUSE, CAR AN' RADIO! ALL I GET OUT O' LIFE IS WORK, SLEEP AN' EAT--A GUY IN TH' PEN GETS THAT, DON'T HE? HAH--MORE-MORE!!
I THINK I'LL MOVE--WHAT'S THAT GANG OVER THERE TALKIN' ABOUT? NO, THAT WON'T DO--THEY'RE TALKIN' POLITICS--OR IS IT WAR? YOU SHOULD HAVE PLEASANT CONVERSATION WITH MEALS
IT'S HARD TO FIND THESE DAYS--I THINK THAT'S WHY THERE'S SO MUCH INDIGESTION--LET'S GO OVER TO THAT BUNCH--I HEARD A GUY LAUGH!
J.R. WILLIAMS
THE SOUR HOUR

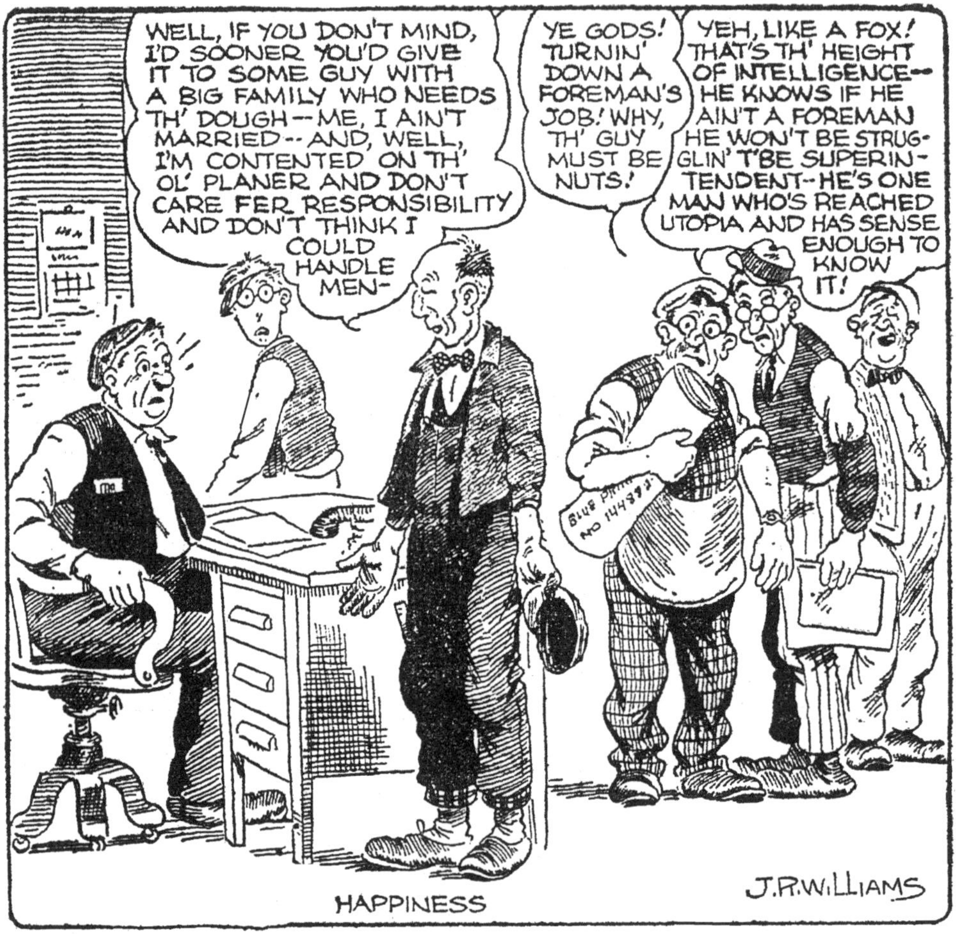
WELL, IF YOU DON'T MIND, I'D SOONER YOU'D GIVE IT TO SOME GUY WITH A BIG FAMILY WHO NEEDS TH' DOUGH -- ME, I AIN'T MARRIED -- AND, WELL, I'M CONTENTED ON TH' OL' PLANER AND DON'T CARE FER RESPONSIBILITY AND DON'T THINK I COULD HANDLE MEN-
YE GODS! TURNIN' DOWN A FOREMAN'S JOB! WHY, TH' GUY MUST BE NUTS!
YEH, LIKE A FOX! THAT'S TH' HEIGHT OF INTELLIGENCE-- HE KNOWS IF HE AIN'T A FOREMAN HE WON'T BE STRUGGLIN' T'BE SUPERINTENDENT-- HE'S ONE MAN WHO'S REACHED UTOPIA AND HAS SENSE ENOUGH TO KNOW IT!
HAPPINESS
J.R.WILLIAMS

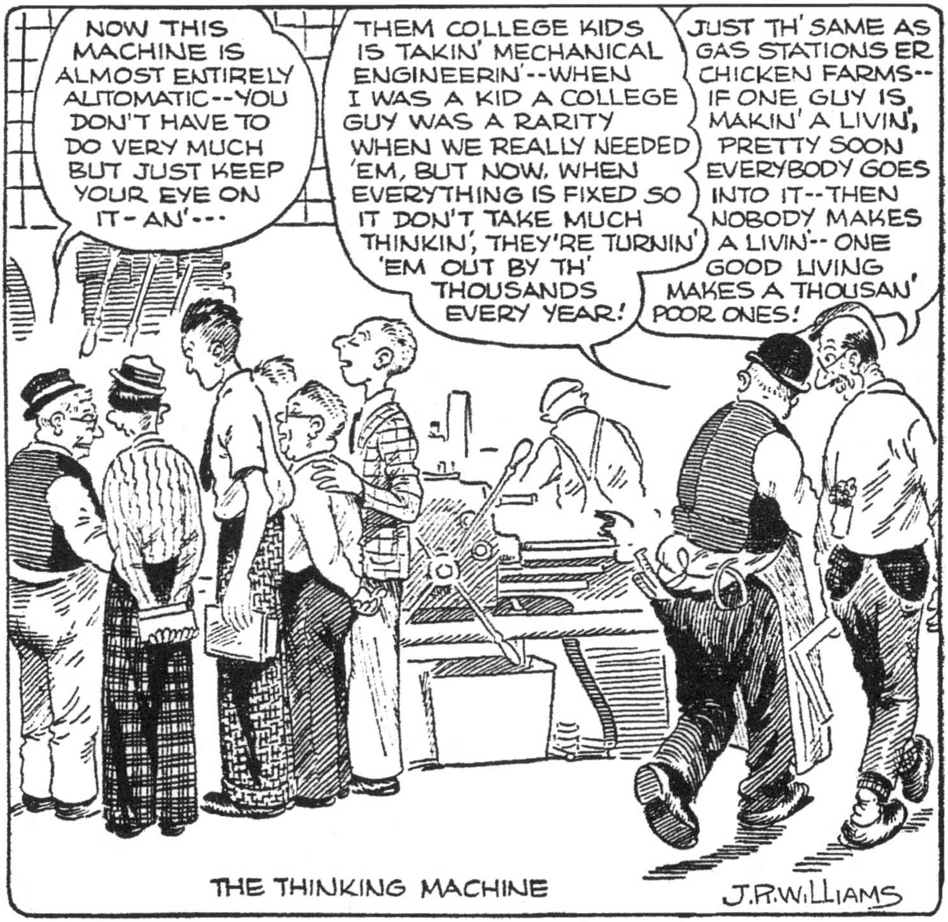
NOW THIS MACHINE IS ALMOST ENTIRELY AUTOMATIC--YOU DON'T HAVE TO DO VERY MUCH BUT JUST KEEP YOUR EYE ON IT-AN'---
THEM COLLEGE KIDS IS TAKIN' MECHANICAL ENGINEERIN'--WHEN I WAS A KID A COLLEGE GUY WAS A RARITY WHEN WE REALLY NEEDED 'EM, BUT NOW, WHEN EVERYTHING IS FIXED SO IT DON'T TAKE MUCH THINKIN', THEY'RE TURNIN' 'EM OUT BY TH' THOUSANDS EVERY YEAR!
JUST TH' SAME AS GAS STATIONS ER CHICKEN FARMS--IF ONE GUY IS MAKIN' A LIVIN', PRETTY SOON EVERYBODY GOES INTO IT--THEN NOBODY MAKES A LIVIN'--ONE GOOD LIVING MAKES A THOUSAN' POOR ONES!
THE THINKING MACHINE
J.R.WILLIAMS

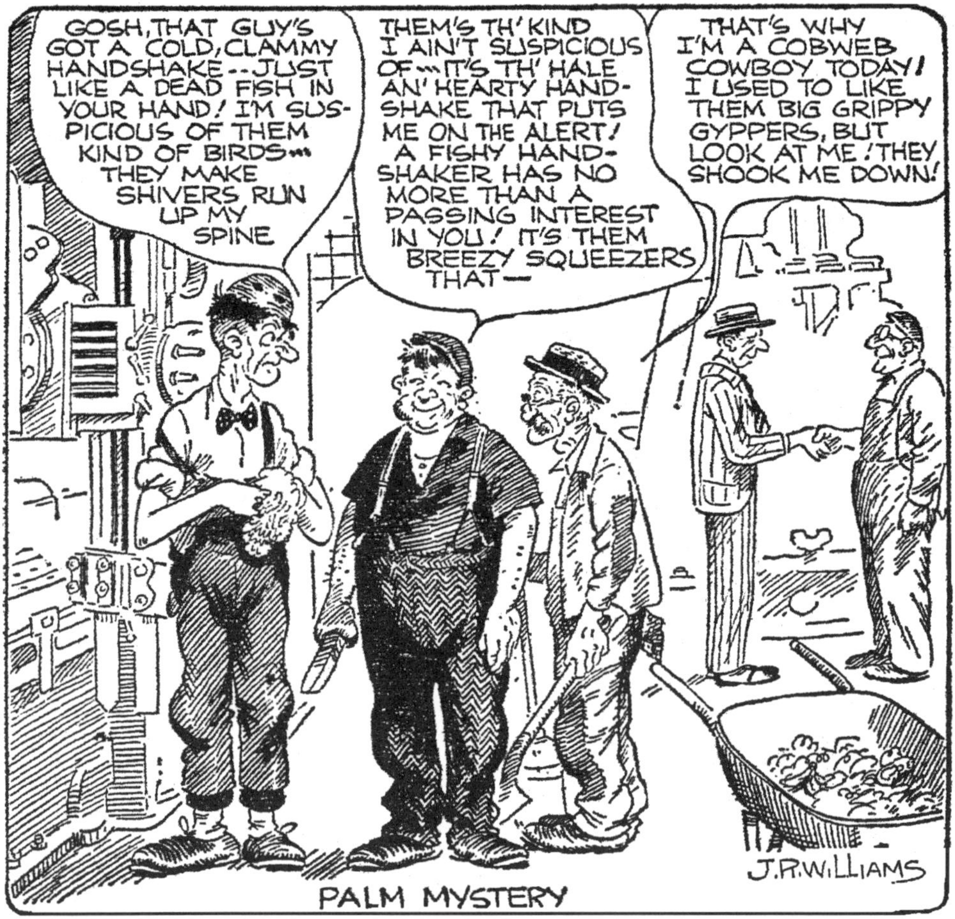
GOSH, THAT GUY'S GOT A COLD, CLAMMY HANDSHAKE--JUST LIKE A DEAD FISH IN YOUR HAND! I'M SUSPICIOUS OF THEM KIND OF BIRDS... THEY MAKE SHIVERS RUN UP MY SPINE
THEM'S TH' KIND I AIN'T SUSPICIOUS OF... IT'S TH' HALE AN' HEARTY HANDSHAKE THAT PUTS ME ON THE ALERT! A FISHY HANDSHAKER HAS NO MORE THAN A PASSING INTEREST IN YOU! IT'S THEM BREEZY SQUEEZERS THAT—
THAT'S WHY I'M A COBWEB COWBOY TODAY! I USED TO LIKE THEM BIG GRIPPY GYPPERS, BUT LOOK AT ME! THEY SHOOK ME DOWN!
J.R.WILLIAMS
PALM MYSTERY

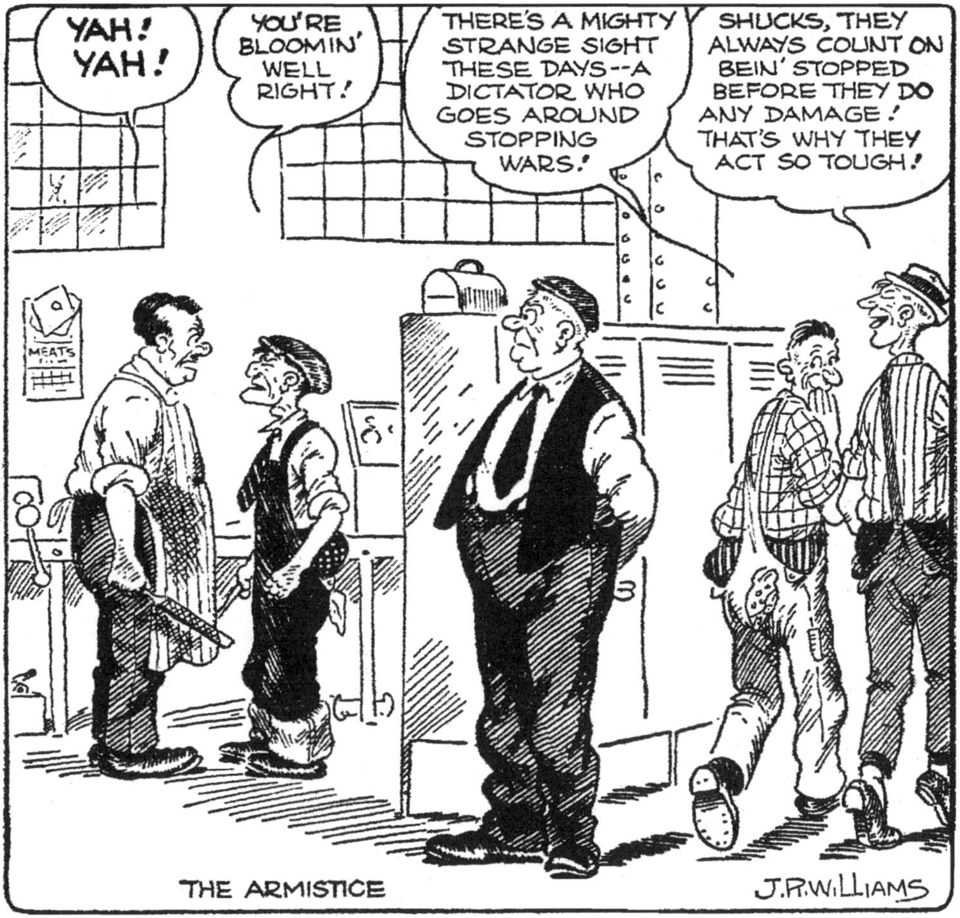
YAH! YAH!
YOU'RE BLOOMIN' WELL RIGHT!
THERE'S A MIGHTY STRANGE SIGHT THESE DAYS--A DICTATOR WHO GOES AROUND STOPPING WARS!
SHUCKS, THEY ALWAYS COUNT ON BEIN' STOPPED BEFORE THEY DO ANY DAMAGE! THAT'S WHY THEY ACT SO TOUGH!
MEATS
THE ARMISTICE
J.R. WILLIAMS

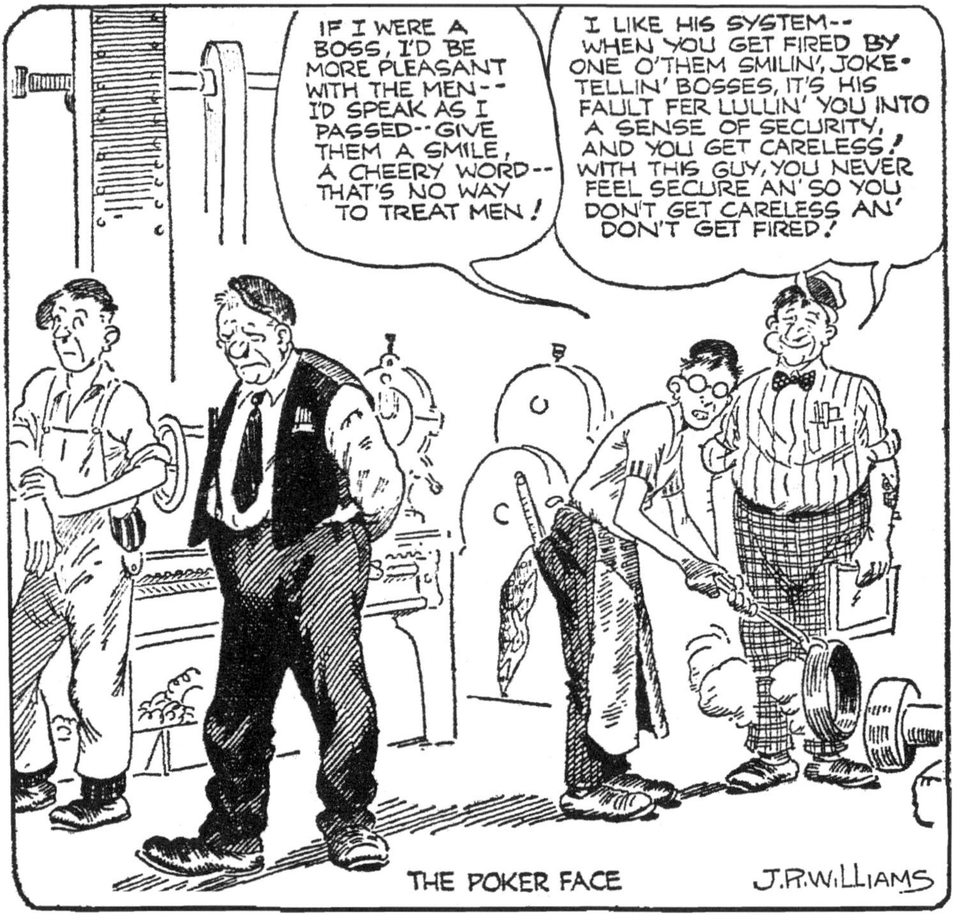
IF I WERE A BOSS, I'D BE MORE PLEASANT WITH THE MEN-- I'D SPEAK AS I PASSED--GIVE THEM A SMILE, A CHEERY WORD-- THAT'S NO WAY TO TREAT MEN!
I LIKE HIS SYSTEM-- WHEN YOU GET FIRED BY ONE O'THEM SMILIN', JOKE-TELLIN' BOSSES, IT'S HIS FAULT FER LULLIN' YOU INTO A SENSE OF SECURITY, AND YOU GET CARELESS! WITH THIS GUY, YOU NEVER FEEL SECURE AN' SO YOU DON'T GET CARELESS AN' DON'T GET FIRED!
THE POKER FACE
J.R.WILLIAMS

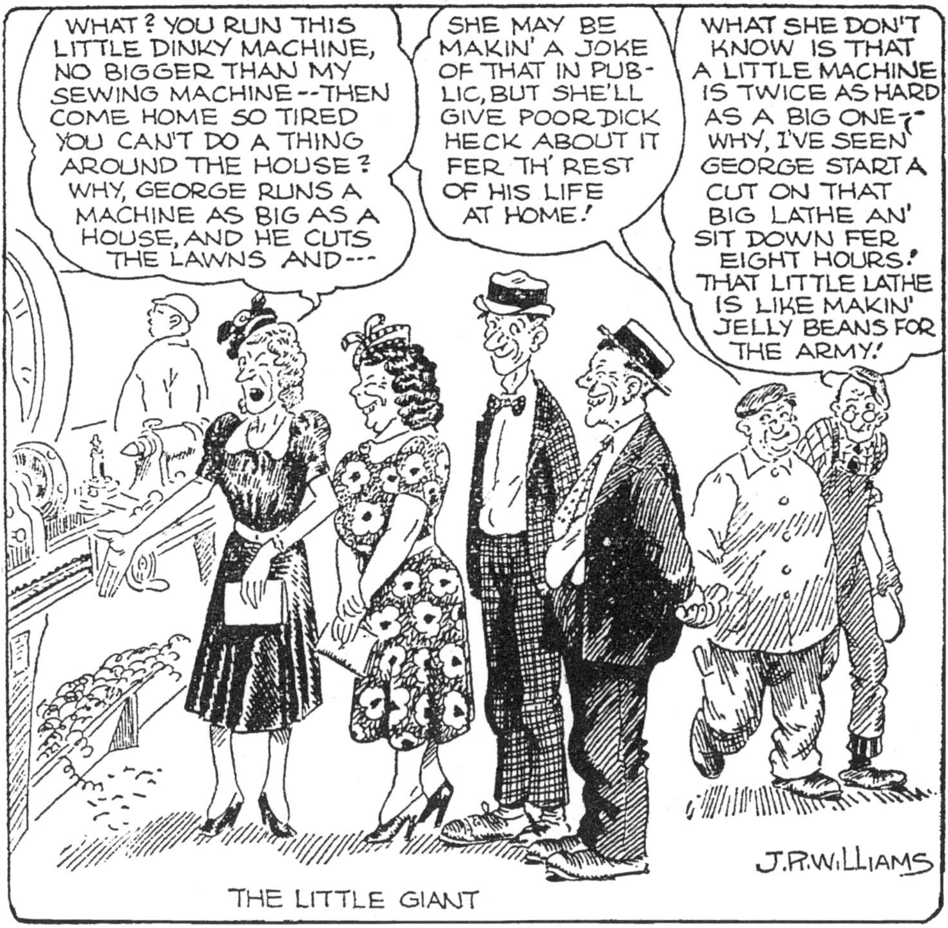
WHAT? YOU RUN THIS LITTLE DINKY MACHINE, NO BIGGER THAN MY SEWING MACHINE--THEN COME HOME SO TIRED YOU CAN'T DO A THING AROUND THE HOUSE? WHY, GEORGE RUNS A MACHINE AS BIG AS A HOUSE, AND HE CUTS THE LAWNS AND---
SHE MAY BE MAKIN' A JOKE OF THAT IN PUB-LIC, BUT SHE'LL GIVE POOR DICK HECK ABOUT IT FER TH' REST OF HIS LIFE AT HOME!
WHAT SHE DON'T KNOW IS THAT A LITTLE MACHINE IS TWICE AS HARD AS A BIG ONE-- WHY, I'VE SEEN GEORGE START A CUT ON THAT BIG LATHE AN' SIT DOWN FER EIGHT HOURS! THAT LITTLE LATHE IS LIKE MAKIN' JELLY BEANS FOR THE ARMY!
J.R.WILLIAMS
THE LITTLE GIANT

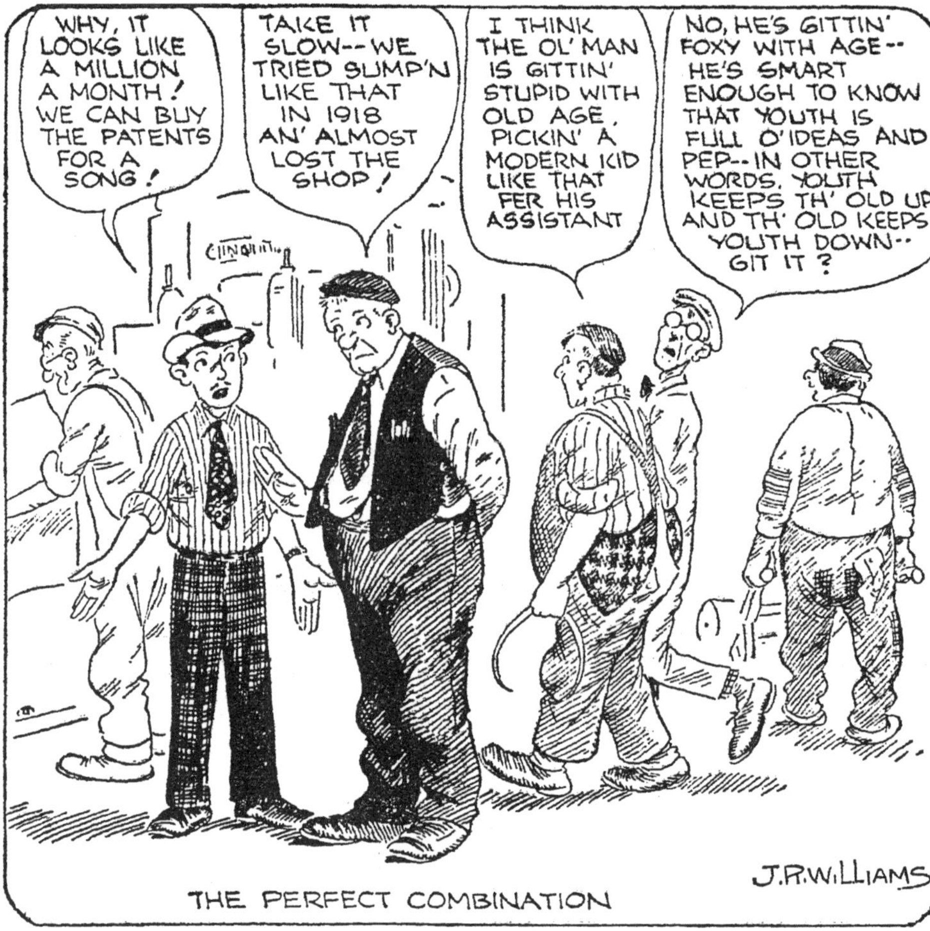
WHY, IT LOOKS LIKE A MILLION A MONTH! WE CAN BUY THE PATENTS FOR A SONG!
TAKE IT SLOW--WE TRIED SUMP'N LIKE THAT IN 1918 AN' ALMOST LOST THE SHOP!
I THINK THE OL' MAN IS GITTIN' STUPID WITH OLD AGE, PICKIN' A MODERN KID LIKE THAT FER HIS ASSISTANT
NO, HE'S GITTIN' FOXY WITH AGE--HE'S SMART ENOUGH TO KNOW THAT YOUTH IS FULL O'IDEAS AND PEP--IN OTHER WORDS, YOUTH KEEPS TH' OLD UP AND TH' OLD KEEPS YOUTH DOWN--GIT IT?
THE PERFECT COMBINATION
J.R.WILLIAMS

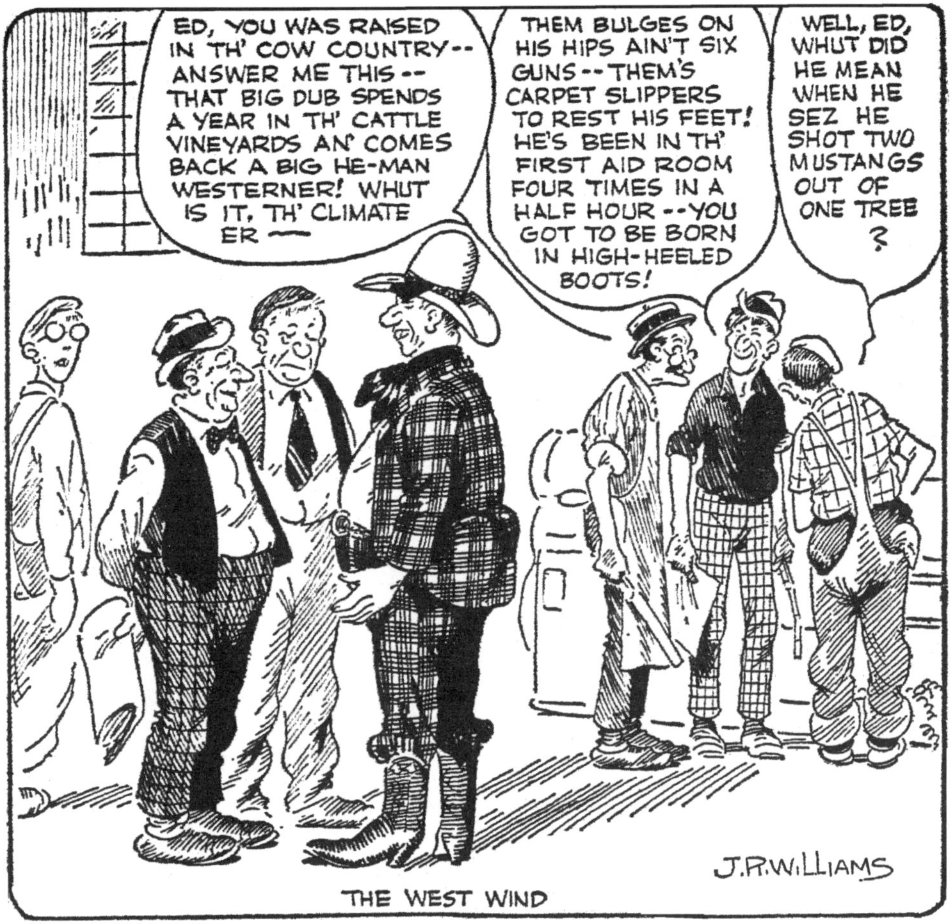
ED, YOU WAS RAISED IN TH' COW COUNTRY-- ANSWER ME THIS-- THAT BIG DUB SPENDS A YEAR IN TH' CATTLE VINEYARDS AN' COMES BACK A BIG HE-MAN WESTERNER! WHUT IS IT, TH' CLIMATE ER—
THEM BULGES ON HIS HIPS AIN'T SIX GUNS--THEM'S CARPET SLIPPERS TO REST HIS FEET! HE'S BEEN IN TH' FIRST AID ROOM FOUR TIMES IN A HALF HOUR--YOU GOT TO BE BORN IN HIGH-HEELED BOOTS!
WELL, ED, WHUT DID HE MEAN WHEN HE SEZ HE SHOT TWO MUSTANGS OUT OF ONE TREE ?
J.R.WILLIAMS
THE WEST WIND

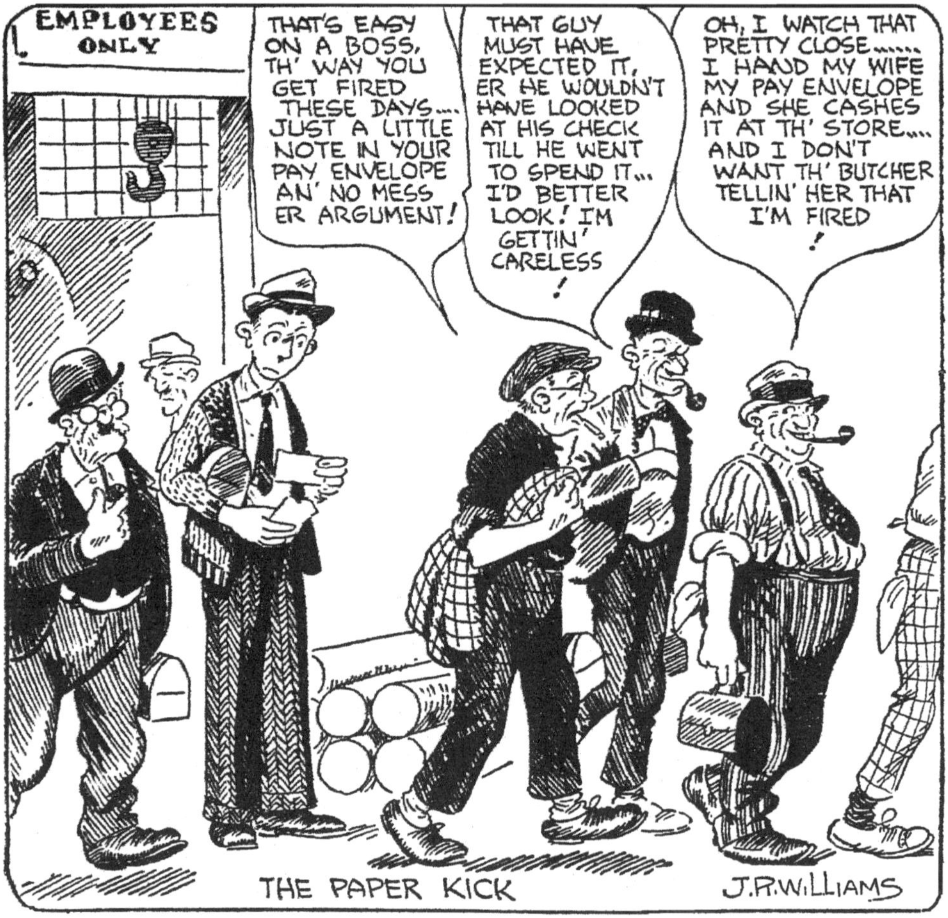
EMPLOYEES ONLY
THAT'S EASY ON A BOSS, TH' WAY YOU GET FIRED THESE DAYS.... JUST A LITTLE NOTE IN YOUR PAY ENVELOPE AN' NO MESS ER ARGUMENT!
THAT GUY MUST HAVE EXPECTED IT, ER HE WOULDN'T HAVE LOOKED AT HIS CHECK TILL HE WENT TO SPEND IT... I'D BETTER LOOK! I'M GETTIN' CARELESS!
OH, I WATCH THAT PRETTY CLOSE...... I HAND MY WIFE MY PAY ENVELOPE AND SHE CASHES IT AT TH' STORE.... AND I DON'T WANT TH' BUTCHER TELLIN' HER THAT I'M FIRED!
THE PAPER KICK
J.R.WILLIAMS

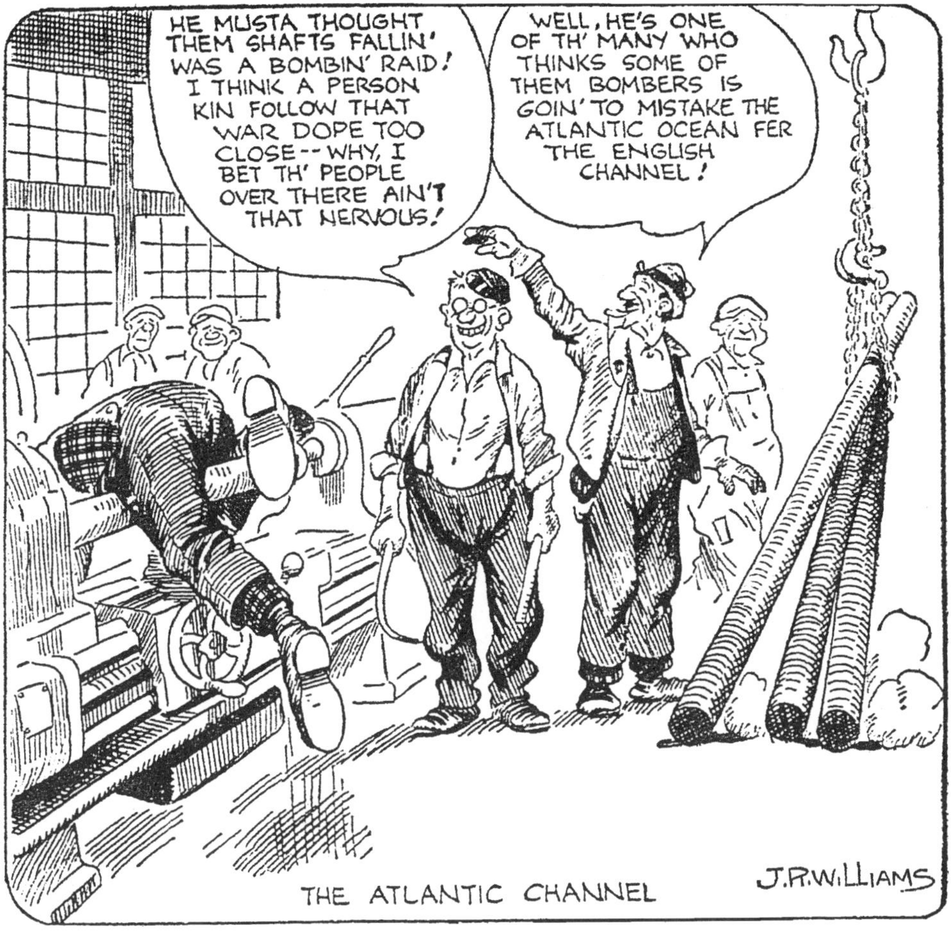
HE MUSTA THOUGHT THEM SHAFTS FALLIN' WAS A BOMBIN' RAID! I THINK A PERSON KIN FOLLOW THAT WAR DOPE TOO CLOSE--WHY, I BET TH' PEOPLE OVER THERE AIN'T THAT NERVOUS!
WELL, HE'S ONE OF TH' MANY WHO THINKS SOME OF THEM BOMBERS IS GOIN' TO MISTAKE THE ATLANTIC OCEAN FER THE ENGLISH CHANNEL!
J.R.WILLIAMS
THE ATLANTIC CHANNEL

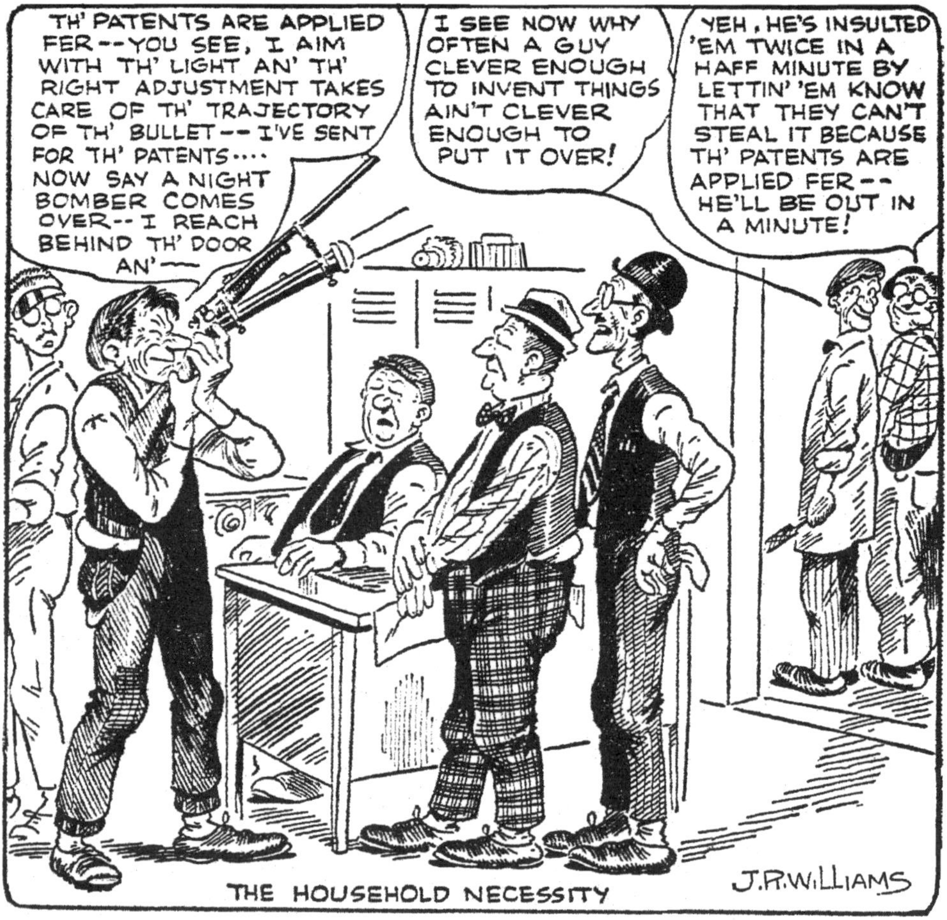
TH' PATENTS ARE APPLIED FER--YOU SEE, I AIM WITH TH' LIGHT AN' TH' RIGHT ADJUSTMENT TAKES CARE OF TH' TRAJECTORY OF TH' BULLET--I'VE SENT FOR TH' PATENTS.... NOW SAY A NIGHT BOMBER COMES OVER--I REACH BEHIND TH' DOOR AN'--
I SEE NOW WHY OFTEN A GUY CLEVER ENOUGH TO INVENT THINGS AIN'T CLEVER ENOUGH TO PUT IT OVER!
YEH, HE'S INSULTED 'EM TWICE IN A HAFF MINUTE BY LETTIN' 'EM KNOW THAT THEY CAN'T STEAL IT BECAUSE TH' PATENTS ARE APPLIED FER-- HE'LL BE OUT IN A MINUTE!
THE HOUSEHOLD NECESSITY
J.R.WILLIAMS

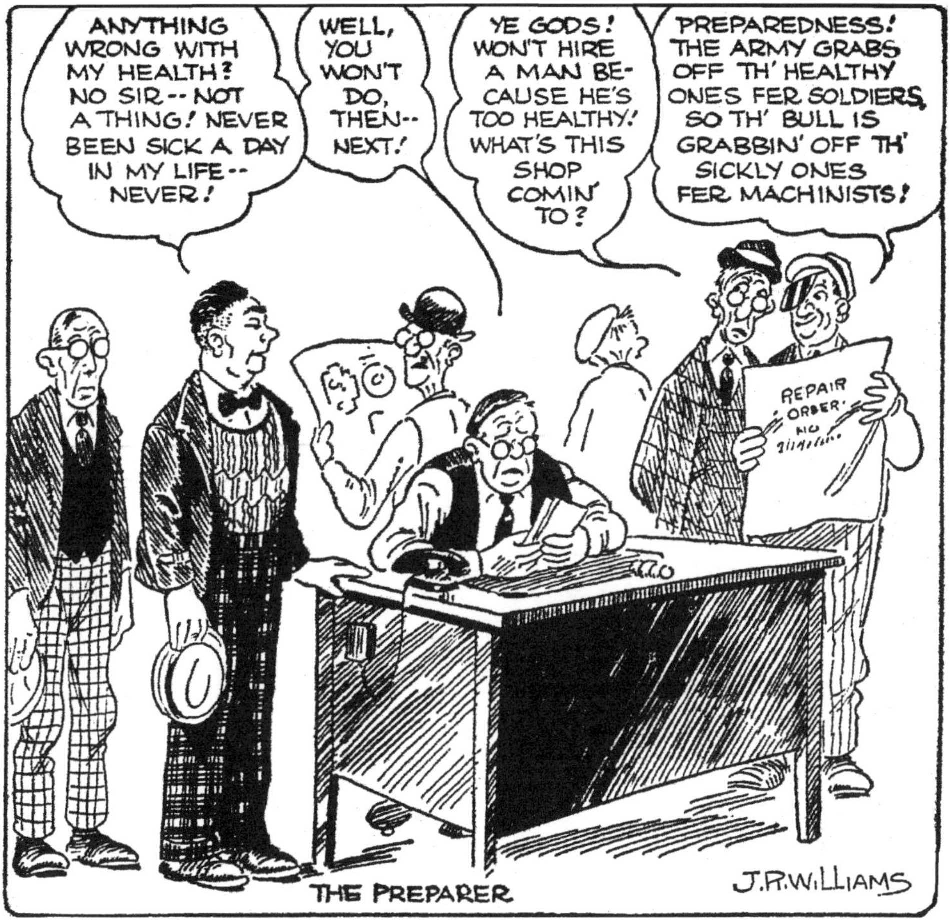
ANYTHING WRONG WITH MY HEALTH? NO SIR--NOT A THING! NEVER BEEN SICK A DAY IN MY LIFE--NEVER!
WELL, YOU WON'T DO, THEN--NEXT!
YE GODS! WON'T HIRE A MAN BE-CAUSE HE'S TOO HEALTHY! WHAT'S THIS SHOP COMIN' TO?
PREPAREDNESS! THE ARMY GRABS OFF TH' HEALTHY ONES FER SOLDIERS, SO TH' BULL IS GRABBIN' OFF TH' SICKLY ONES FER MACHINISTS!
REPAIR ORDER NO
THE PREPARER
J.R. WILLIAMS

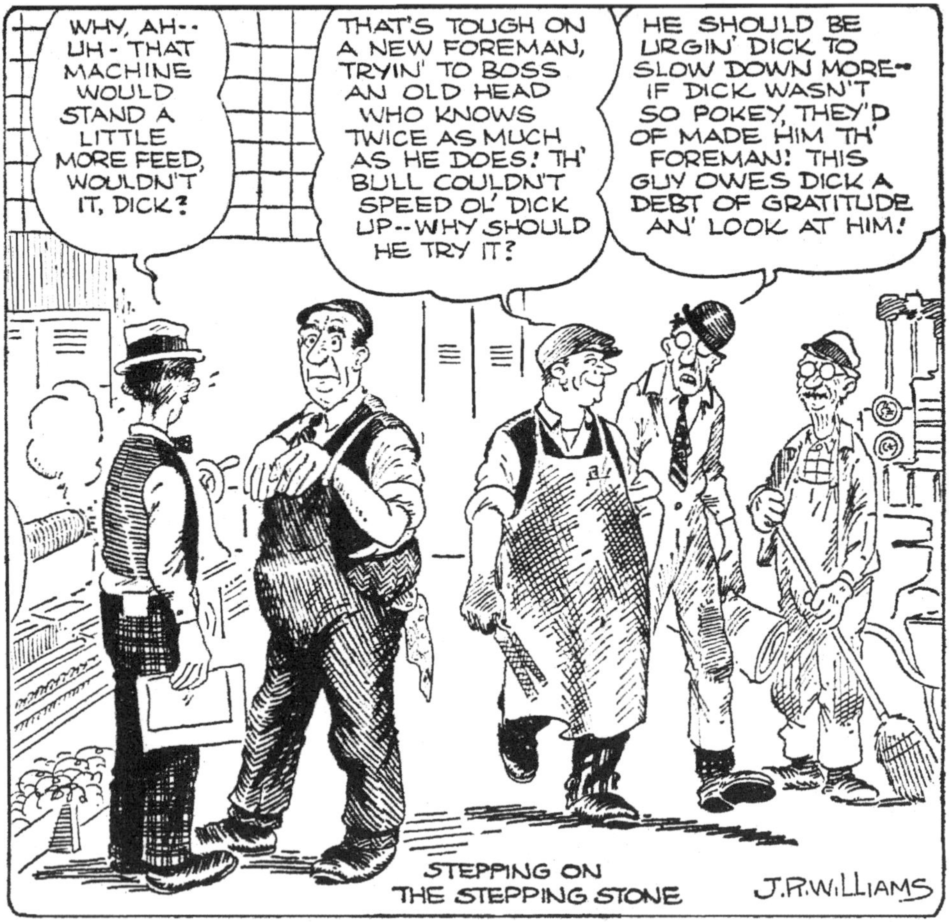
WHY, AH-- UH- THAT MACHINE WOULD STAND A LITTLE MORE FEED, WOULDN'T IT, DICK?
THAT'S TOUGH ON A NEW FOREMAN, TRYIN' TO BOSS AN OLD HEAD WHO KNOWS TWICE AS MUCH AS HE DOES! TH' BULL COULDN'T SPEED OL' DICK UP--WHY SHOULD HE TRY IT?
HE SHOULD BE URGIN' DICK TO SLOW DOWN MORE-- IF DICK WASN'T SO POKEY, THEY'D OF MADE HIM TH' FOREMAN! THIS GUY OWES DICK A DEBT OF GRATITUDE AN' LOOK AT HIM!
STEPPING ON THE STEPPING STONE
J.R.WILLIAMS

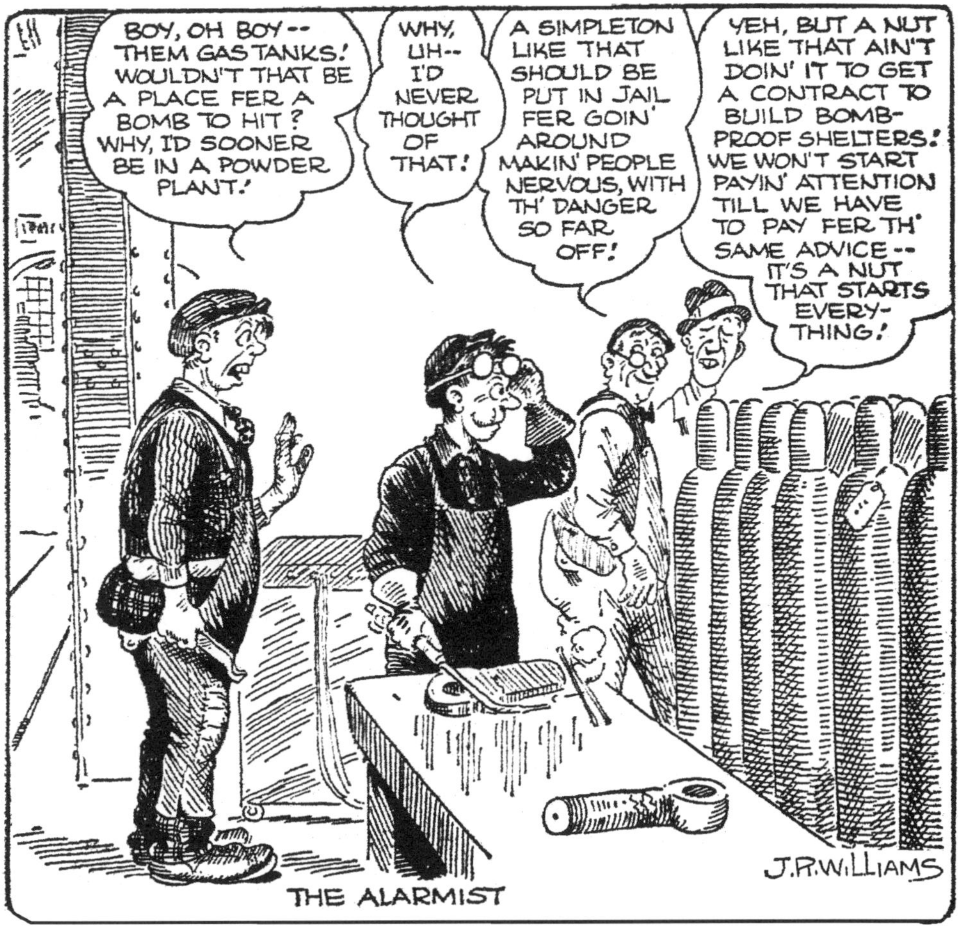
BOY, OH BOY -- THEM GAS TANKS! WOULDN'T THAT BE A PLACE FER A BOMB TO HIT? WHY, I'D SOONER BE IN A POWDER PLANT!
WHY, UH-- I'D NEVER THOUGHT OF THAT!
A SIMPLETON LIKE THAT SHOULD BE PUT IN JAIL FER GOIN' AROUND MAKIN' PEOPLE NERVOUS, WITH TH' DANGER SO FAR OFF!
YEH, BUT A NUT LIKE THAT AIN'T DOIN' IT TO GET A CONTRACT TO BUILD BOMB-PROOF SHELTERS! WE WON'T START PAYIN' ATTENTION TILL WE HAVE TO PAY FER TH' SAME ADVICE -- IT'S A NUT THAT STARTS EVERY-THING!
J.R. WILLIAMS
THE ALARMIST

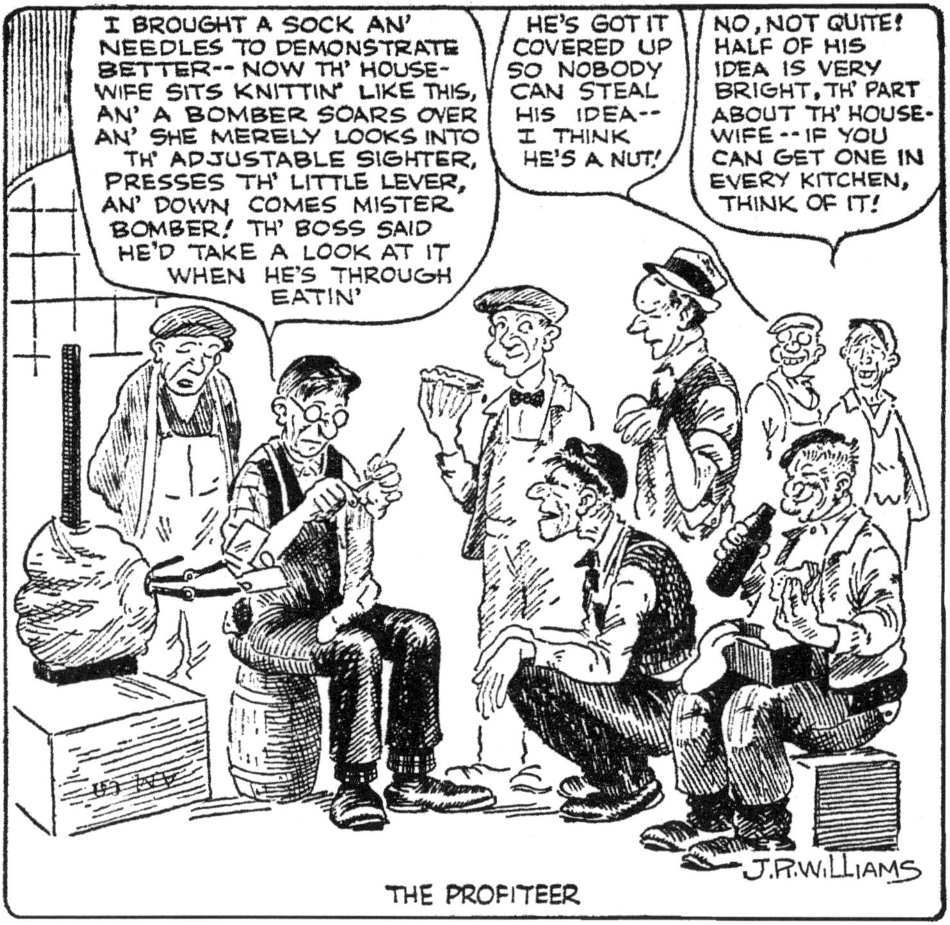
I BROUGHT A SOCK AN' NEEDLES TO DEMONSTRATE BETTER-- NOW TH' HOUSE-WIFE SITS KNITTIN' LIKE THIS, AN' A BOMBER SOARS OVER AN' SHE MERELY LOOKS INTO TH' ADJUSTABLE SIGHTER, PRESSES TH' LITTLE LEVER, AN' DOWN COMES MISTER BOMBER! TH' BOSS SAID HE'D TAKE A LOOK AT IT WHEN HE'S THROUGH EATIN'
HE'S GOT IT COVERED UP SO NOBODY CAN STEAL HIS IDEA-- I THINK HE'S A NUT!
NO, NOT QUITE! HALF OF HIS IDEA IS VERY BRIGHT, TH' PART ABOUT TH' HOUSE-WIFE -- IF YOU CAN GET ONE IN EVERY KITCHEN, THINK OF IT!
J.R. WILLIAMS
THE PROFITEER

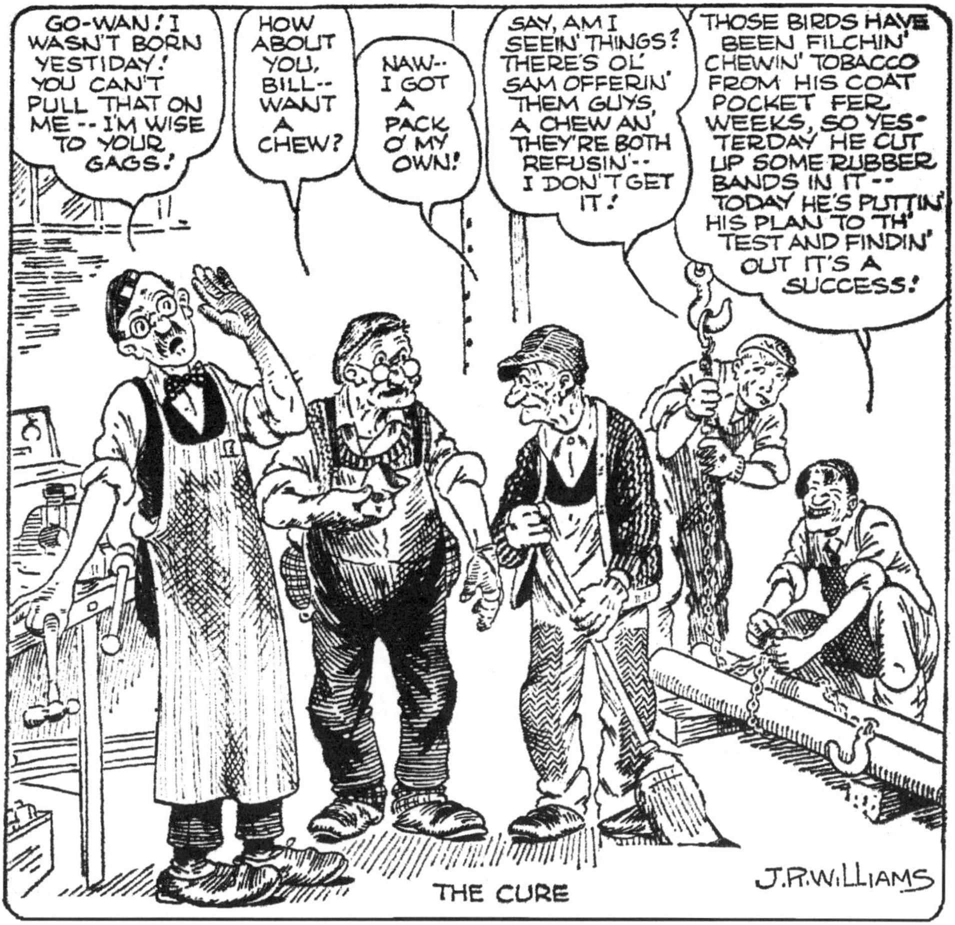
GO-WAN! I WASN'T BORN YESTIDAY! YOU CAN'T PULL THAT ON ME -- I'M WISE TO YOUR GAGS!
HOW ABOUT YOU, BILL-- WANT A CHEW?
NAW-- I GOT A PACK O' MY OWN!
SAY, AM I SEEIN' THINGS? THERE'S OL' SAM OFFERIN' THEM GUYS A CHEW AN' THEY'RE BOTH REFUSIN'-- I DON'T GET IT!
THOSE BIRDS HAVE BEEN FILCHIN' CHEWIN' TOBACCO FROM HIS COAT POCKET FER WEEKS, SO YESTERDAY HE CUT UP SOME RUBBER BANDS IN IT -- TODAY HE'S PUTTIN' HIS PLAN TO TH' TEST AND FINDIN' OUT IT'S A SUCCESS!
THE CURE
J.R.WILLIAMS

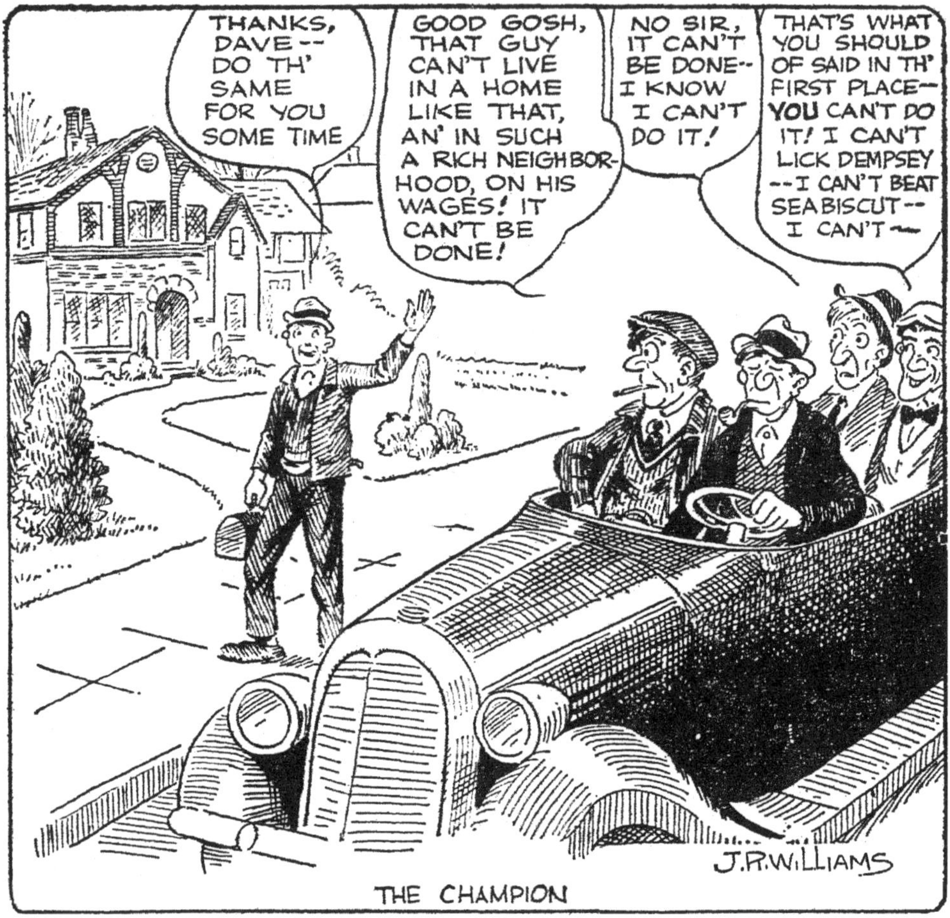
THANKS, DAVE -- DO TH' SAME FOR YOU SOME TIME
GOOD GOSH, THAT GUY CAN'T LIVE IN A HOME LIKE THAT, AN' IN SUCH A RICH NEIGHBOR-HOOD, ON HIS WAGES! IT CAN'T BE DONE!
NO SIR, IT CAN'T BE DONE-- I KNOW I CAN'T DO IT!
THAT'S WHAT YOU SHOULD OF SAID IN TH' FIRST PLACE-- YOU CAN'T DO IT! I CAN'T LICK DEMPSEY --I CAN'T BEAT SEABISCUT-- I CAN'T--
J.R.WILLIAMS
THE CHAMPION

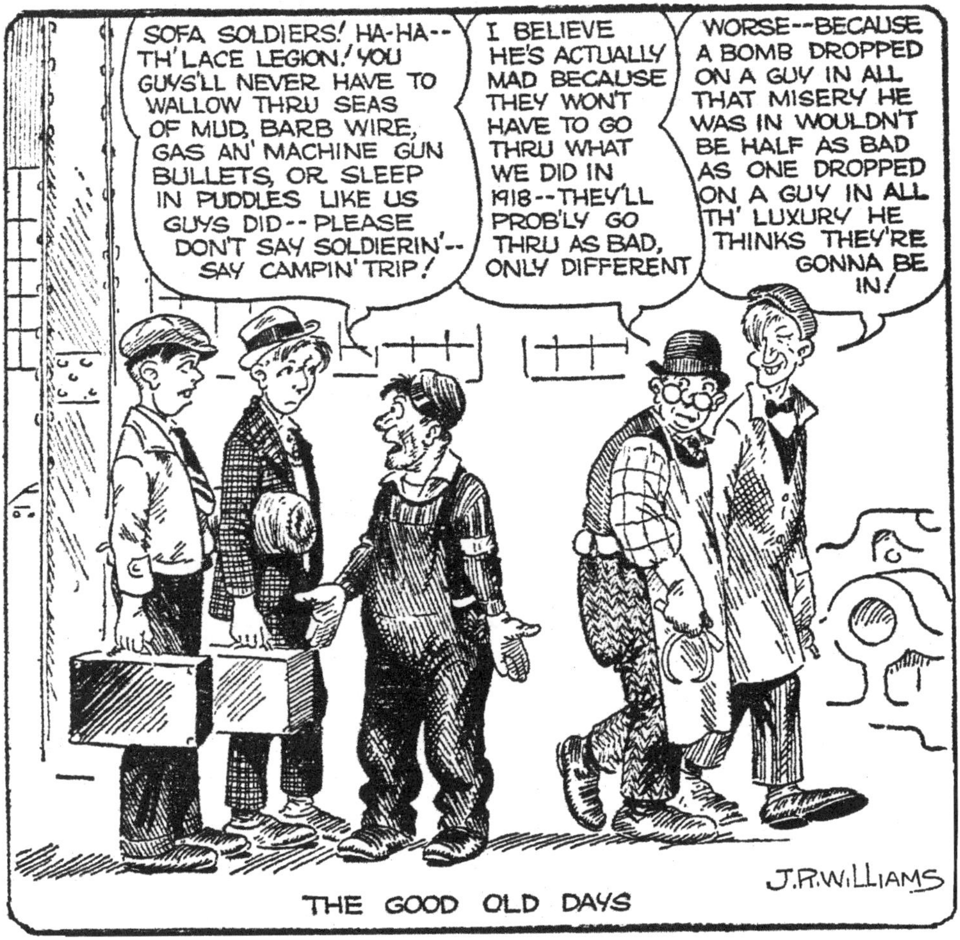
SOFA SOLDIERS! HA-HA-- TH' LACE LEGION! YOU GUYS'LL NEVER HAVE TO WALLOW THRU SEAS OF MUD, BARB WIRE, GAS AN' MACHINE GUN BULLETS, OR SLEEP IN PUDDLES LIKE US GUYS DID--PLEASE DON'T SAY SOLDIERIN'-- SAY CAMPIN' TRIP!
I BELIEVE HE'S ACTUALLY MAD BECAUSE THEY WON'T HAVE TO GO THRU WHAT WE DID IN 1918--THEY'LL PROB'LY GO THRU AS BAD, ONLY DIFFERENT
WORSE--BECAUSE A BOMB DROPPED ON A GUY IN ALL THAT MISERY HE WAS IN WOULDN'T BE HALF AS BAD AS ONE DROPPED ON A GUY IN ALL TH' LUXURY HE THINKS THEY'RE GONNA BE IN!
J.R.WILLIAMS
THE GOOD OLD DAYS

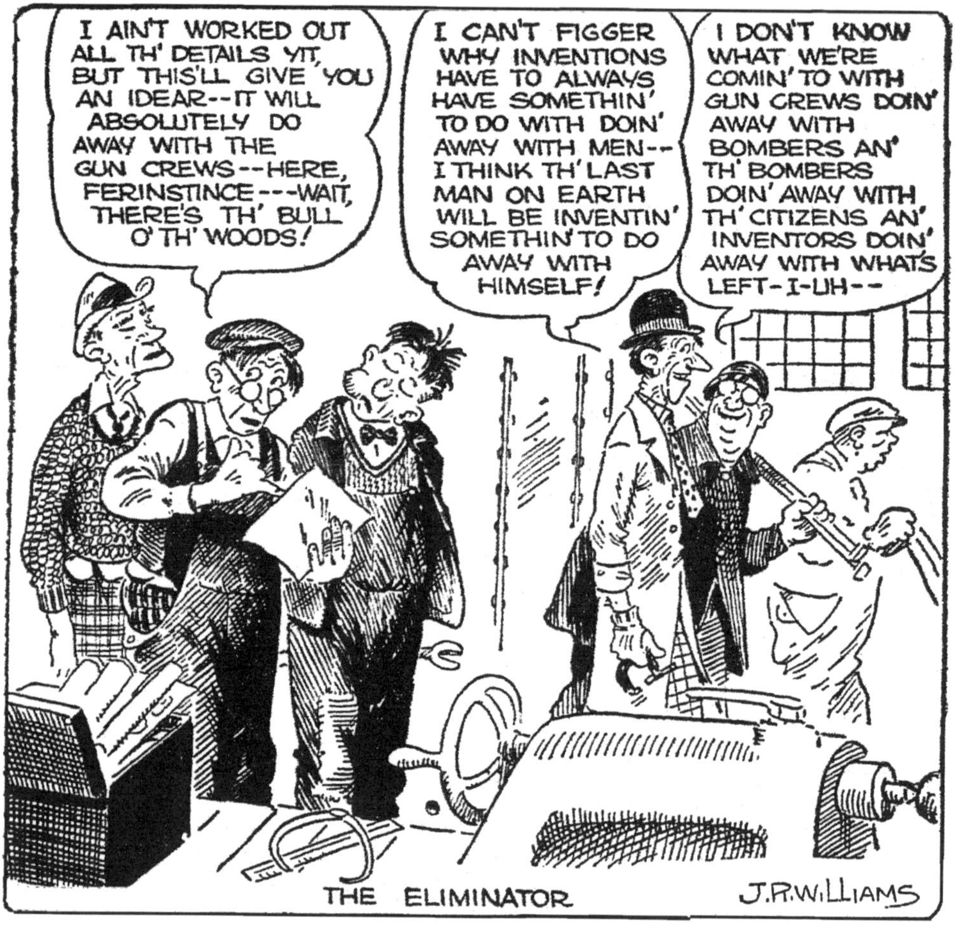
I AIN'T WORKED OUT ALL TH' DETAILS YIT, BUT THIS'LL GIVE YOU AN IDEAR--IT WILL ABSOLUTELY DO AWAY WITH THE GUN CREWS--HERE, FERINSTINCE---WAIT, THERE'S TH' BULL O'TH' WOODS!
I CAN'T FIGGER WHY INVENTIONS HAVE TO ALWAYS HAVE SOMETHIN' TO DO WITH DOIN' AWAY WITH MEN--I THINK TH' LAST MAN ON EARTH WILL BE INVENTIN' SOMETHIN' TO DO AWAY WITH HIMSELF!
I DON'T KNOW WHAT WE'RE COMIN' TO WITH GUN CREWS DOIN' AWAY WITH BOMBERS AN' TH' BOMBERS DOIN' AWAY WITH TH' CITIZENS AN' INVENTORS DOIN' AWAY WITH WHAT'S LEFT-I-UH--
THE ELIMINATOR
J.R.WILLIAMS

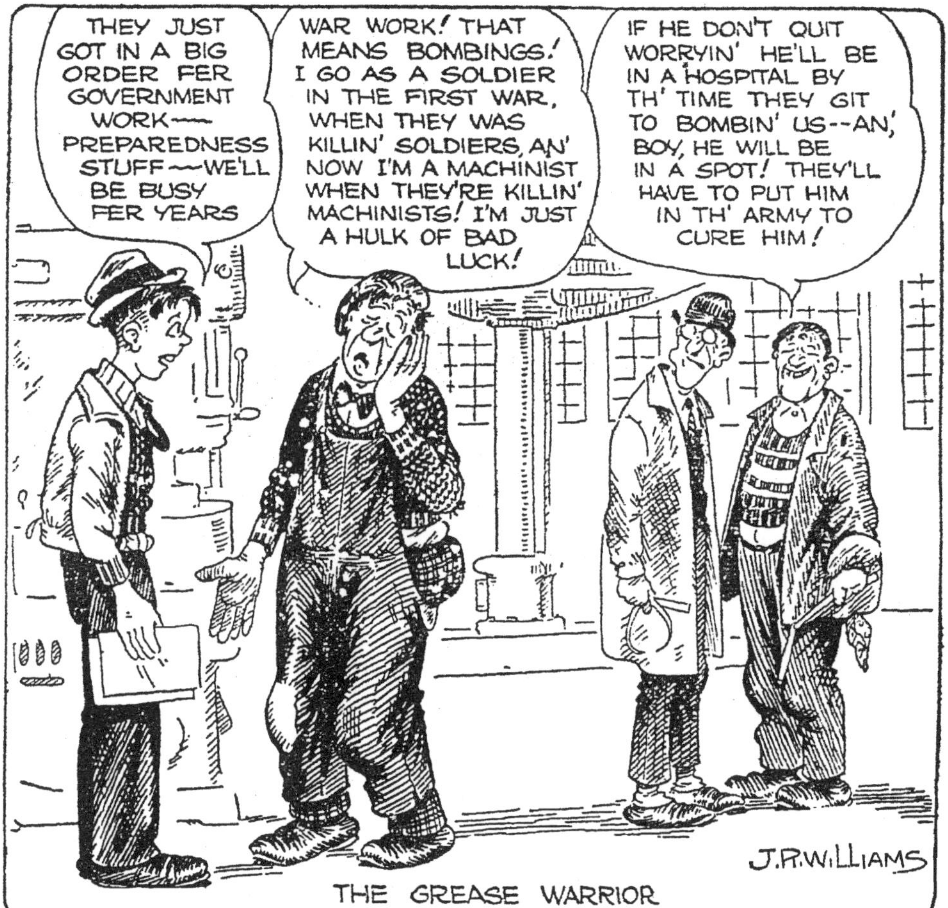
THEY JUST GOT IN A BIG ORDER FER GOVERNMENT WORK—— PREPAREDNESS STUFF——WE'LL BE BUSY FER YEARS
WAR WORK! THAT MEANS BOMBINGS! I GO AS A SOLDIER IN THE FIRST WAR, WHEN THEY WAS KILLIN' SOLDIERS, AN' NOW I'M A MACHINIST WHEN THEY'RE KILLIN' MACHINISTS! I'M JUST A HULK OF BAD LUCK!
IF HE DON'T QUIT WORRYIN' HE'LL BE IN A HOSPITAL BY TH' TIME THEY GIT TO BOMBIN' US--AN', BOY, HE WILL BE IN A SPOT! THEY'LL HAVE TO PUT HIM IN TH' ARMY TO CURE HIM!
J.R.WILLIAMS
THE GREASE WARRIOR

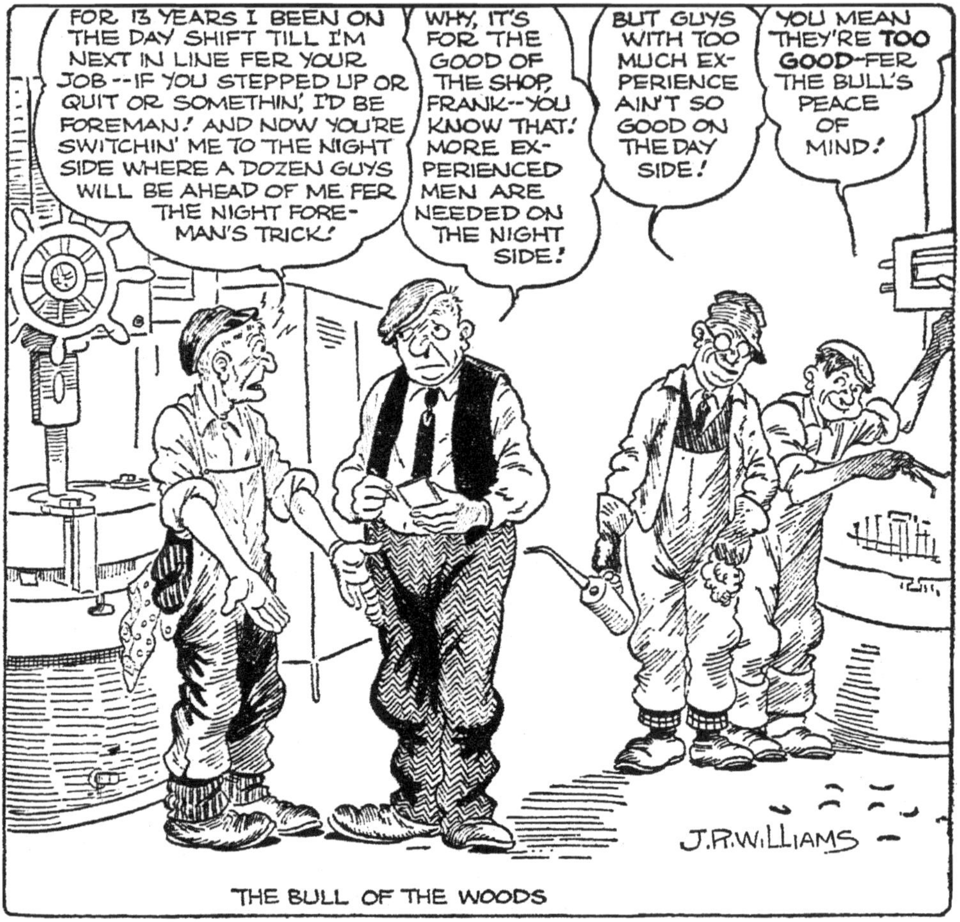
FOR 13 YEARS I BEEN ON THE DAY SHIFT TILL I'M NEXT IN LINE FER YOUR JOB --IF YOU STEPPED UP OR QUIT OR SOMETHIN', I'D BE FOREMAN! AND NOW YOU'RE SWITCHIN' ME TO THE NIGHT SIDE WHERE A DOZEN GUYS WILL BE AHEAD OF ME FER THE NIGHT FORE-MAN'S TRICK!
WHY, IT'S FOR THE GOOD OF THE SHOP, FRANK--YOU KNOW THAT! MORE EX-PERIENCED MEN ARE NEEDED ON THE NIGHT SIDE!
BUT GUYS WITH TOO MUCH EX-PERIENCE AIN'T SO GOOD ON THE DAY SIDE!
YOU MEAN THEY'RE **TOO GOOD**-FER THE BULL'S PEACE OF MIND!
J.R.WILLIAMS
THE BULL OF THE WOODS

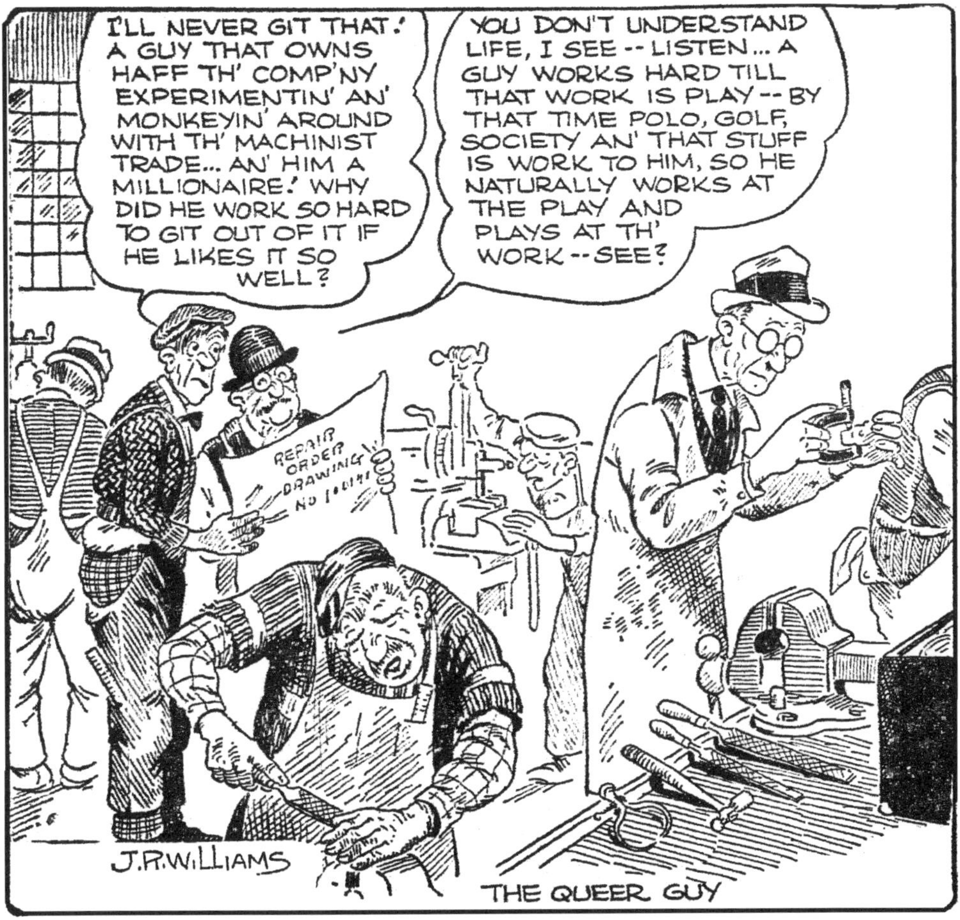
I'LL NEVER GIT THAT! A GUY THAT OWNS HAFF TH' COMP'NY EXPERIMENTIN' AN' MONKEYIN' AROUND WITH TH' MACHINIST TRADE... AN' HIM A MILLIONAIRE! WHY DID HE WORK SO HARD TO GIT OUT OF IT IF HE LIKES IT SO WELL?
YOU DON'T UNDERSTAND LIFE, I SEE -- LISTEN... A GUY WORKS HARD TILL THAT WORK IS PLAY -- BY THAT TIME POLO, GOLF, SOCIETY AN' THAT STUFF IS WORK TO HIM, SO HE NATURALLY WORKS AT THE PLAY AND PLAYS AT TH' WORK -- SEE?
REPAIR ORDER DRAWING
J.R. WILLIAMS
THE QUEER GUY

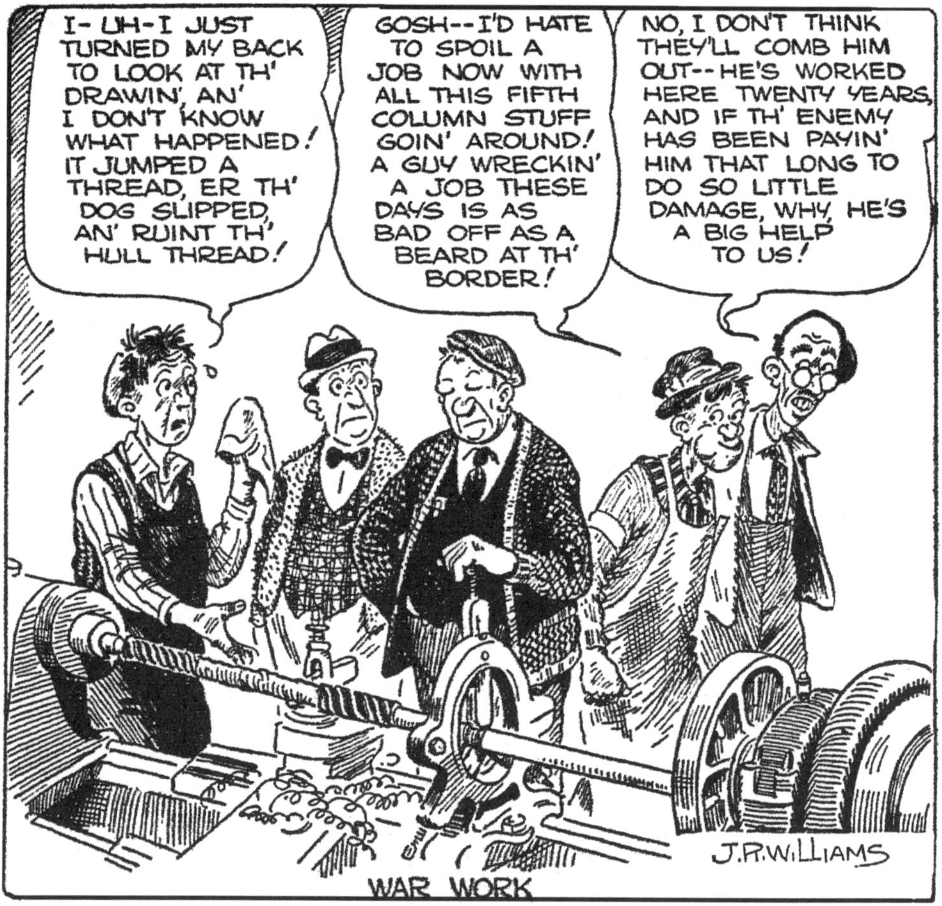
I- UH-I JUST TURNED MY BACK TO LOOK AT TH' DRAWIN', AN' I DON'T KNOW WHAT HAPPENED! IT JUMPED A THREAD, ER TH' DOG SLIPPED, AN' RUINT TH' HULL THREAD!
GOSH--I'D HATE TO SPOIL A JOB NOW WITH ALL THIS FIFTH COLUMN STUFF GOIN' AROUND! A GUY WRECKIN' A JOB THESE DAYS IS AS BAD OFF AS A BEARD AT TH' BORDER!
NO, I DON'T THINK THEY'LL COMB HIM OUT--HE'S WORKED HERE TWENTY YEARS, AND IF TH' ENEMY HAS BEEN PAYIN' HIM THAT LONG TO DO SO LITTLE DAMAGE, WHY, HE'S A BIG HELP TO US!
J.R.WILLIAMS
WAR WORK

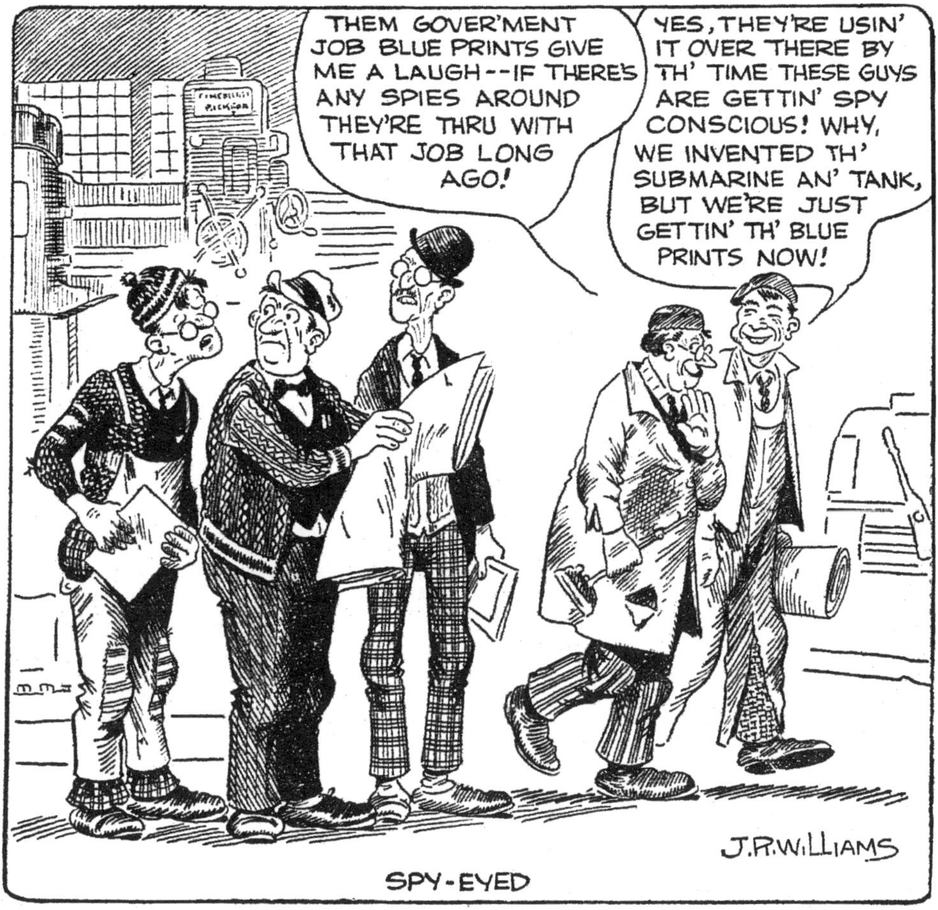
THEM GOVER'MENT JOB BLUE PRINTS GIVE ME A LAUGH--IF THERE'S ANY SPIES AROUND THEY'RE THRU WITH THAT JOB LONG AGO!
YES, THEY'RE USIN' IT OVER THERE BY TH' TIME THESE GUYS ARE GETTIN' SPY CONSCIOUS! WHY, WE INVENTED TH' SUBMARINE AN' TANK, BUT WE'RE JUST GETTIN' TH' BLUE PRINTS NOW!
J.R.WILLIAMS
SPY-EYED

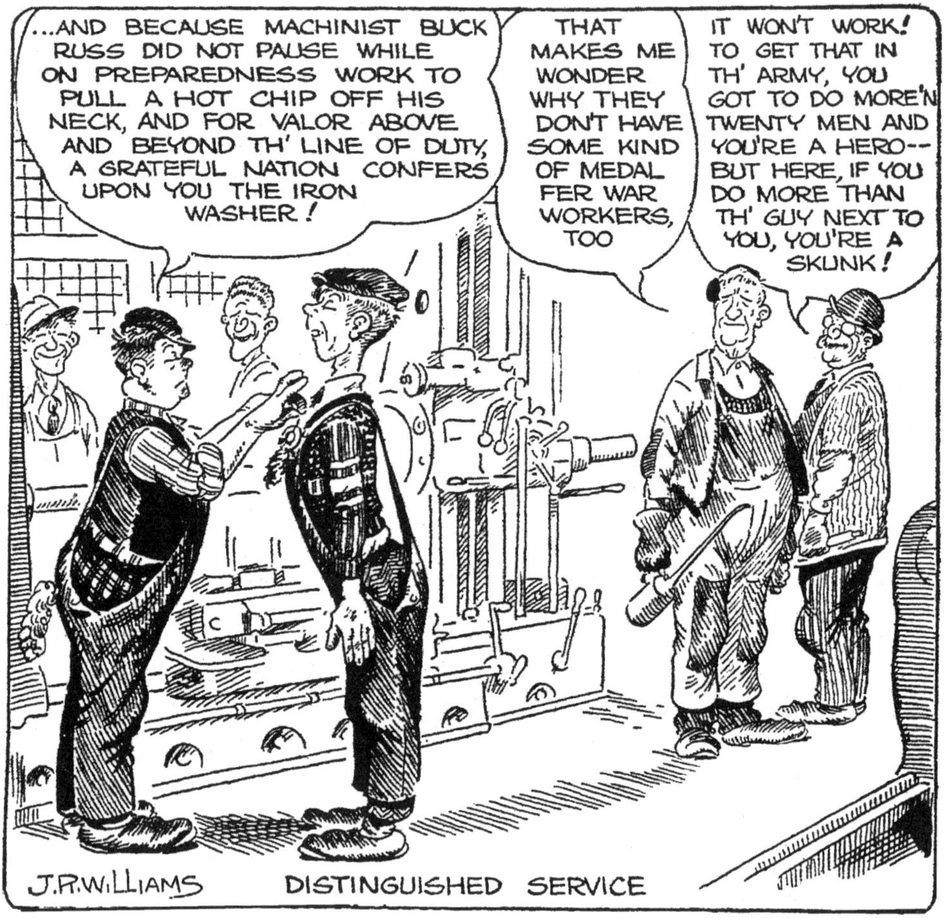
...AND BECAUSE MACHINIST BUCK RUSS DID NOT PAUSE WHILE ON PREPAREDNESS WORK TO PULL A HOT CHIP OFF HIS NECK, AND FOR VALOR ABOVE AND BEYOND TH' LINE OF DUTY, A GRATEFUL NATION CONFERS UPON YOU THE IRON WASHER!
THAT MAKES ME WONDER WHY THEY DON'T HAVE SOME KIND OF MEDAL FER WAR WORKERS, TOO
IT WON'T WORK! TO GET THAT IN TH' ARMY, YOU GOT TO DO MORE'N TWENTY MEN AND YOU'RE A HERO-- BUT HERE, IF YOU DO MORE THAN TH' GUY NEXT TO YOU, YOU'RE A SKUNK!
J.R.WILLIAMS
DISTINGUISHED SERVICE

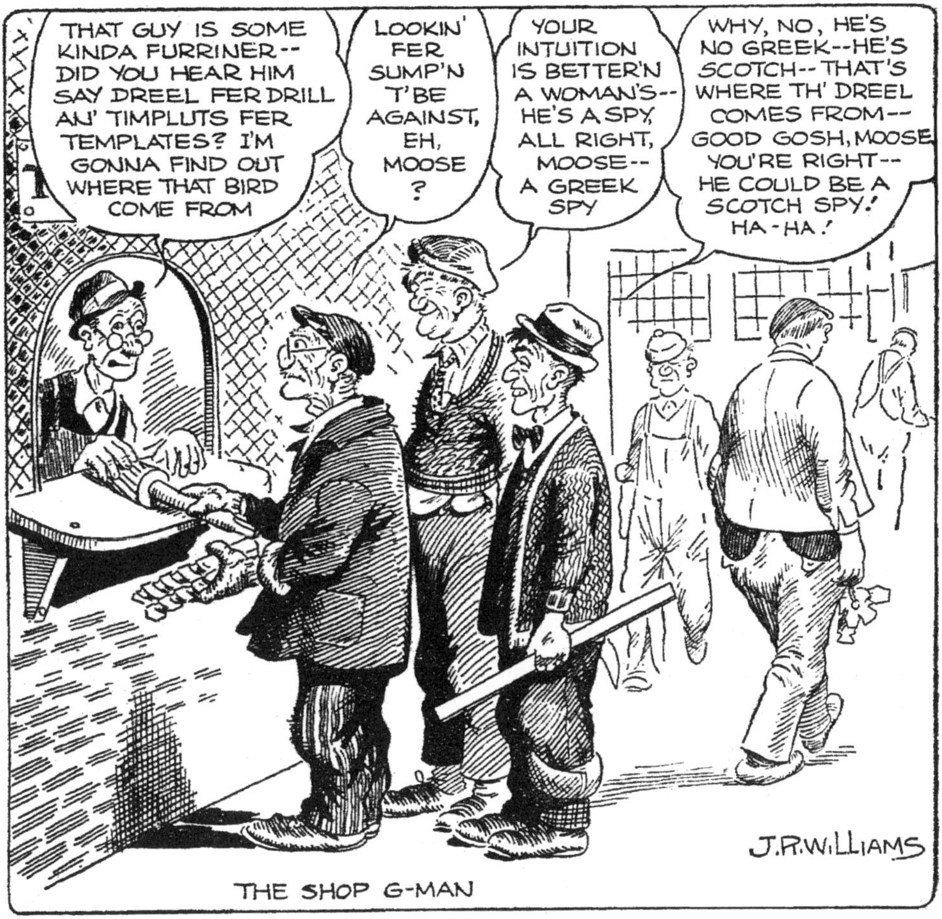
THAT GUY IS SOME KINDA FURRINER-- DID YOU HEAR HIM SAY DREEL FER DRILL AN' TIMPLUTS FER TEMPLATES? I'M GONNA FIND OUT WHERE THAT BIRD COME FROM
LOOKIN' FER SUMP'N T'BE AGAINST, EH, MOOSE ?
YOUR INTUITION IS BETTER'N A WOMAN'S-- HE'S A SPY, ALL RIGHT, MOOSE-- A GREEK SPY
WHY, NO, HE'S NO GREEK--HE'S SCOTCH-- THAT'S WHERE TH' DREEL COMES FROM-- GOOD GOSH, MOOSE YOU'RE RIGHT-- HE COULD BE A SCOTCH SPY! HA-HA!
J.R.WILLIAMS
THE SHOP G-MAN

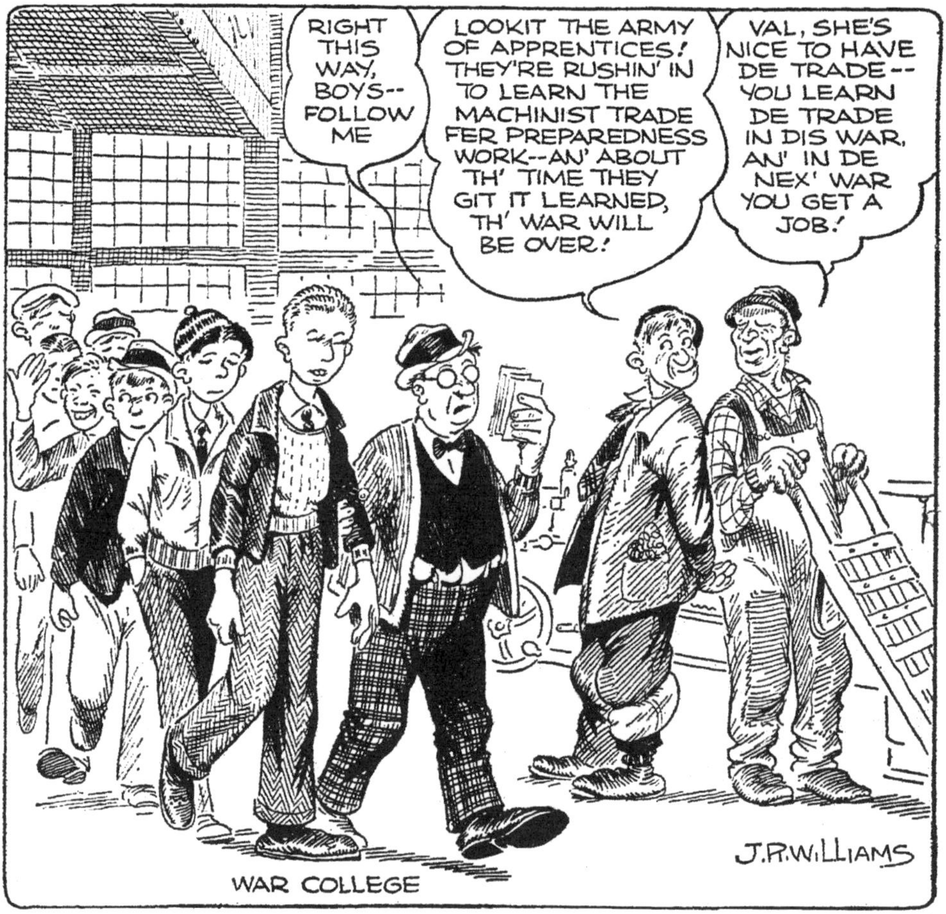
RIGHT THIS WAY, BOYS-- FOLLOW ME
LOOKIT THE ARMY OF APPRENTICES! THEY'RE RUSHIN' IN TO LEARN THE MACHINIST TRADE FER PREPAREDNESS WORK--AN' ABOUT TH' TIME THEY GIT IT LEARNED, TH' WAR WILL BE OVER!
VAL, SHE'S NICE TO HAVE DE TRADE-- YOU LEARN DE TRADE IN DIS WAR, AN' IN DE NEX' WAR YOU GET A JOB!
J.R.WILLIAMS
WAR COLLEGE

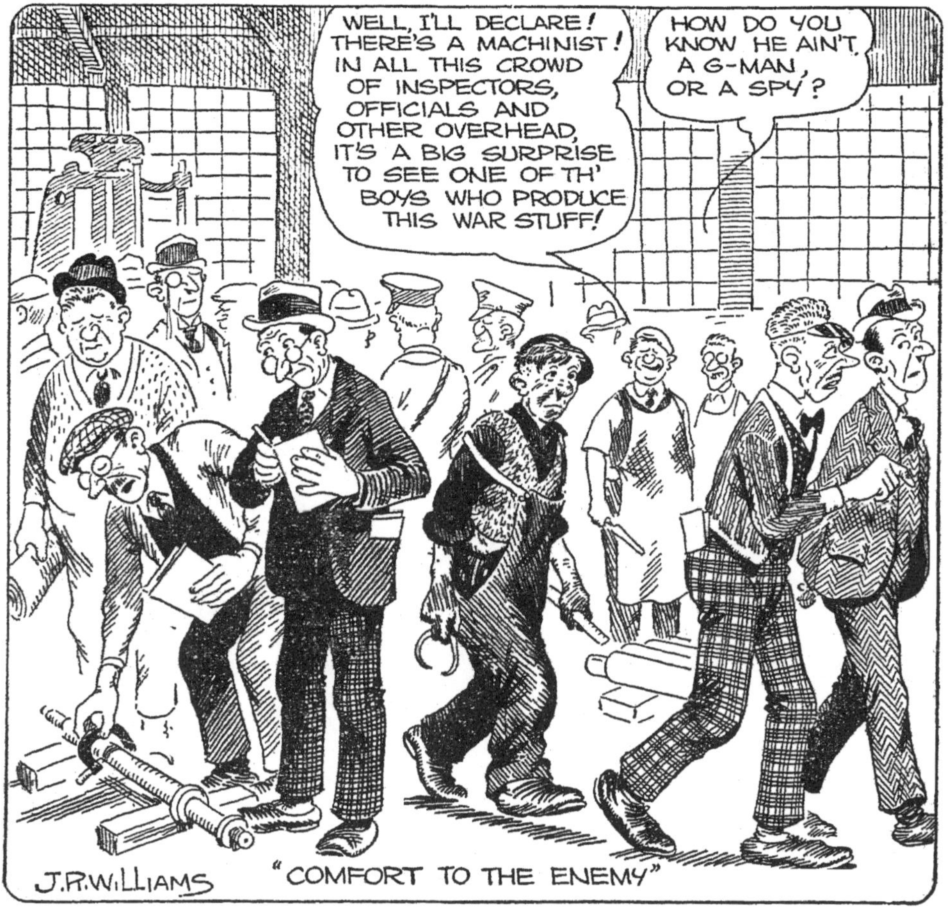
WELL, I'LL DECLARE! THERE'S A MACHINIST! IN ALL THIS CROWD OF INSPECTORS, OFFICIALS AND OTHER OVERHEAD, IT'S A BIG SURPRISE TO SEE ONE OF TH' BOYS WHO PRODUCE THIS WAR STUFF!
HOW DO YOU KNOW HE AIN'T A G-MAN, OR A SPY?
J.R.WILLIAMS
"COMFORT TO THE ENEMY"

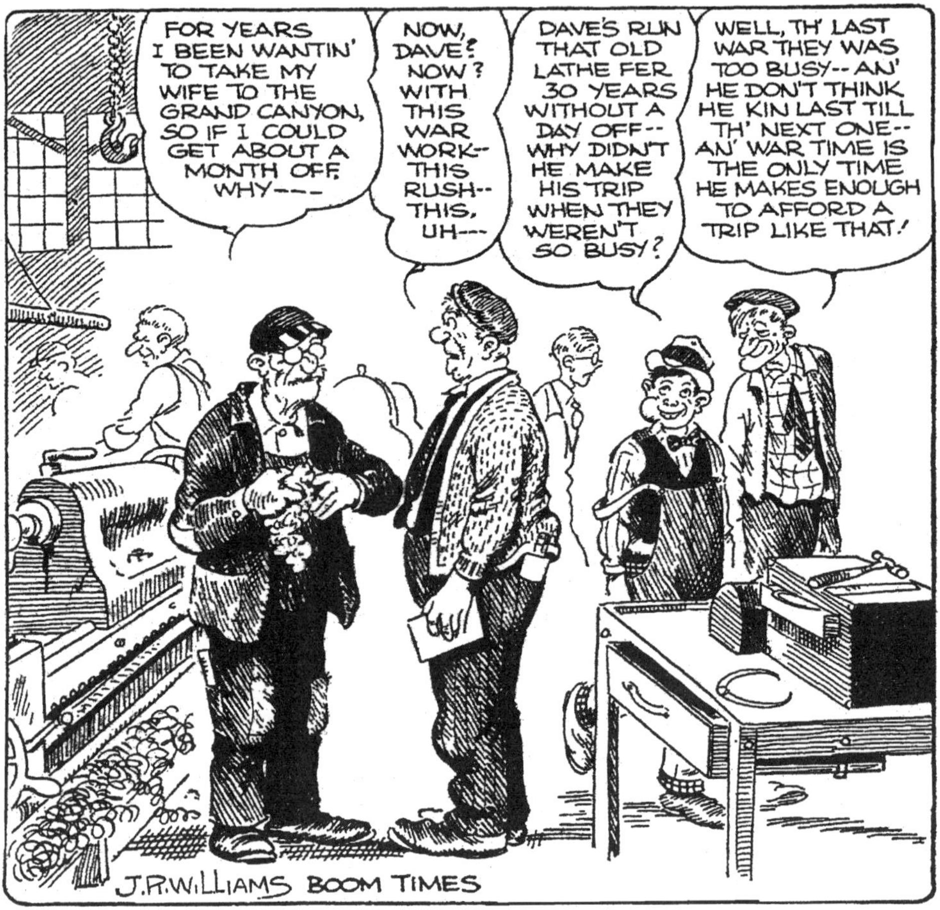
FOR YEARS I BEEN WANTIN' TO TAKE MY WIFE TO THE GRAND CANYON, SO IF I COULD GET ABOUT A MONTH OFF, WHY---
NOW, DAVE? NOW? WITH THIS WAR WORK-- THIS RUSH-- THIS, UH---
DAVE'S RUN THAT OLD LATHE FER 30 YEARS WITHOUT A DAY OFF-- WHY DIDN'T HE MAKE HIS TRIP WHEN THEY WEREN'T SO BUSY?
WELL, TH' LAST WAR THEY WAS TOO BUSY-- AN' HE DON'T THINK HE KIN LAST TILL TH' NEXT ONE-- AN' WAR TIME IS THE ONLY TIME HE MAKES ENOUGH TO AFFORD A TRIP LIKE THAT!
J.R. WILLIAMS BOOM TIMES

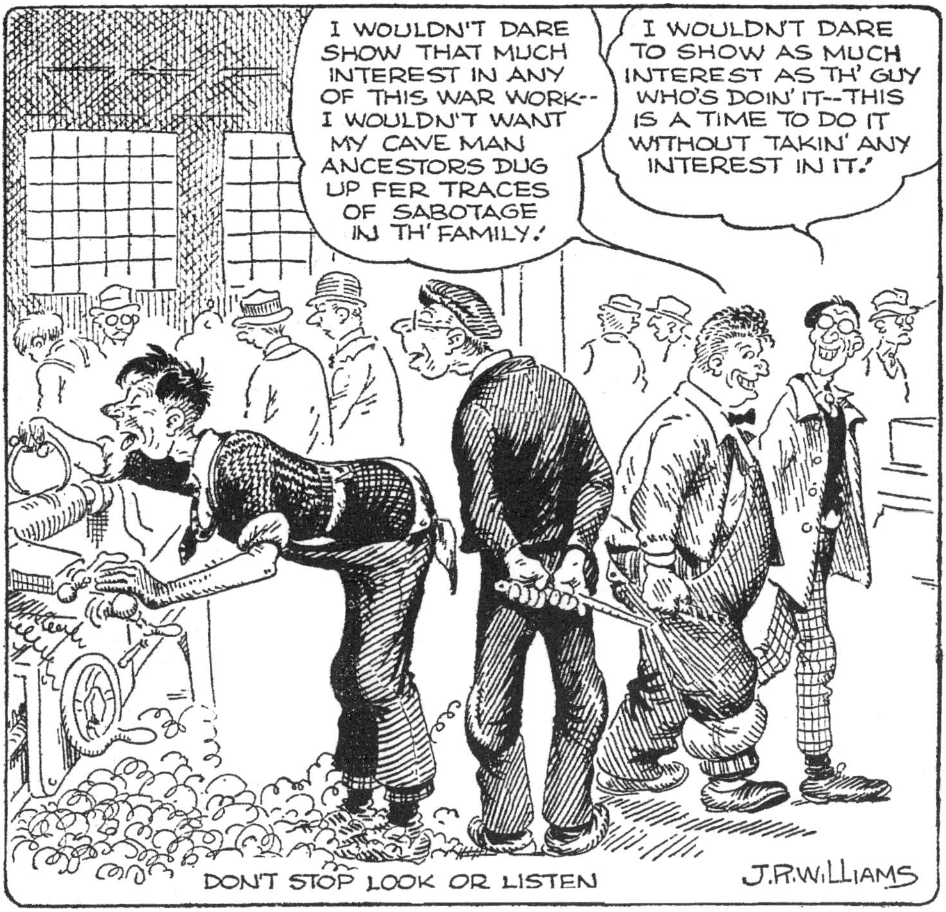
I WOULDN'T DARE SHOW THAT MUCH INTEREST IN ANY OF THIS WAR WORK-- I WOULDN'T WANT MY CAVE MAN ANCESTORS DUG UP FER TRACES OF SABOTAGE IN TH' FAMILY!
I WOULDN'T DARE TO SHOW AS MUCH INTEREST AS TH' GUY WHO'S DOIN' IT--THIS IS A TIME TO DO IT WITHOUT TAKIN' ANY INTEREST IN IT!
DON'T STOP LOOK OR LISTEN
J.R.WILLIAMS

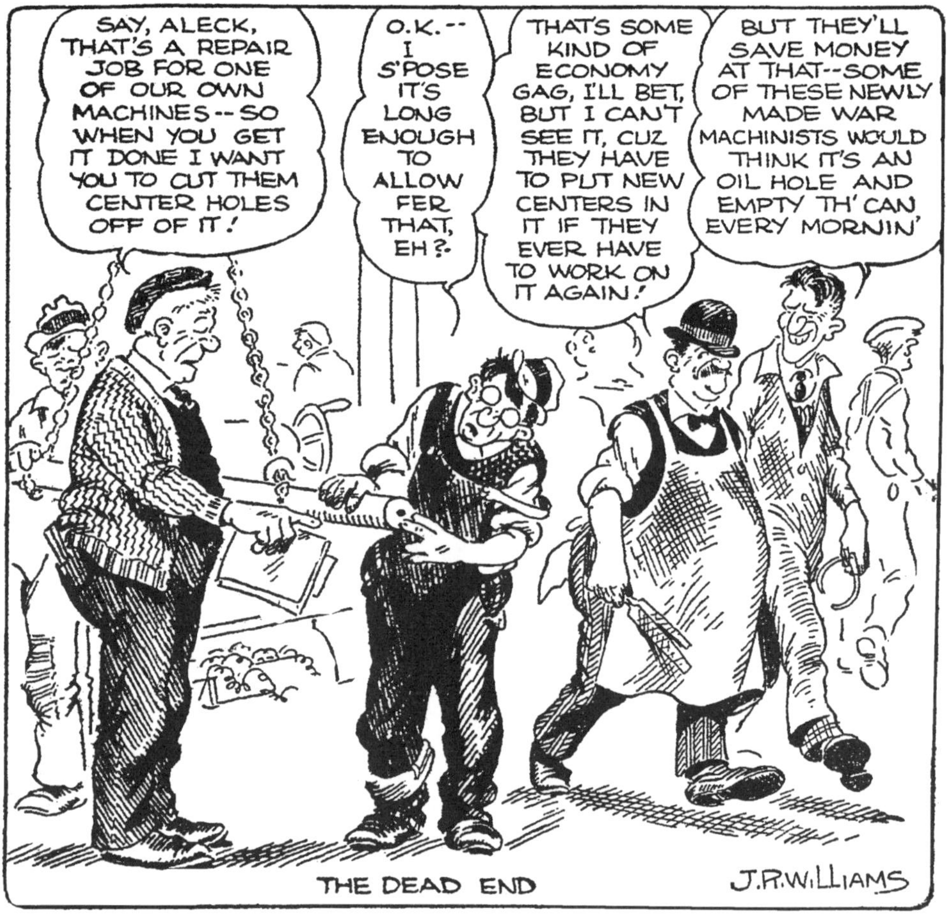
SAY, ALECK, THAT'S A REPAIR JOB FOR ONE OF OUR OWN MACHINES -- SO WHEN YOU GET IT DONE I WANT YOU TO CUT THEM CENTER HOLES OFF OF IT!
O.K. -- I S'POSE IT'S LONG ENOUGH TO ALLOW FER THAT, EH?-
THAT'S SOME KIND OF ECONOMY GAG, I'LL BET, BUT I CAN'T SEE IT, CUZ THEY HAVE TO PUT NEW CENTERS IN IT IF THEY EVER HAVE TO WORK ON IT AGAIN!
BUT THEY'LL SAVE MONEY AT THAT -- SOME OF THESE NEWLY MADE WAR MACHINISTS WOULD THINK IT'S AN OIL HOLE AND EMPTY TH' CAN EVERY MORNIN'
THE DEAD END
J.R.WILLIAMS

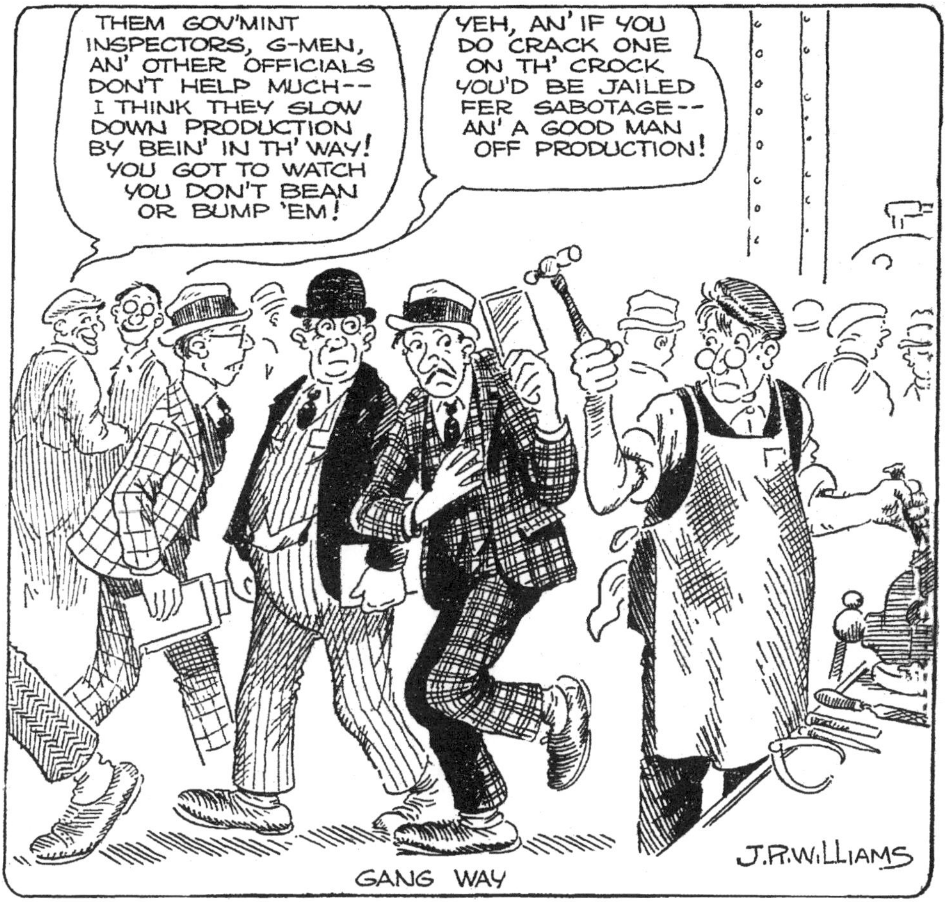
THEM GOV'MINT INSPECTORS, G-MEN, AN' OTHER OFFICIALS DON'T HELP MUCH-- I THINK THEY SLOW DOWN PRODUCTION BY BEIN' IN TH' WAY! YOU GOT TO WATCH YOU DON'T BEAN OR BUMP 'EM!
YEH, AN' IF YOU DO CRACK ONE ON TH' CROCK YOU'D BE JAILED FER SABOTAGE-- AN' A GOOD MAN OFF PRODUCTION!
J.R.WILLIAMS

GANG WAY

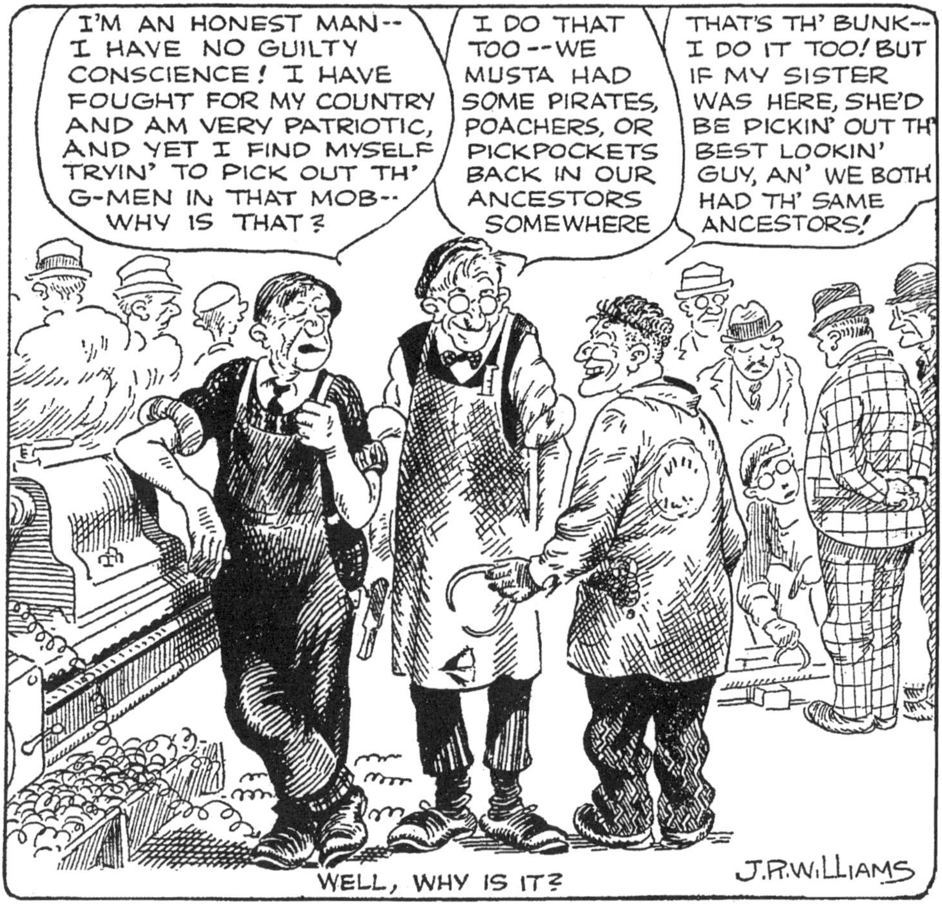
I'M AN HONEST MAN-- I HAVE NO GUILTY CONSCIENCE! I HAVE FOUGHT FOR MY COUNTRY AND AM VERY PATRIOTIC, AND YET I FIND MYSELF TRYIN' TO PICK OUT TH' G-MEN IN THAT MOB-- WHY IS THAT?
I DO THAT TOO--WE MUSTA HAD SOME PIRATES, POACHERS, OR PICKPOCKETS BACK IN OUR ANCESTORS SOMEWHERE
THAT'S TH' BUNK-- I DO IT TOO! BUT IF MY SISTER WAS HERE, SHE'D BE PICKIN' OUT TH' BEST LOOKIN' GUY, AN' WE BOTH HAD TH' SAME ANCESTORS!
WELL, WHY IS IT?
J.R.WILLIAMS

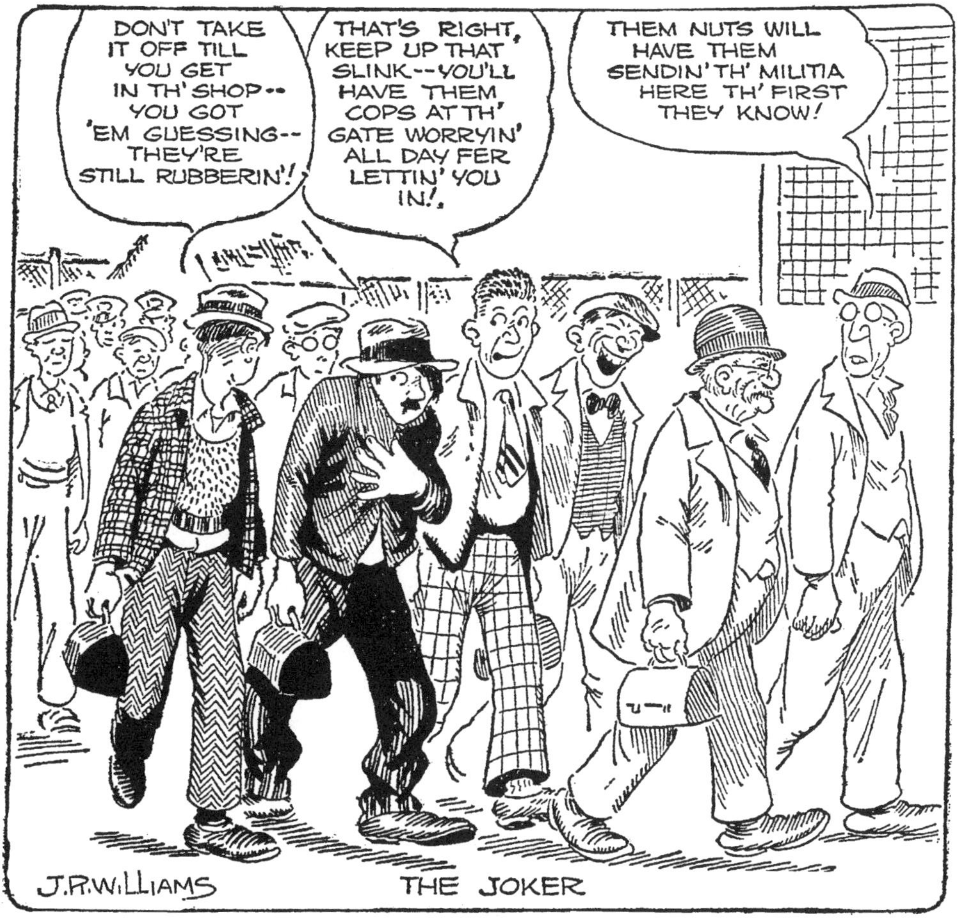
DON'T TAKE IT OFF TILL YOU GET IN TH' SHOP -- YOU GOT 'EM GUESSING -- THEY'RE STILL RUBBERIN'!
THAT'S RIGHT, KEEP UP THAT SLINK -- YOU'LL HAVE THEM COPS AT TH' GATE WORRYIN' ALL DAY FER LETTIN' YOU IN!
THEM NUTS WILL HAVE THEM SENDIN' TH' MILITIA HERE TH' FIRST THEY KNOW!
J.R.WILLIAMS
THE JOKER

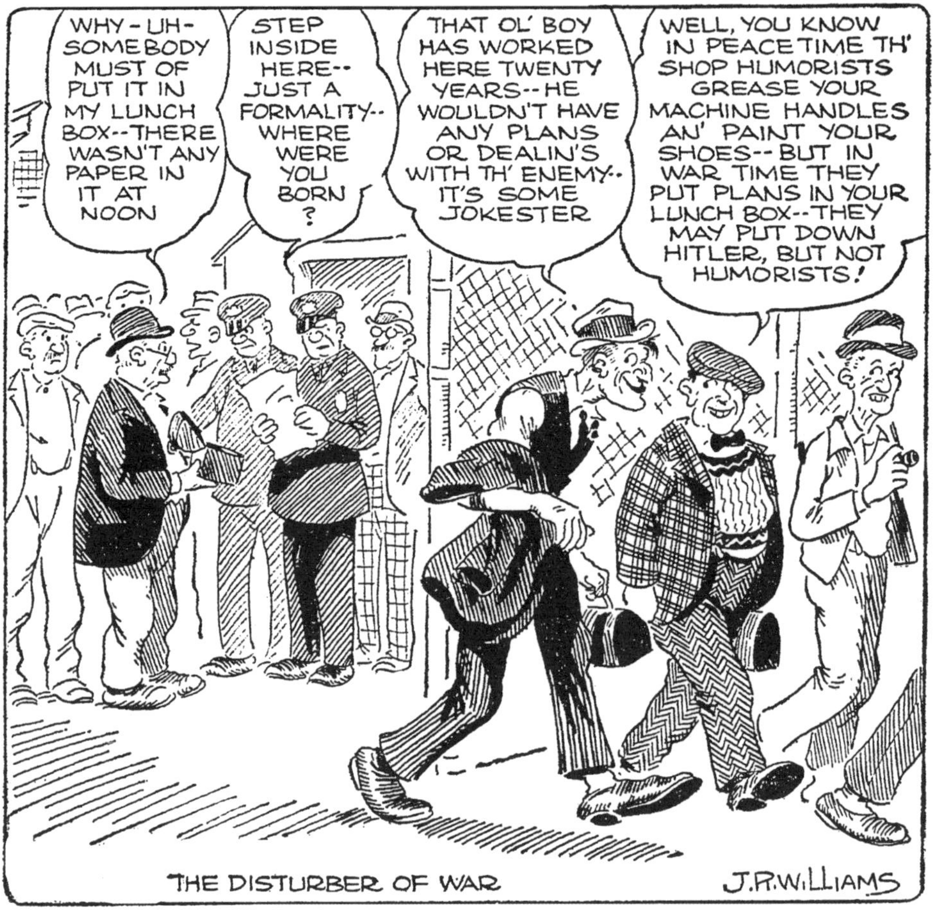
WHY - UH - SOMEBODY MUST OF PUT IT IN MY LUNCH BOX--THERE WASN'T ANY PAPER IN IT AT NOON
STEP INSIDE HERE--JUST A FORMALITY--WHERE WERE YOU BORN ?
THAT OL' BOY HAS WORKED HERE TWENTY YEARS--HE WOULDN'T HAVE ANY PLANS OR DEALIN'S WITH TH' ENEMY--IT'S SOME JOKESTER
WELL, YOU KNOW IN PEACE TIME TH' SHOP HUMORISTS GREASE YOUR MACHINE HANDLES AN' PAINT YOUR SHOES--BUT IN WAR TIME THEY PUT PLANS IN YOUR LUNCH BOX--THEY MAY PUT DOWN HITLER, BUT NOT HUMORISTS!
THE DISTURBER OF WAR
J.R.WILLIAMS

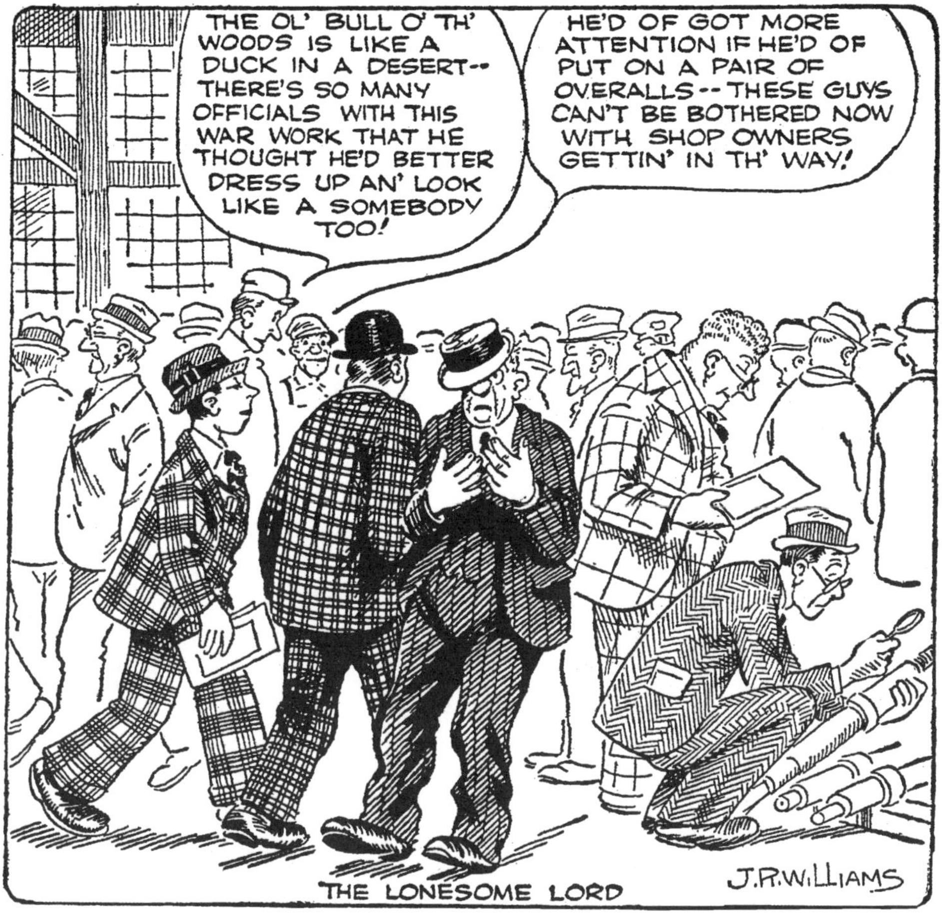
THE OL' BULL O' TH' WOODS IS LIKE A DUCK IN A DESERT-- THERE'S SO MANY OFFICIALS WITH THIS WAR WORK THAT HE THOUGHT HE'D BETTER DRESS UP AN' LOOK LIKE A SOMEBODY TOO!
HE'D OF GOT MORE ATTENTION IF HE'D OF PUT ON A PAIR OF OVERALLS -- THESE GUYS CAN'T BE BOTHERED NOW WITH SHOP OWNERS GETTIN' IN TH' WAY!
THE LONESOME LORD
J.R.WILLIAMS

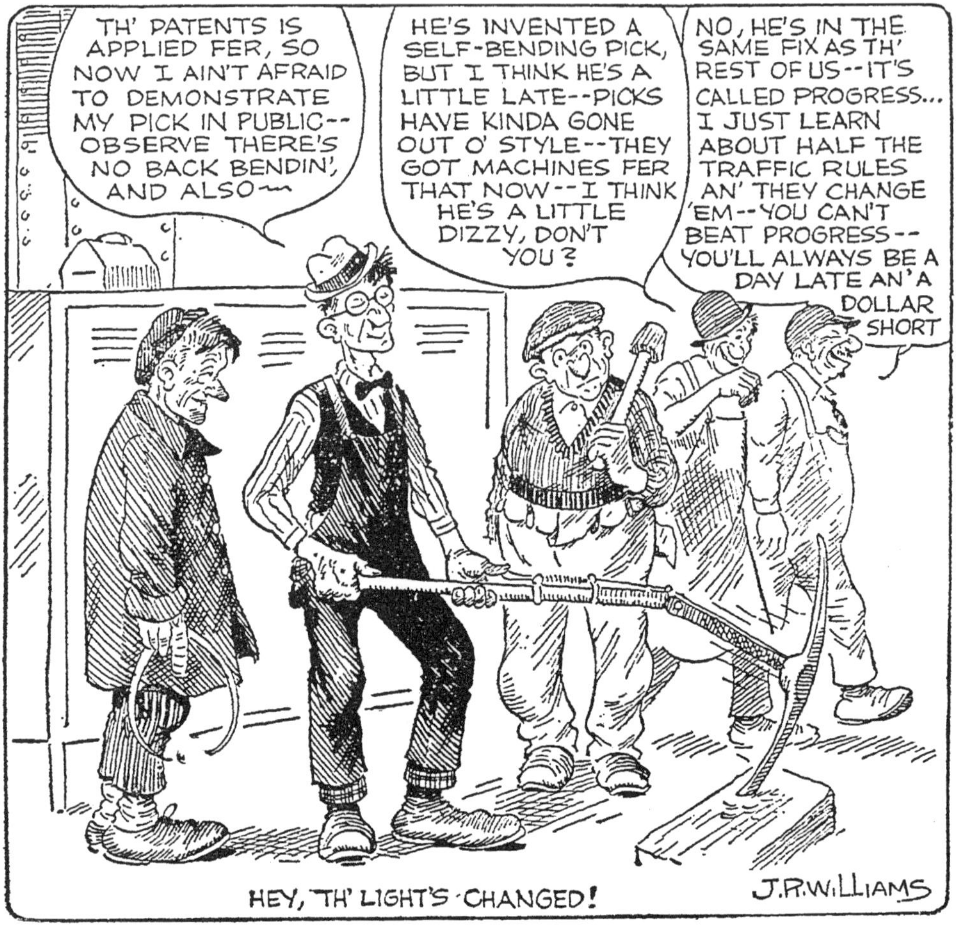
TH' PATENTS IS APPLIED FER, SO NOW I AIN'T AFRAID TO DEMONSTRATE MY PICK IN PUBLIC-- OBSERVE THERE'S NO BACK BENDIN', AND ALSO--
HE'S INVENTED A SELF-BENDING PICK, BUT I THINK HE'S A LITTLE LATE--PICKS HAVE KINDA GONE OUT O' STYLE--THEY GOT MACHINES FER THAT NOW--I THINK HE'S A LITTLE DIZZY, DON'T YOU?
NO, HE'S IN THE SAME FIX AS TH' REST OF US--IT'S CALLED PROGRESS... I JUST LEARN ABOUT HALF THE TRAFFIC RULES AN' THEY CHANGE 'EM--YOU CAN'T BEAT PROGRESS--YOU'LL ALWAYS BE A DAY LATE AN' A DOLLAR SHORT
HEY, TH' LIGHT'S CHANGED!
J.R.WILLIAMS

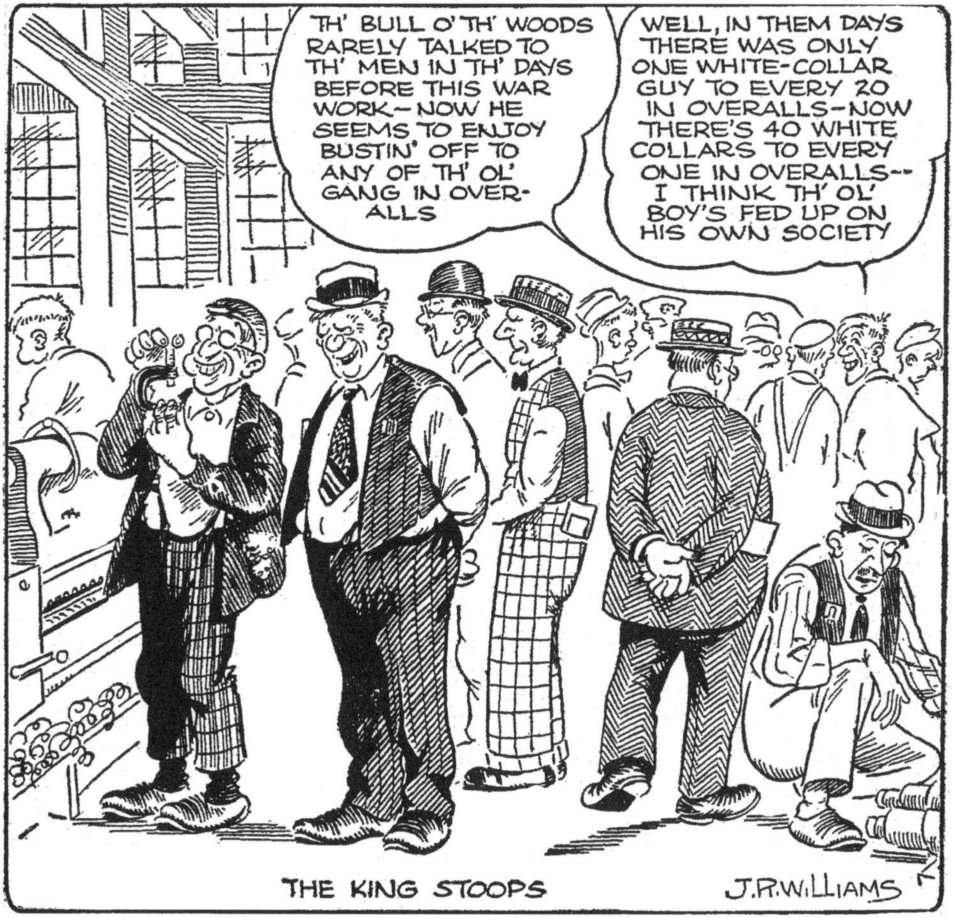
TH' BULL O'TH' WOODS RARELY TALKED TO TH' MEN IN TH' DAYS BEFORE THIS WAR WORK—NOW HE SEEMS TO ENJOY BUSTIN' OFF TO ANY OF TH' OL' GANG IN OVER-ALLS
WELL, IN THEM DAYS THERE WAS ONLY ONE WHITE-COLLAR GUY TO EVERY 20 IN OVERALLS—NOW THERE'S 40 WHITE COLLARS TO EVERY ONE IN OVERALLS-- I THINK TH' OL' BOY'S FED UP ON HIS OWN SOCIETY
THE KING STOOPS
J.R.WILLIAMS

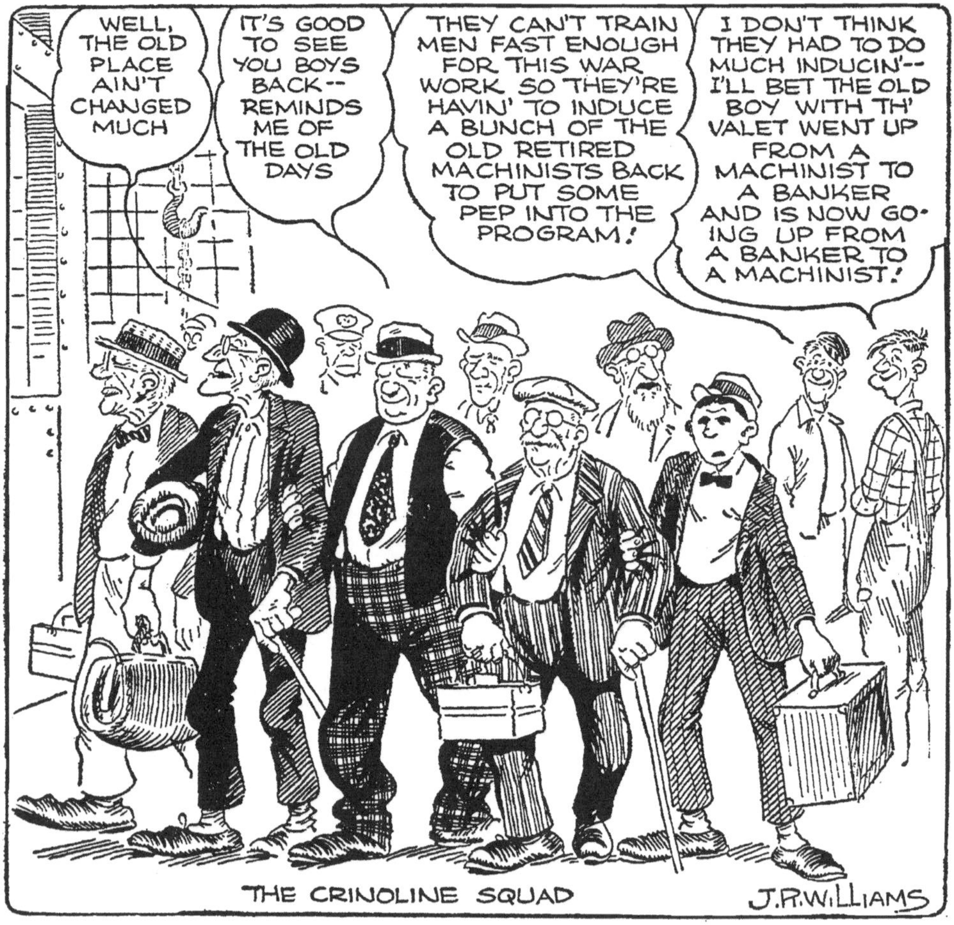
WELL, THE OLD PLACE AIN'T CHANGED MUCH
IT'S GOOD TO SEE YOU BOYS BACK-- REMINDS ME OF THE OLD DAYS
THEY CAN'T TRAIN MEN FAST ENOUGH FOR THIS WAR WORK SO THEY'RE HAVIN' TO INDUCE A BUNCH OF THE OLD RETIRED MACHINISTS BACK TO PUT SOME PEP INTO THE PROGRAM!
I DON'T THINK THEY HAD TO DO MUCH INDUCIN'-- I'LL BET THE OLD BOY WITH TH' VALET WENT UP FROM A MACHINIST TO A BANKER AND IS NOW GO-ING UP FROM A BANKER TO A MACHINIST!
THE CRINOLINE SQUAD
J.R.WILLIAMS

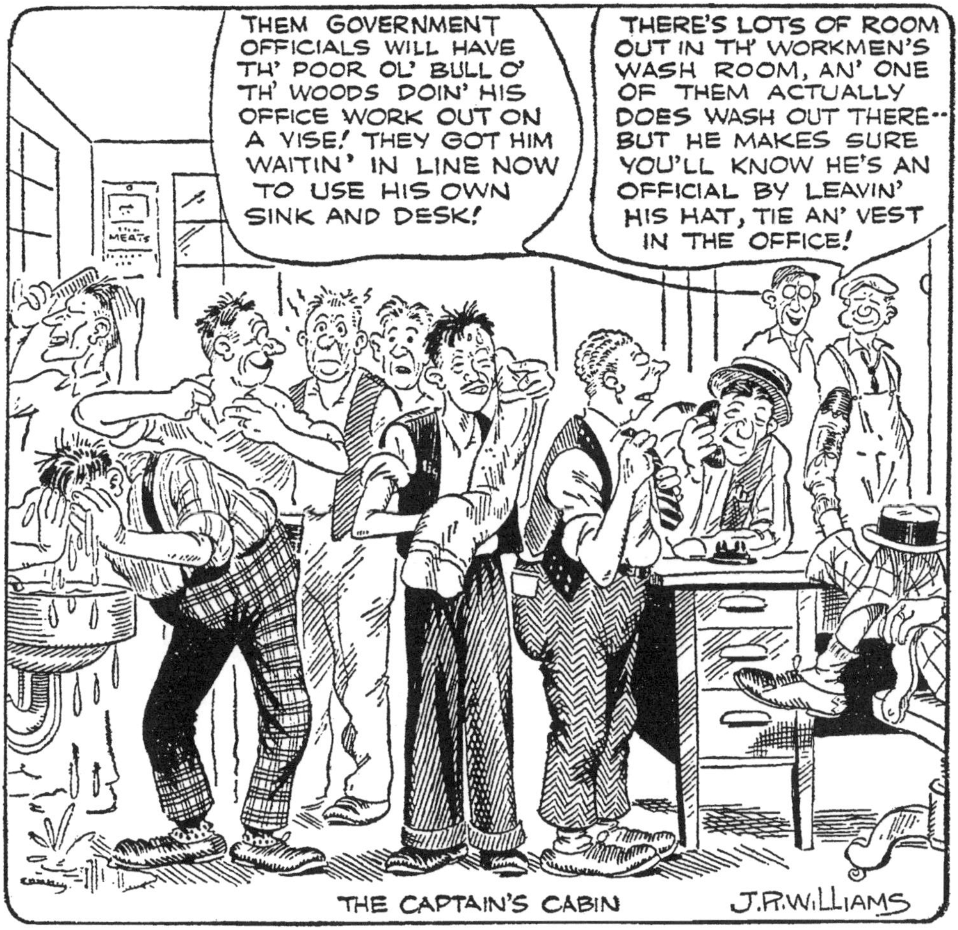
THEM GOVERNMENT OFFICIALS WILL HAVE TH' POOR OL' BULL O' TH' WOODS DOIN' HIS OFFICE WORK OUT ON A VISE! THEY GOT HIM WAITIN' IN LINE NOW TO USE HIS OWN SINK AND DESK!
THERE'S LOTS OF ROOM OUT IN TH' WORKMEN'S WASH ROOM, AN' ONE OF THEM ACTUALLY DOES WASH OUT THERE-- BUT HE MAKES SURE YOU'LL KNOW HE'S AN OFFICIAL BY LEAVIN' HIS HAT, TIE AN' VEST IN THE OFFICE!
MEATS
THE CAPTAIN'S CABIN
J.R.WILLIAMS

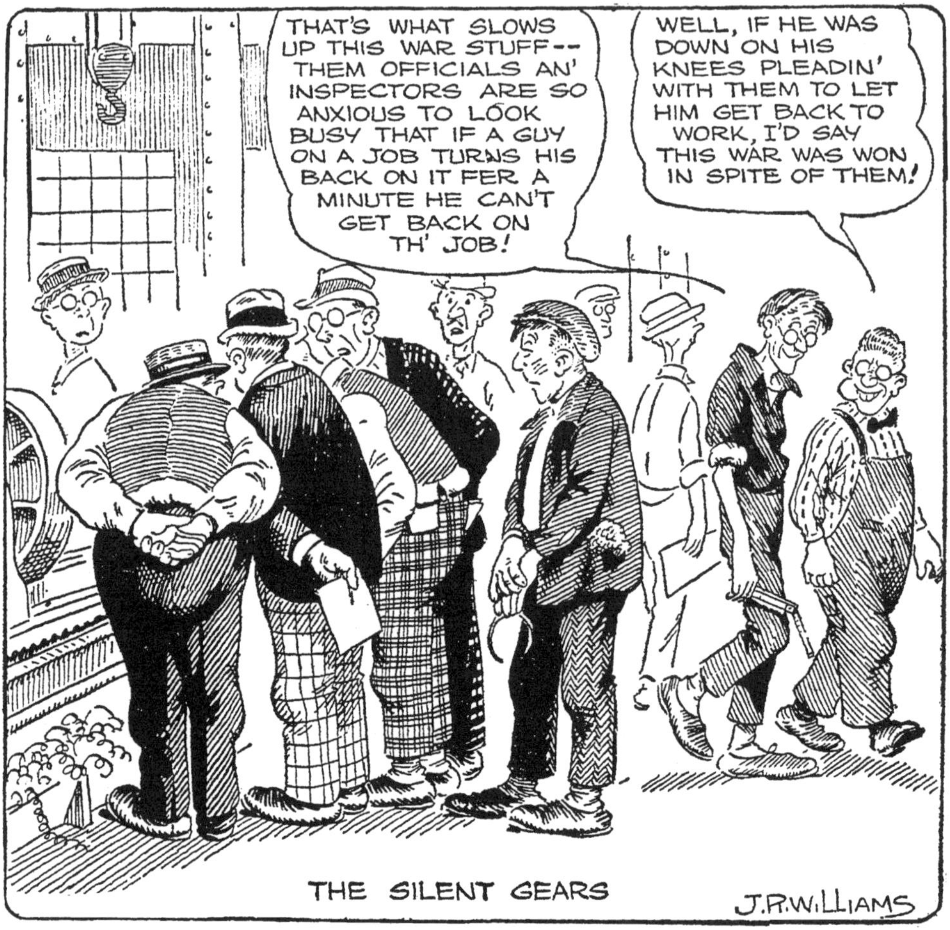
THAT'S WHAT SLOWS UP THIS WAR STUFF-- THEM OFFICIALS AN' INSPECTORS ARE SO ANXIOUS TO LOOK BUSY THAT IF A GUY ON A JOB TURNS HIS BACK ON IT FER A MINUTE HE CAN'T GET BACK ON TH' JOB!
WELL, IF HE WAS DOWN ON HIS KNEES PLEADIN' WITH THEM TO LET HIM GET BACK TO WORK, I'D SAY THIS WAR WAS WON IN SPITE OF THEM!
THE SILENT GEARS
J.R.WILLIAMS

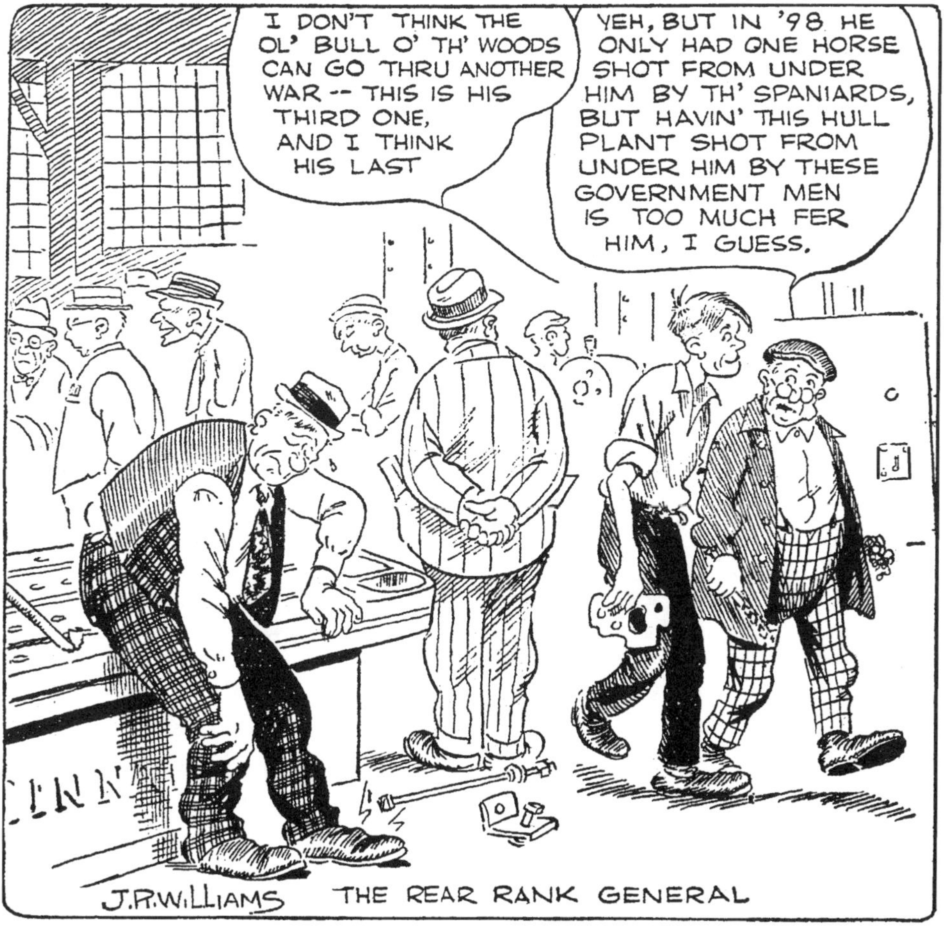
I DON'T THINK THE OL' BULL O' TH' WOODS CAN GO THRU ANOTHER WAR -- THIS IS HIS THIRD ONE, AND I THINK HIS LAST
YEH, BUT IN '98 HE ONLY HAD ONE HORSE SHOT FROM UNDER HIM BY TH' SPANIARDS, BUT HAVIN' THIS HULL PLANT SHOT FROM UNDER HIM BY THESE GOVERNMENT MEN IS TOO MUCH FER HIM, I GUESS.
J.R.WILLIAMS
THE REAR RANK GENERAL

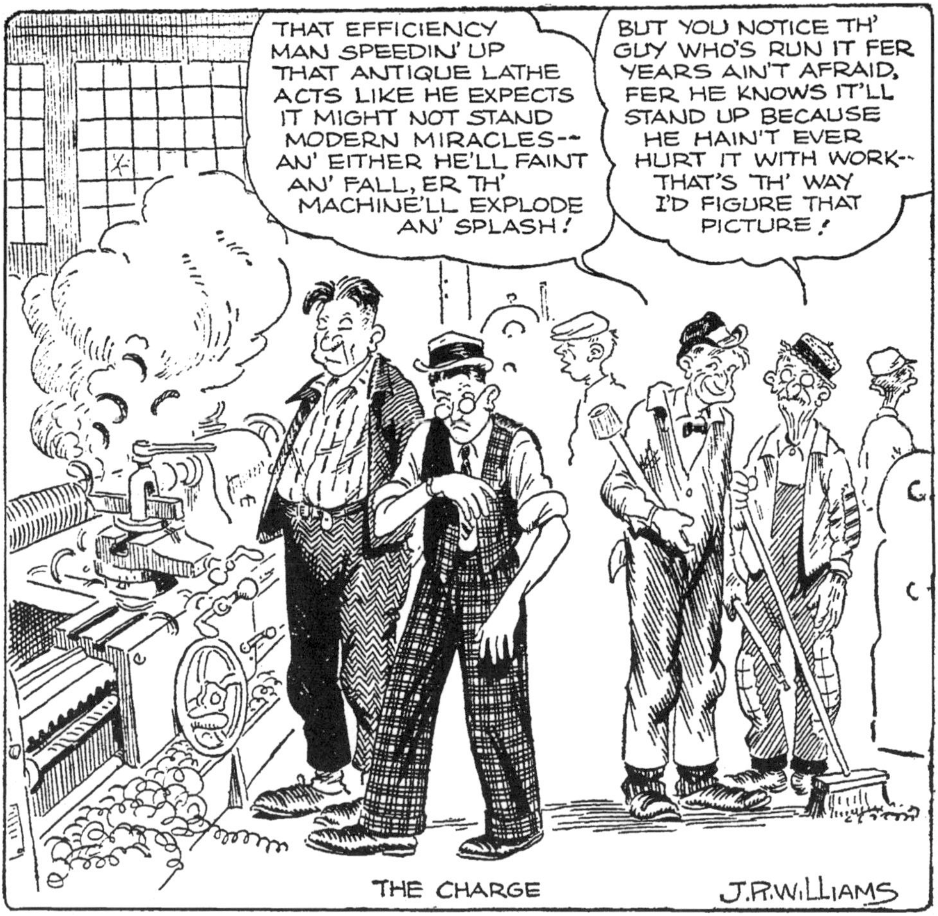
THAT EFFICIENCY MAN SPEEDIN' UP THAT ANTIQUE LATHE ACTS LIKE HE EXPECTS IT MIGHT NOT STAND MODERN MIRACLES-- AN' EITHER HE'LL FAINT AN' FALL, ER TH' MACHINE'LL EXPLODE AN' SPLASH!
BUT YOU NOTICE TH' GUY WHO'S RUN IT FER YEARS AIN'T AFRAID, FER HE KNOWS IT'LL STAND UP BECAUSE HE HAIN'T EVER HURT IT WITH WORK-- THAT'S TH' WAY I'D FIGURE THAT PICTURE!
THE CHARGE
J.R.WILLIAMS

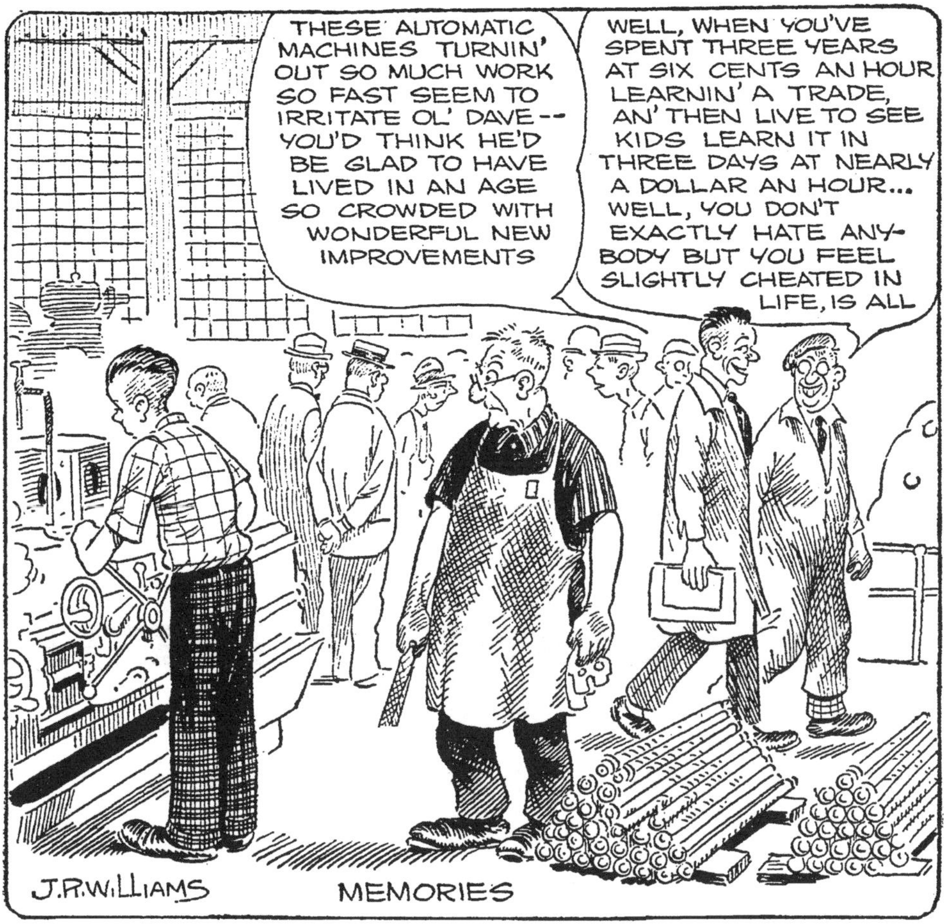
THESE AUTOMATIC MACHINES TURNIN' OUT SO MUCH WORK SO FAST SEEM TO IRRITATE OL' DAVE-- YOU'D THINK HE'D BE GLAD TO HAVE LIVED IN AN AGE SO CROWDED WITH WONDERFUL NEW IMPROVEMENTS
WELL, WHEN YOU'VE SPENT THREE YEARS AT SIX CENTS AN HOUR LEARNIN' A TRADE, AN' THEN LIVE TO SEE KIDS LEARN IT IN THREE DAYS AT NEARLY A DOLLAR AN HOUR... WELL, YOU DON'T EXACTLY HATE ANY-BODY BUT YOU FEEL SLIGHTLY CHEATED IN LIFE, IS ALL
J.R.WILLIAMS
MEMORIES

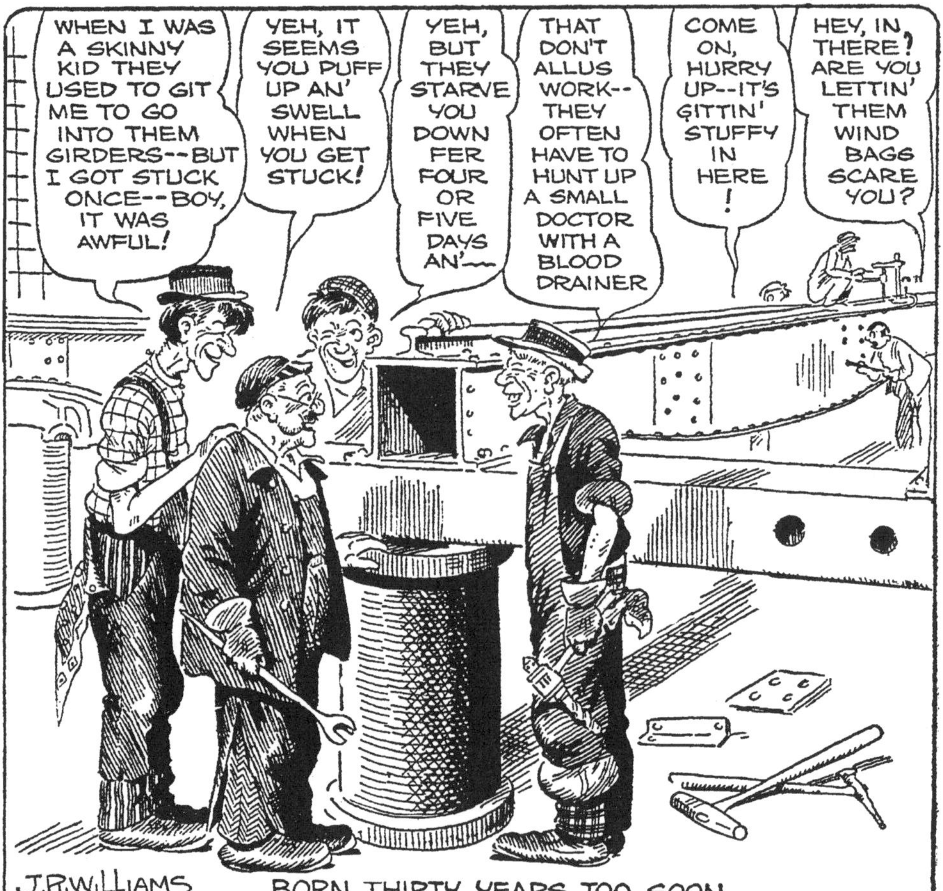
WHEN I WAS A SKINNY KID THEY USED TO GIT ME TO GO INTO THEM GIRDERS--BUT I GOT STUCK ONCE--BOY, IT WAS AWFUL!
YEH, IT SEEMS YOU PUFF UP AN' SWELL WHEN YOU GET STUCK!
YEH, BUT THEY STARVE YOU DOWN FER FOUR OR FIVE DAYS AN'—
THAT DON'T ALLUS WORK--THEY OFTEN HAVE TO HUNT UP A SMALL DOCTOR WITH A BLOOD DRAINER
COME ON, HURRY UP--IT'S GITTIN' STUFFY IN HERE!
HEY, IN, THERE! ARE YOU LETTIN' THEM WIND BAGS SCARE YOU?
J.R.WILLIAMS
BORN THIRTY YEARS TOO SOON

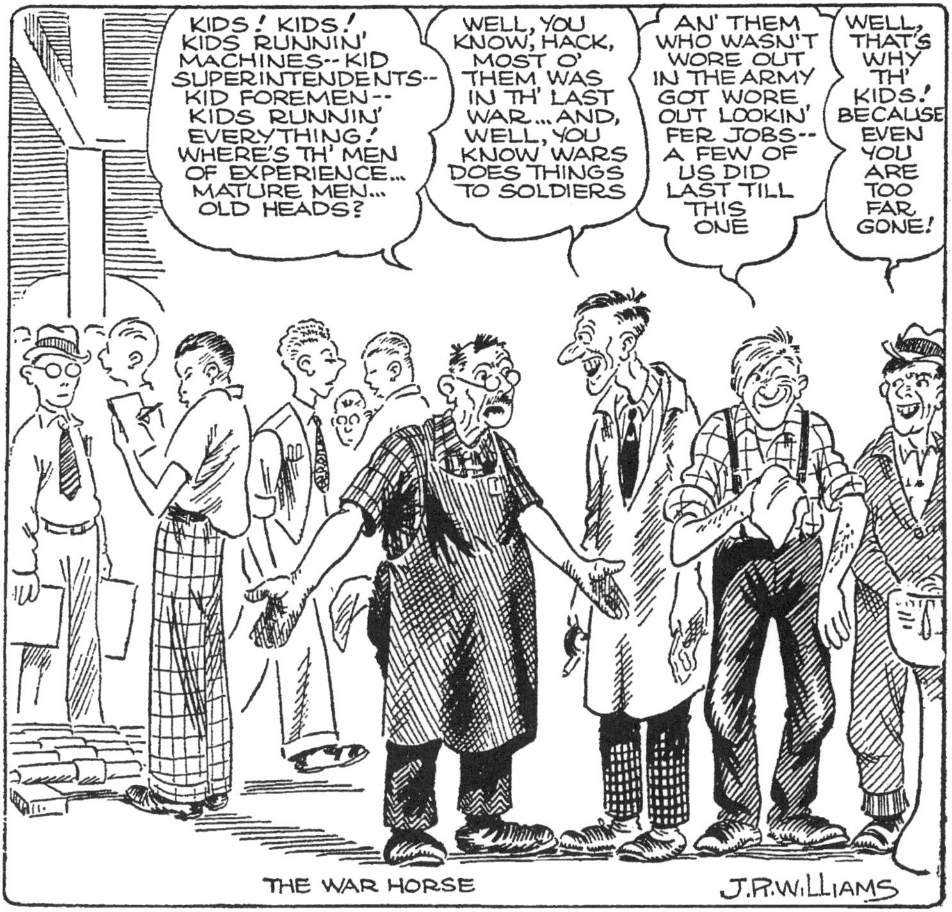
KIDS! KIDS! KIDS RUNNIN' MACHINES--KID SUPERINTENDENTS--KID FOREMEN--KIDS RUNNIN' EVERYTHING! WHERE'S TH' MEN OF EXPERIENCE... MATURE MEN... OLD HEADS?
WELL, YOU KNOW, HACK, MOST O' THEM WAS IN TH' LAST WAR... AND, WELL, YOU KNOW WARS DOES THINGS TO SOLDIERS
AN' THEM WHO WASN'T WORE OUT IN THE ARMY GOT WORE OUT LOOKIN' FER JOBS-- A FEW OF US DID LAST TILL THIS ONE
WELL, THAT'S WHY TH' KIDS! BECAUSE EVEN YOU ARE TOO FAR GONE!
THE WAR HORSE
J.R. WILLIAMS

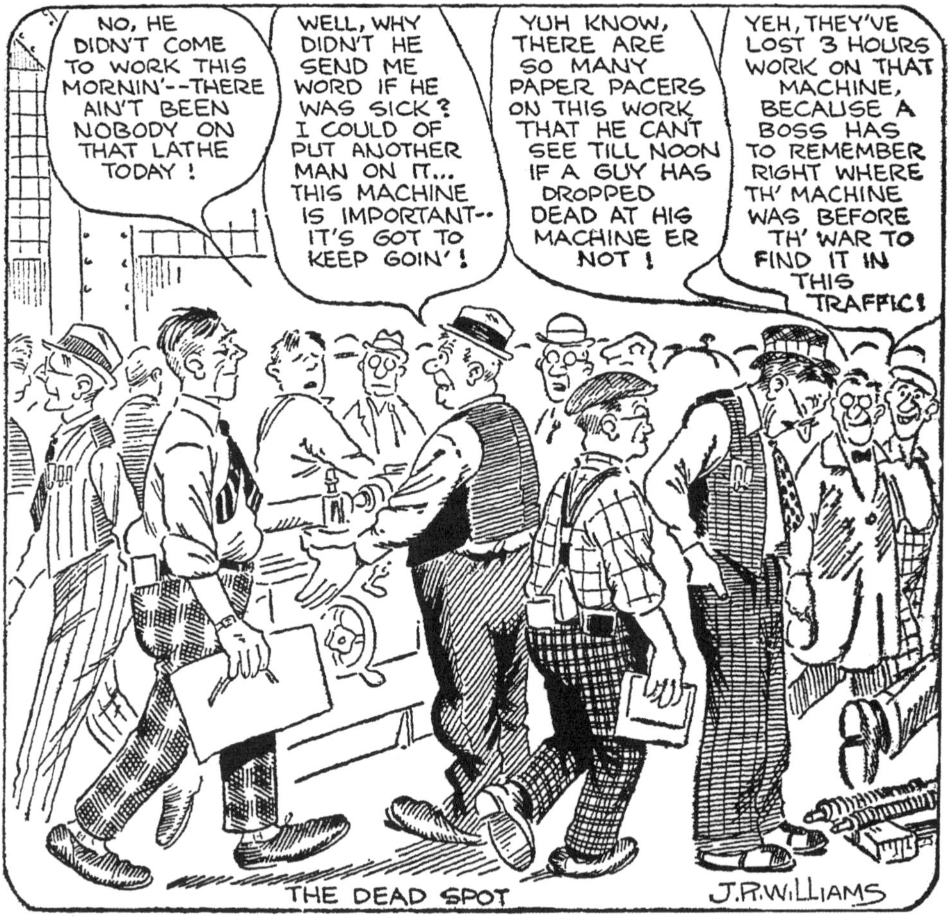
NO, HE DIDN'T COME TO WORK THIS MORNIN'--THERE AIN'T BEEN NOBODY ON THAT LATHE TODAY!
WELL, WHY DIDN'T HE SEND ME WORD IF HE WAS SICK? I COULD OF PUT ANOTHER MAN ON IT... THIS MACHINE IS IMPORTANT-- IT'S GOT TO KEEP GOIN'!
YUH KNOW, THERE ARE SO MANY PAPER PACERS ON THIS WORK THAT HE CAN'T SEE TILL NOON IF A GUY HAS DROPPED DEAD AT HIS MACHINE ER NOT!
YEH, THEY'VE LOST 3 HOURS WORK ON THAT MACHINE, BECAUSE A BOSS HAS TO REMEMBER RIGHT WHERE TH' MACHINE WAS BEFORE TH' WAR TO FIND IT IN THIS TRAFFIC!
THE DEAD SPOT
J.R. WILLIAMS

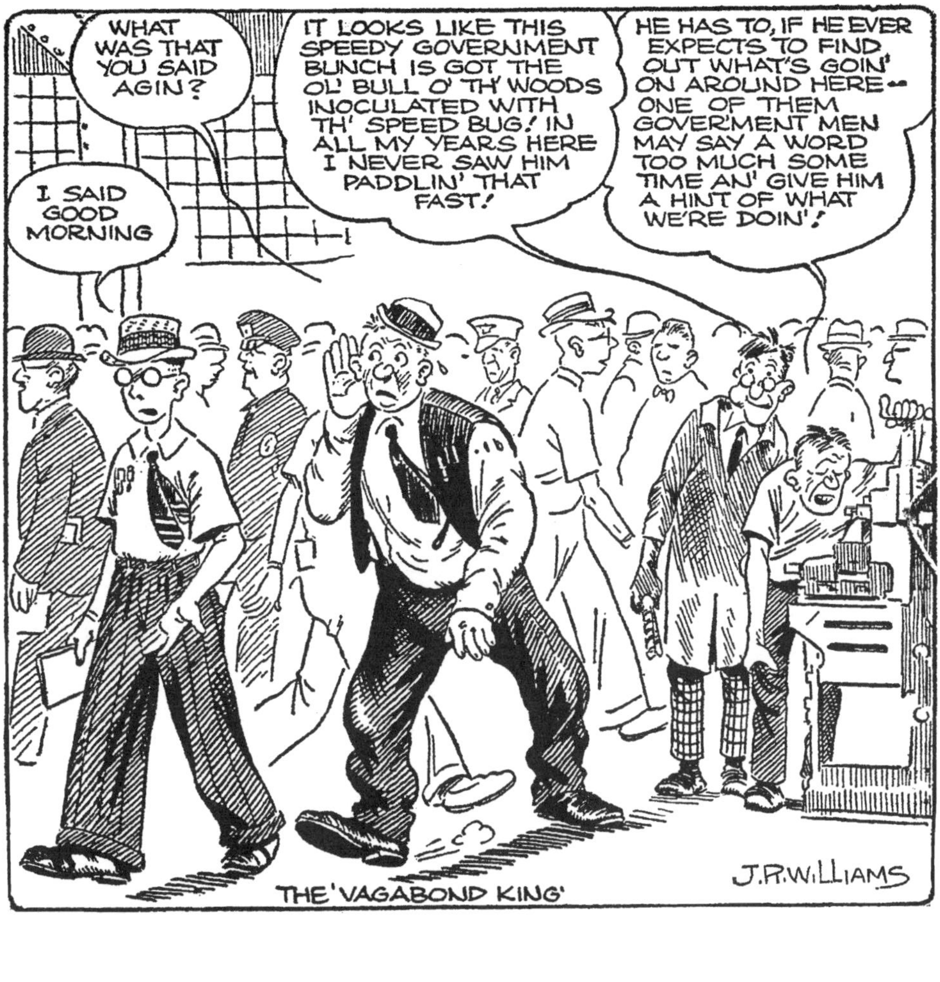
WHAT WAS THAT YOU SAID AGIN?
I SAID GOOD MORNING
IT LOOKS LIKE THIS SPEEDY GOVERNMENT BUNCH IS GOT THE OL' BULL O' TH' WOODS INOCULATED WITH TH' SPEED BUG! IN ALL MY YEARS HERE I NEVER SAW HIM PADDLIN' THAT FAST!
HE HAS TO, IF HE EVER EXPECTS TO FIND OUT WHAT'S GOIN' ON AROUND HERE-- ONE OF THEM GOVER'MENT MEN MAY SAY A WORD TOO MUCH SOME TIME AN' GIVE HIM A HINT OF WHAT WE'RE DOIN'!
THE 'VAGABOND KING'
J.R.WILLIAMS

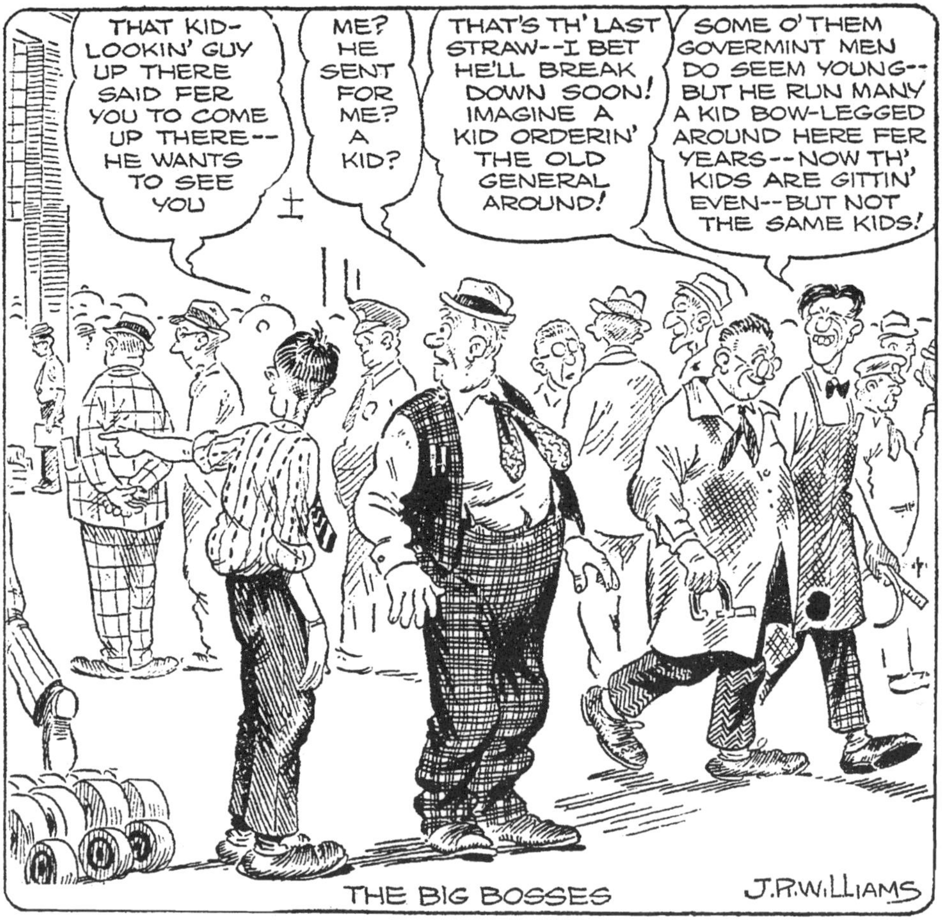
THAT KID-LOOKIN' GUY UP THERE SAID FER YOU TO COME UP THERE--HE WANTS TO SEE YOU
ME? HE SENT FOR ME? A KID?
THAT'S TH' LAST STRAW--I BET HE'LL BREAK DOWN SOON! IMAGINE A KID ORDERIN' THE OLD GENERAL AROUND!
SOME O'THEM GOVERMINT MEN DO SEEM YOUNG--BUT HE RUN MANY A KID BOW-LEGGED AROUND HERE FER YEARS--NOW TH' KIDS ARE GITTIN' EVEN--BUT NOT THE SAME KIDS!
THE BIG BOSSES
J.R.WILLIAMS

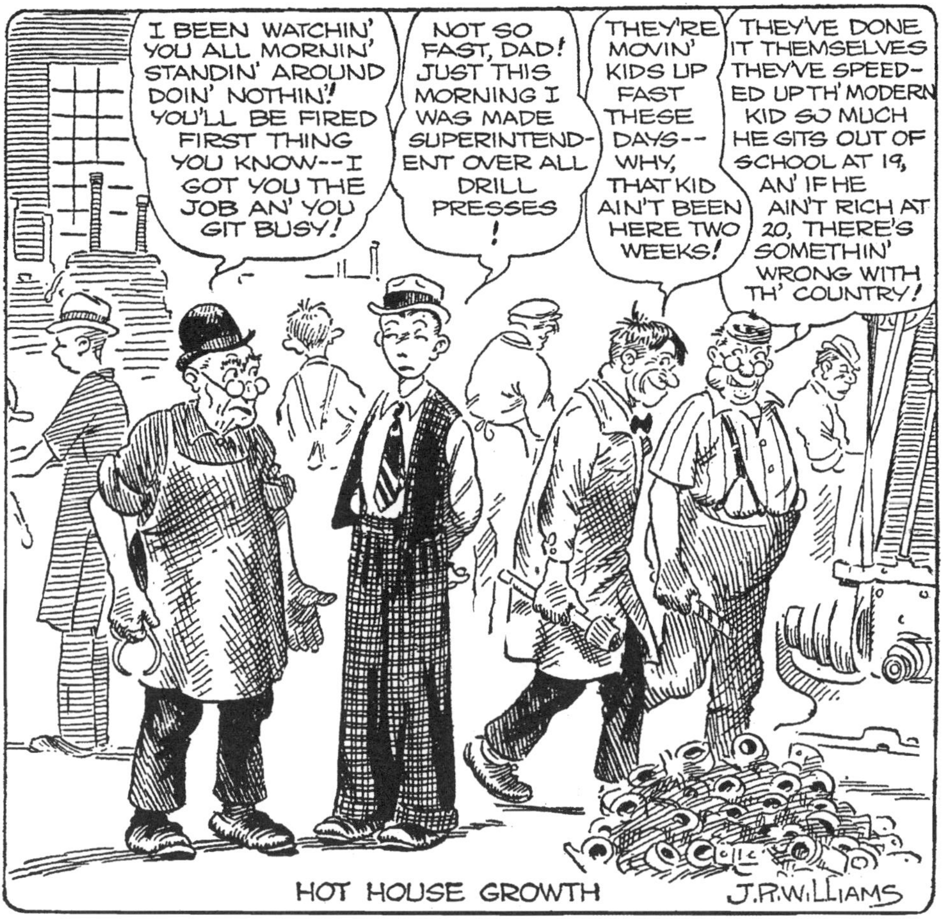
I BEEN WATCHIN' YOU ALL MORNIN' STANDIN' AROUND DOIN' NOTHIN'! YOU'LL BE FIRED FIRST THING YOU KNOW--I GOT YOU THE JOB AN' YOU GIT BUSY!
NOT SO FAST, DAD! JUST THIS MORNING I WAS MADE SUPERINTENDENT OVER ALL DRILL PRESSES!
THEY'RE MOVIN' KIDS UP FAST THESE DAYS--WHY, THAT KID AIN'T BEEN HERE TWO WEEKS!
THEY'VE DONE IT THEMSELVES THEY'VE SPEEDED UP TH' MODERN KID SO MUCH HE GITS OUT OF SCHOOL AT 19, AN' IF HE AIN'T RICH AT 20, THERE'S SOMETHIN' WRONG WITH TH' COUNTRY!
HOT HOUSE GROWTH
J.R.WILLIAMS

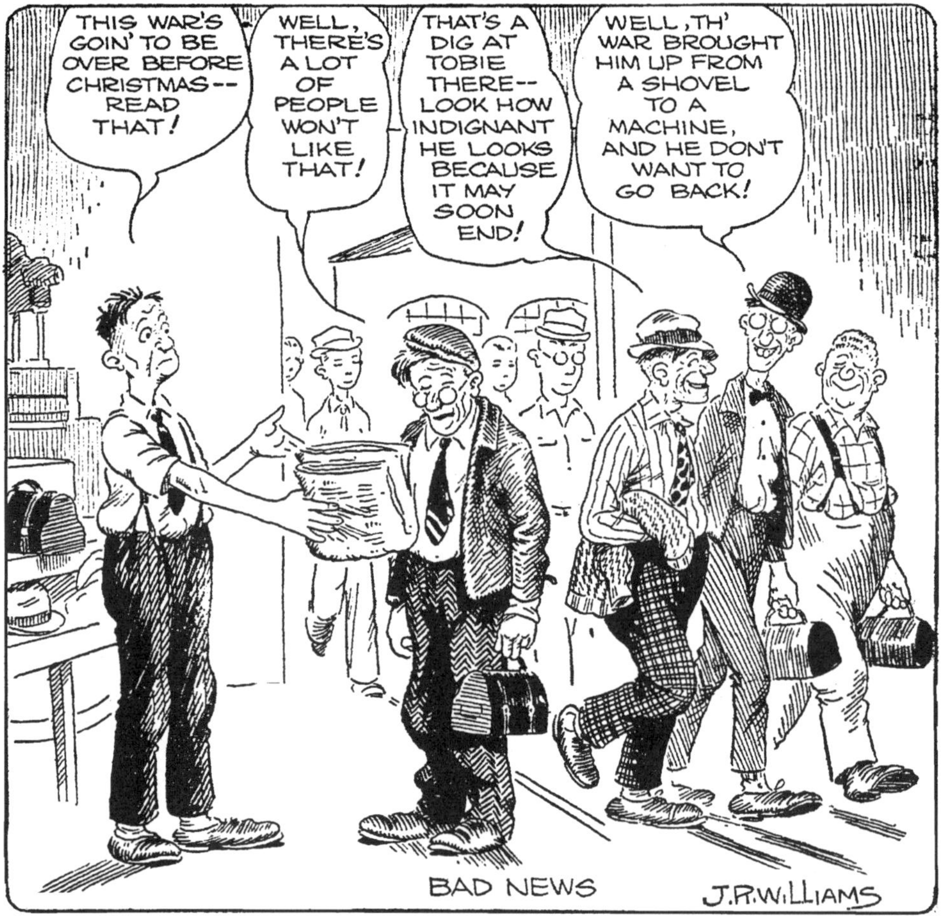
THIS WAR'S GOIN' TO BE OVER BEFORE CHRISTMAS-- READ THAT!
WELL, THERE'S A LOT OF PEOPLE WON'T LIKE THAT!
THAT'S A DIG AT TOBIE THERE-- LOOK HOW INDIGNANT HE LOOKS BECAUSE IT MAY SOON END!
WELL, TH' WAR BROUGHT HIM UP FROM A SHOVEL TO A MACHINE, AND HE DON'T WANT TO GO BACK!
BAD NEWS
J.R.WILLIAMS

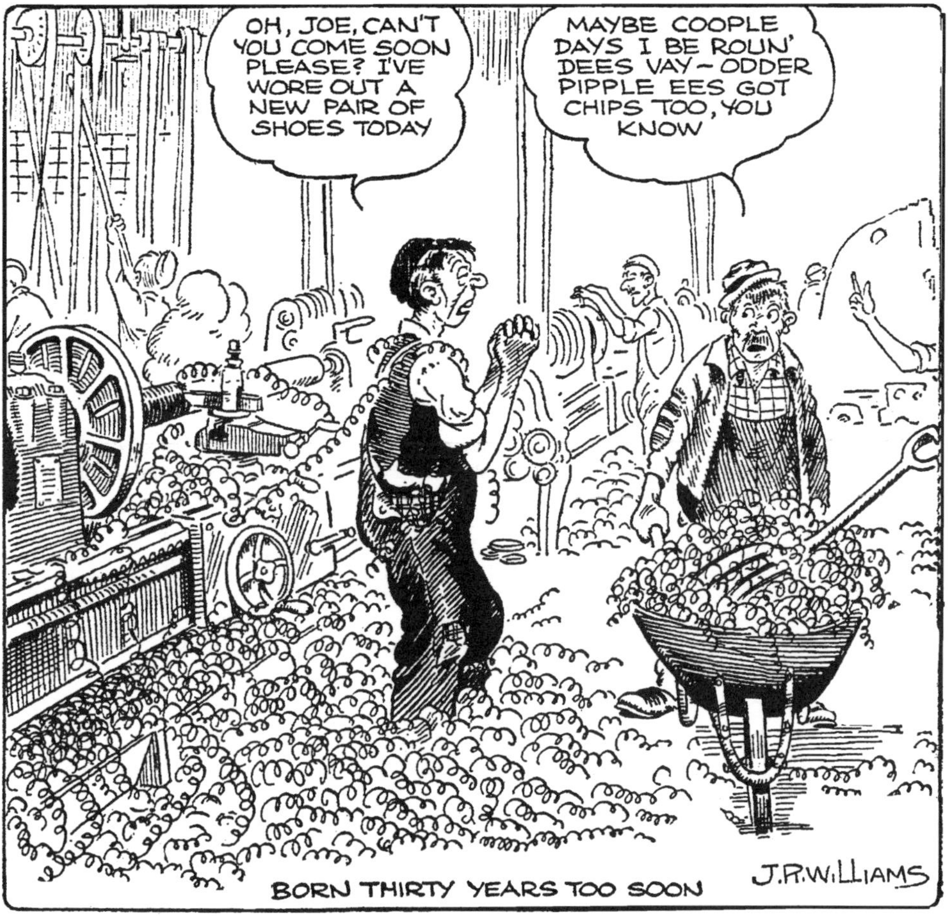
OH, JOE, CAN'T YOU COME SOON PLEASE? I'VE WORE OUT A NEW PAIR OF SHOES TODAY
MAYBE COOPLE DAYS I BE ROUN' DEES VAY – ODDER PIPPLE EES GOT CHIPS TOO, YOU KNOW
BORN THIRTY YEARS TOO SOON
J.R.WILLIAMS

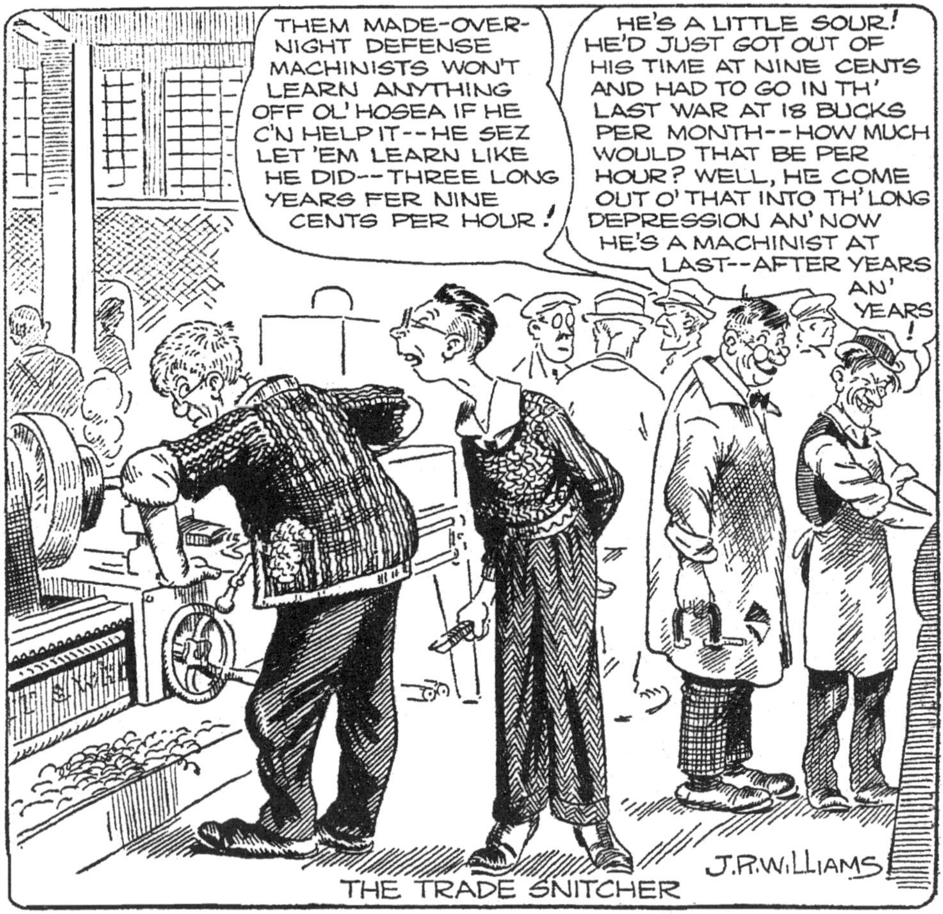
THEM MADE-OVER-NIGHT DEFENSE MACHINISTS WON'T LEARN ANYTHING OFF OL' HOSEA IF HE C'N HELP IT--HE SEZ LET 'EM LEARN LIKE HE DID--THREE LONG YEARS FER NINE CENTS PER HOUR!
HE'S A LITTLE SOUR! HE'D JUST GOT OUT OF HIS TIME AT NINE CENTS AND HAD TO GO IN TH' LAST WAR AT 18 BUCKS PER MONTH--HOW MUCH WOULD THAT BE PER HOUR? WELL, HE COME OUT O' THAT INTO TH' LONG DEPRESSION AN' NOW HE'S A MACHINIST AT LAST--AFTER YEARS AN' YEARS!
J.R.WILLIAMS
THE TRADE SNITCHER

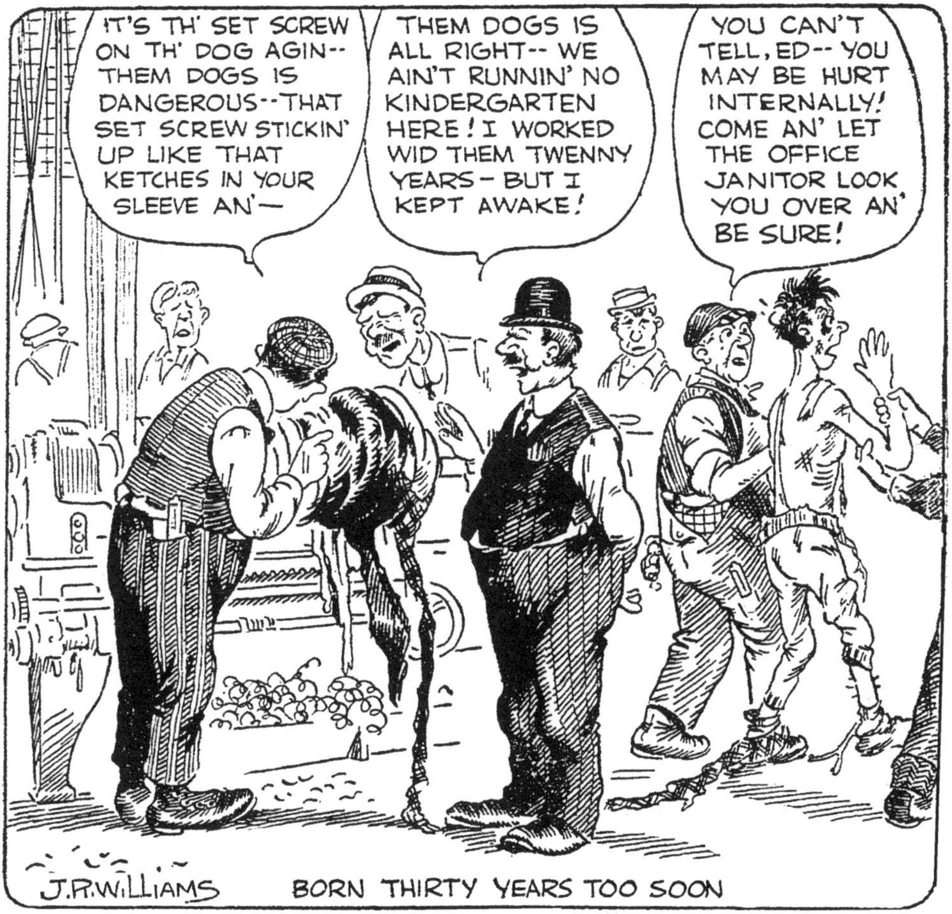
IT'S TH' SET SCREW ON TH' DOG AGIN-- THEM DOGS IS DANGEROUS--THAT SET SCREW STICKIN' UP LIKE THAT KETCHES IN YOUR SLEEVE AN'—
THEM DOGS IS ALL RIGHT-- WE AIN'T RUNNIN' NO KINDERGARTEN HERE! I WORKED WID THEM TWENNY YEARS – BUT I KEPT AWAKE!
YOU CAN'T TELL, ED-- YOU MAY BE HURT INTERNALLY! COME AN' LET THE OFFICE JANITOR LOOK YOU OVER AN' BE SURE!
J.R.WILLIAMS
BORN THIRTY YEARS TOO SOON

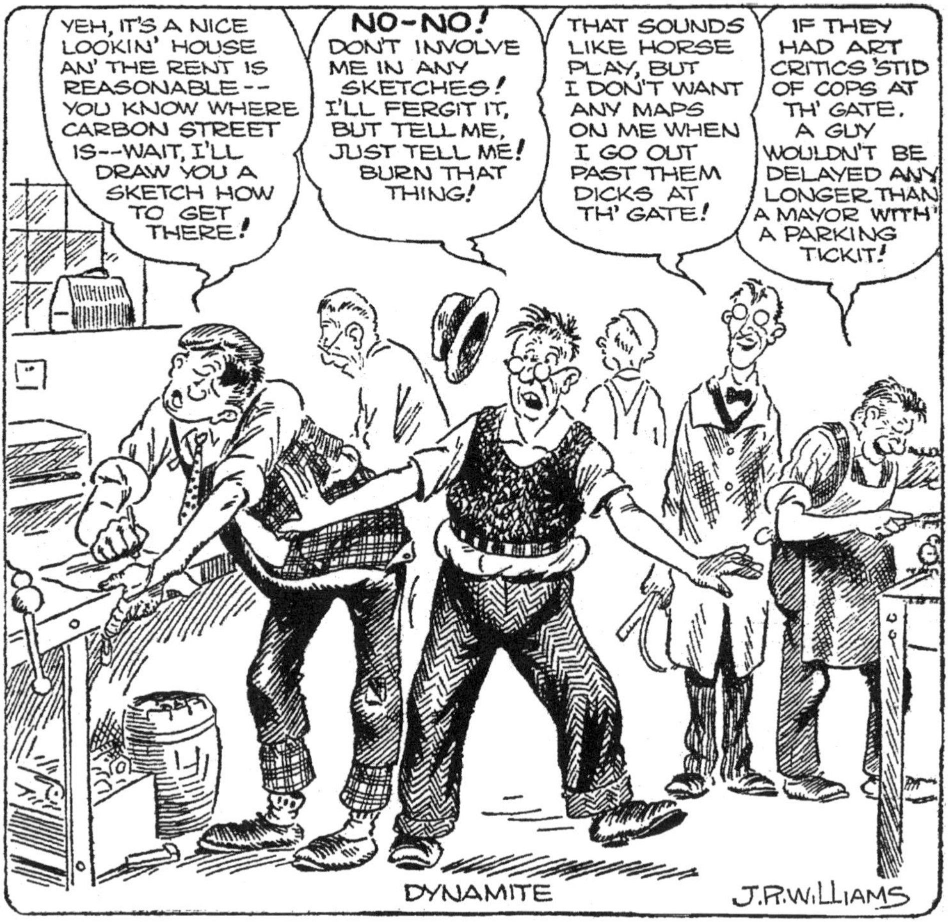
YEH, IT'S A NICE LOOKIN' HOUSE AN' THE RENT IS REASONABLE-- YOU KNOW WHERE CARBON STREET IS--WAIT, I'LL DRAW YOU A SKETCH HOW TO GET THERE!
NO-NO! DON'T INVOLVE ME IN ANY SKETCHES! I'LL FERGIT IT, BUT TELL ME, JUST TELL ME! BURN THAT THING!
THAT SOUNDS LIKE HORSE PLAY, BUT I DON'T WANT ANY MAPS ON ME WHEN I GO OUT PAST THEM DICKS AT TH' GATE!
IF THEY HAD ART CRITICS 'STID OF COPS AT TH' GATE. A GUY WOULDN'T BE DELAYED ANY LONGER THAN A MAYOR WITH A PARKING TICKIT!
DYNAMITE
J.R.WILLIAMS

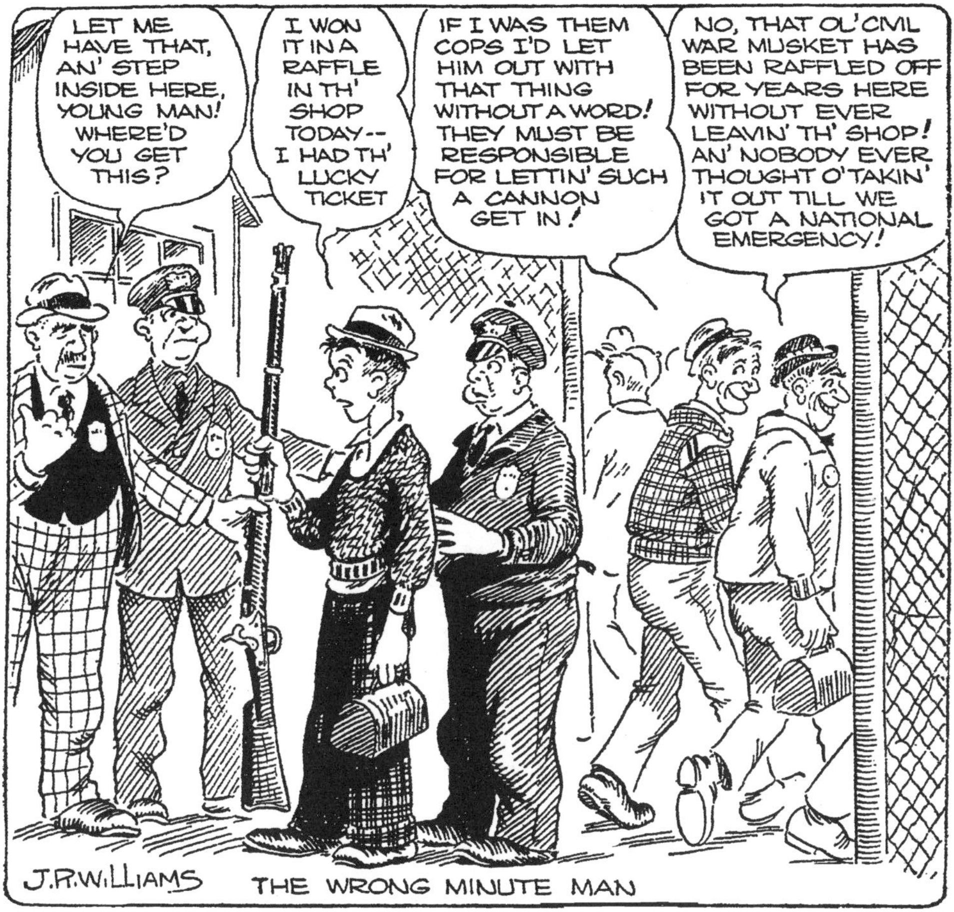
LET ME HAVE THAT, AN' STEP INSIDE HERE, YOUNG MAN! WHERE'D YOU GET THIS?
I WON IT IN A RAFFLE IN TH' SHOP TODAY-- I HAD TH' LUCKY TICKET
IF I WAS THEM COPS I'D LET HIM OUT WITH THAT THING WITHOUT A WORD! THEY MUST BE RESPONSIBLE FOR LETTIN' SUCH A CANNON GET IN!
NO, THAT OL' CIVIL WAR MUSKET HAS BEEN RAFFLED OFF FOR YEARS HERE WITHOUT EVER LEAVIN' TH' SHOP! AN' NOBODY EVER THOUGHT O'TAKIN' IT OUT TILL WE GOT A NATIONAL EMERGENCY!
J.R.WILLIAMS
THE WRONG MINUTE MAN

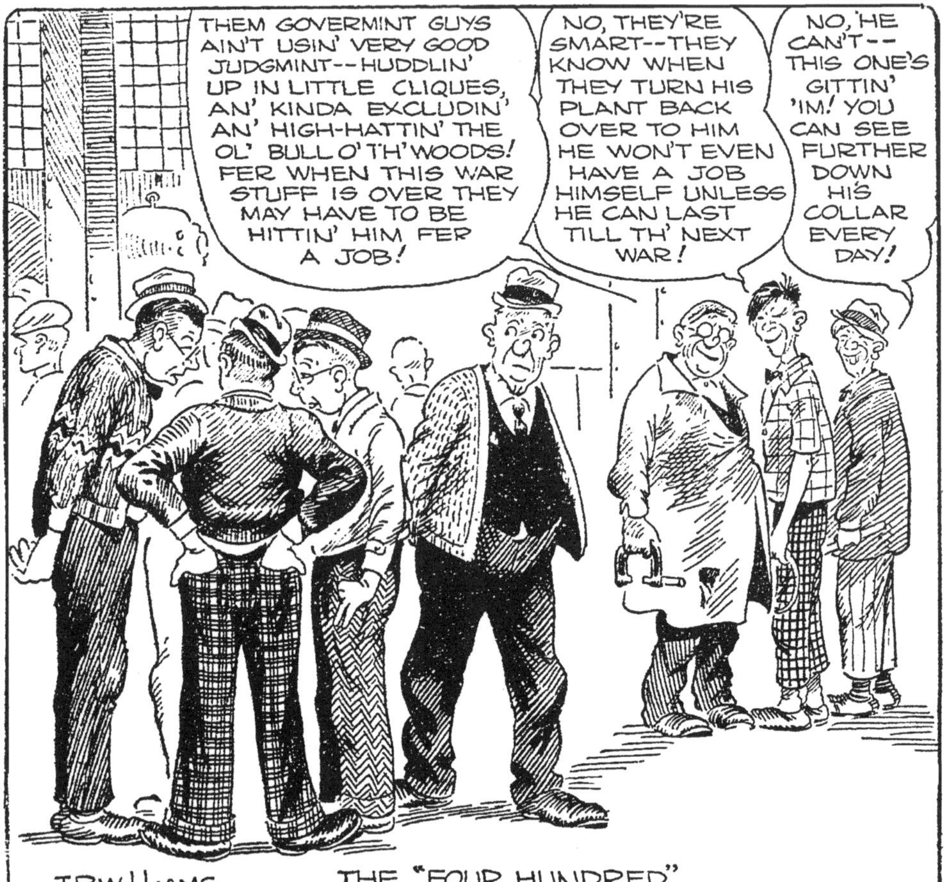
THEM GOVERMINT GUYS AIN'T USIN' VERY GOOD JUDGMINT--HUDDLIN' UP IN LITTLE CLIQUES, AN' KINDA EXCLUDIN' AN' HIGH-HATTIN' THE OL' BULL O' TH' WOODS! FER WHEN THIS WAR STUFF IS OVER THEY MAY HAVE TO BE HITTIN' HIM FER A JOB!
NO, THEY'RE SMART--THEY KNOW WHEN THEY TURN HIS PLANT BACK OVER TO HIM HE WON'T EVEN HAVE A JOB HIMSELF UNLESS HE CAN LAST TILL TH' NEXT WAR!
NO, HE CAN'T-- THIS ONE'S GITTIN' 'IM! YOU CAN SEE FURTHER DOWN HIS COLLAR EVERY DAY!
J.R.WILLIAMS

THE "FOUR HUNDRED"

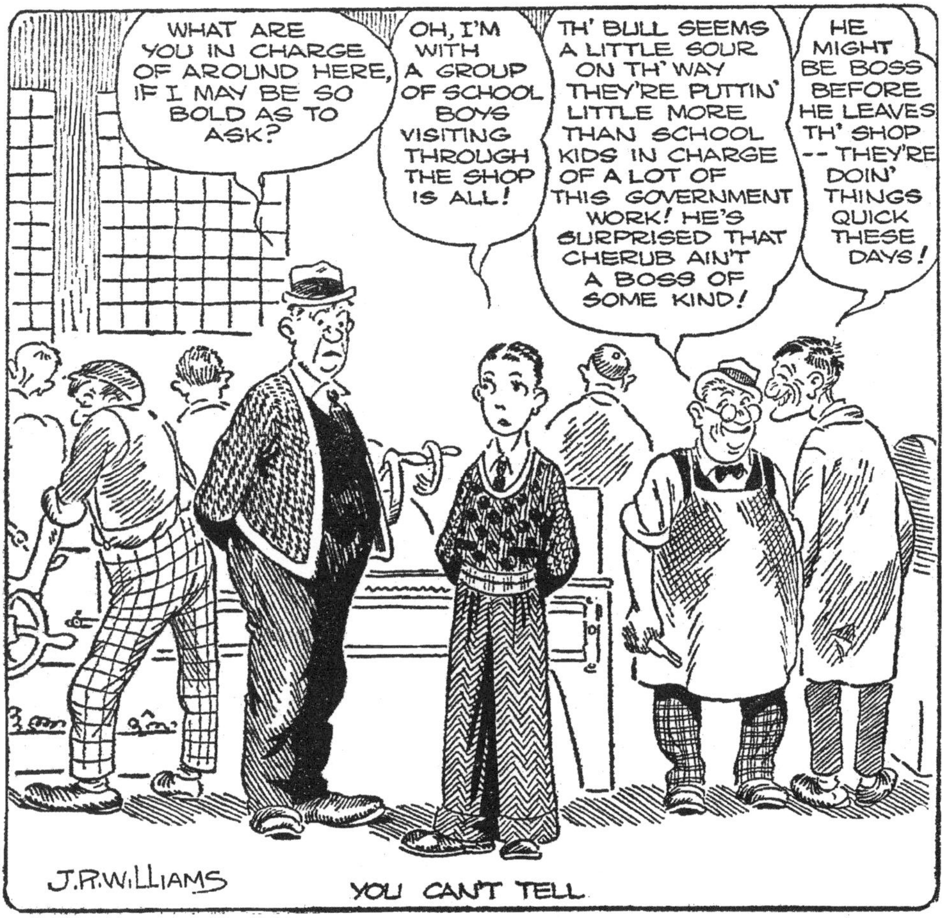
WHAT ARE YOU IN CHARGE OF AROUND HERE, IF I MAY BE SO BOLD AS TO ASK?
OH, I'M WITH A GROUP OF SCHOOL BOYS VISITING THROUGH THE SHOP IS ALL!
TH' BULL SEEMS A LITTLE SOUR ON TH' WAY THEY'RE PUTTIN' LITTLE MORE THAN SCHOOL KIDS IN CHARGE OF A LOT OF THIS GOVERNMENT WORK! HE'S SURPRISED THAT CHERUB AIN'T A BOSS OF SOME KIND!
HE MIGHT BE BOSS BEFORE HE LEAVES TH' SHOP -- THEY'RE DOIN' THINGS QUICK THESE DAYS!
J.R.WILLIAMS
YOU CAN'T TELL

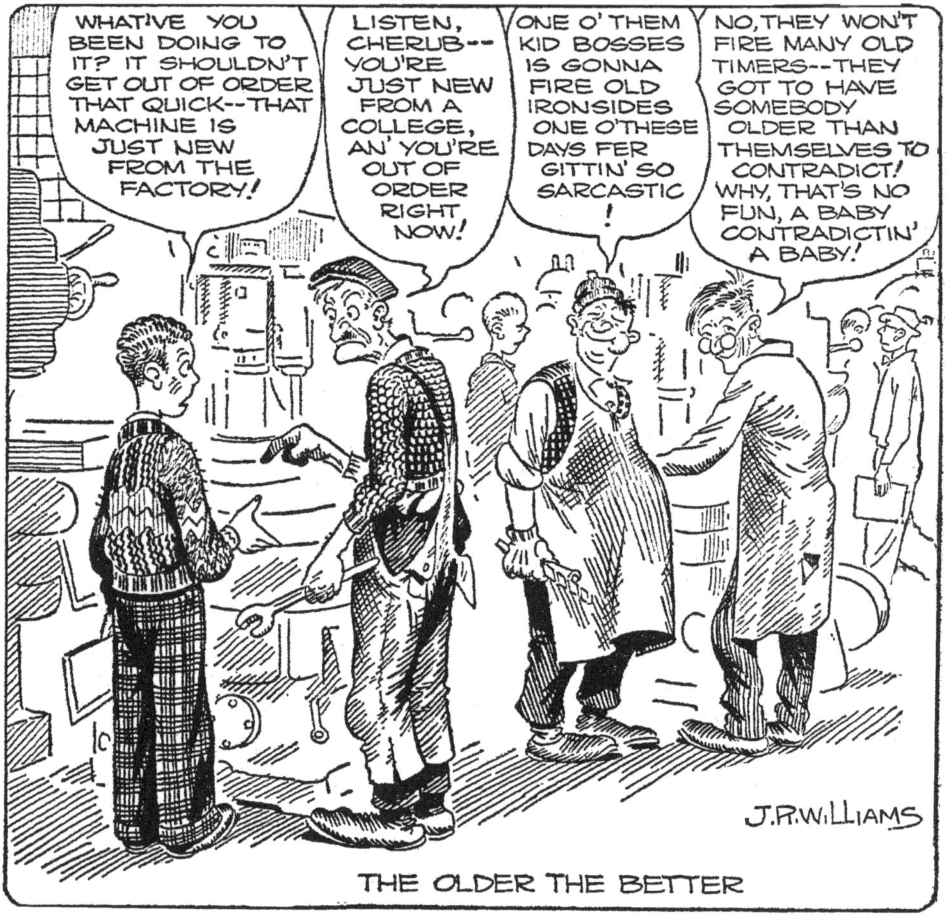
WHAT'VE YOU BEEN DOING TO IT? IT SHOULDN'T GET OUT OF ORDER THAT QUICK--THAT MACHINE IS JUST NEW FROM THE FACTORY!
LISTEN, CHERUB-- YOU'RE JUST NEW FROM A COLLEGE, AN' YOU'RE OUT OF ORDER RIGHT NOW!
ONE O' THEM KID BOSSES IS GONNA FIRE OLD IRONSIDES ONE O'THESE DAYS FER GITTIN' SO SARCASTIC!
NO, THEY WON'T FIRE MANY OLD TIMERS--THEY GOT TO HAVE SOMEBODY OLDER THAN THEMSELVES TO CONTRADICT! WHY, THAT'S NO FUN, A BABY CONTRADICTIN' A BABY!
J.R.WILLIAMS
THE OLDER THE BETTER

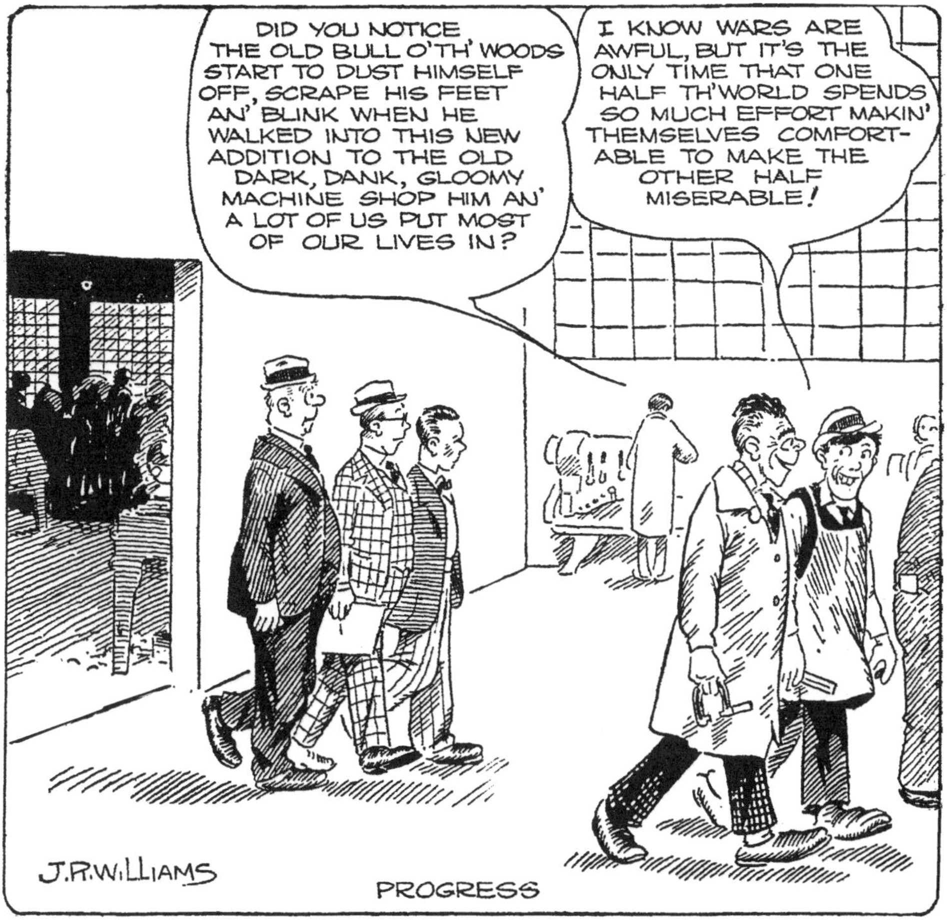
DID YOU NOTICE THE OLD BULL O'TH' WOODS START TO DUST HIMSELF OFF, SCRAPE HIS FEET AN' BLINK WHEN HE WALKED INTO THIS NEW ADDITION TO THE OLD DARK, DANK, GLOOMY MACHINE SHOP HIM AN' A LOT OF US PUT MOST OF OUR LIVES IN?
I KNOW WARS ARE AWFUL, BUT IT'S THE ONLY TIME THAT ONE HALF TH'WORLD SPENDS SO MUCH EFFORT MAKIN' THEMSELVES COMFORTABLE TO MAKE THE OTHER HALF MISERABLE!
J.R.WILLIAMS
PROGRESS

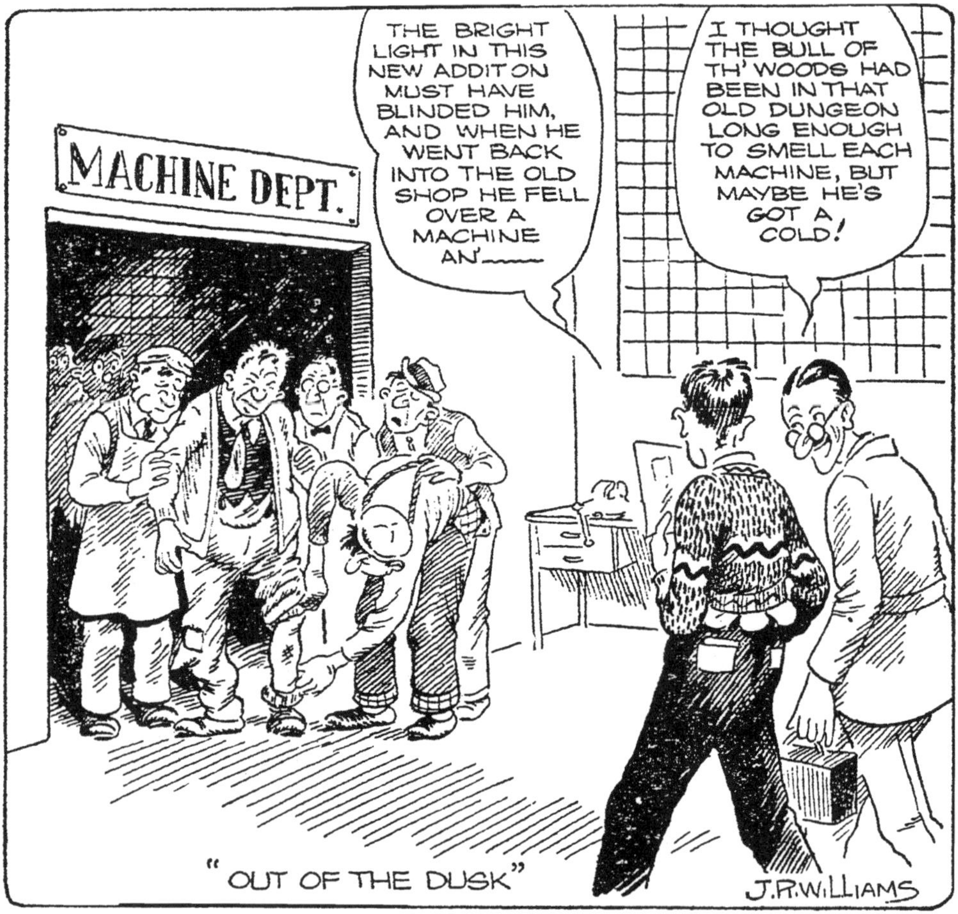
MACHINE DEPT.
THE BRIGHT LIGHT IN THIS NEW ADDIT ON MUST HAVE BLINDED HIM, AND WHEN HE WENT BACK INTO THE OLD SHOP HE FELL OVER A MACHINE AN'____
I THOUGHT THE BULL OF TH' WOODS HAD BEEN IN THAT OLD DUNGEON LONG ENOUGH TO SMELL EACH MACHINE, BUT MAYBE HE'S GOT A COLD!
"OUT OF THE DUSK"
J.R.WILLIAMS

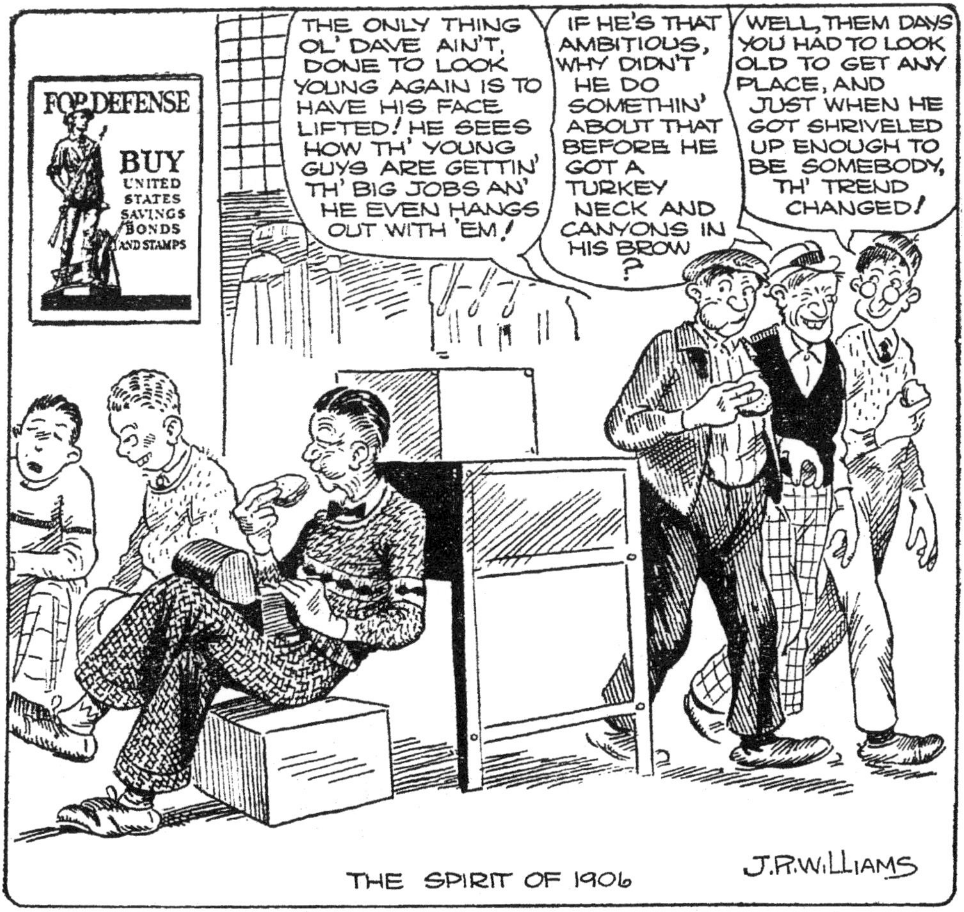
FOR DEFENSE
BUY
UNITED STATES SAVINGS BONDS AND STAMPS
THE ONLY THING OL' DAVE AIN'T, DONE TO LOOK YOUNG AGAIN IS TO HAVE HIS FACE LIFTED! HE SEES HOW TH' YOUNG GUYS ARE GETTIN' TH' BIG JOBS AN' HE EVEN HANGS OUT WITH 'EM!
IF HE'S THAT AMBITIOUS, WHY DIDN'T HE DO SOMETHIN' ABOUT THAT BEFORE HE GOT A TURKEY NECK AND CANYONS IN HIS BROW ?
WELL, THEM DAYS YOU HAD TO LOOK OLD TO GET ANY PLACE, AND JUST WHEN HE GOT SHRIVELED UP ENOUGH TO BE SOMEBODY, TH' TREND CHANGED!
J.R.WILLIAMS
THE SPIRIT OF 1906

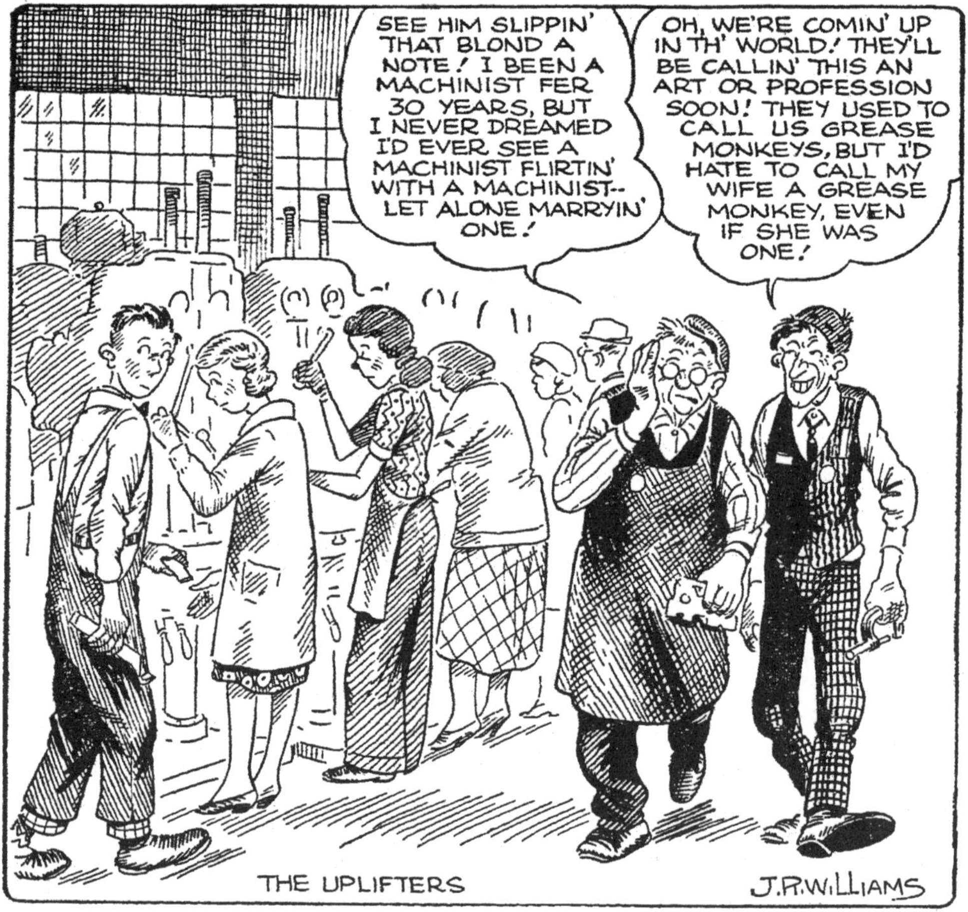
SEE HIM SLIPPIN' THAT BLOND A NOTE! I BEEN A MACHINIST FER 30 YEARS, BUT I NEVER DREAMED I'D EVER SEE A MACHINIST FLIRTIN' WITH A MACHINIST-- LET ALONE MARRYIN' ONE!
OH, WE'RE COMIN' UP IN TH' WORLD! THEY'LL BE CALLIN' THIS AN ART OR PROFESSION SOON! THEY USED TO CALL US GREASE MONKEYS, BUT I'D HATE TO CALL MY WIFE A GREASE MONKEY, EVEN IF SHE WAS ONE!
THE UPLIFTERS
J.R. WILLIAMS

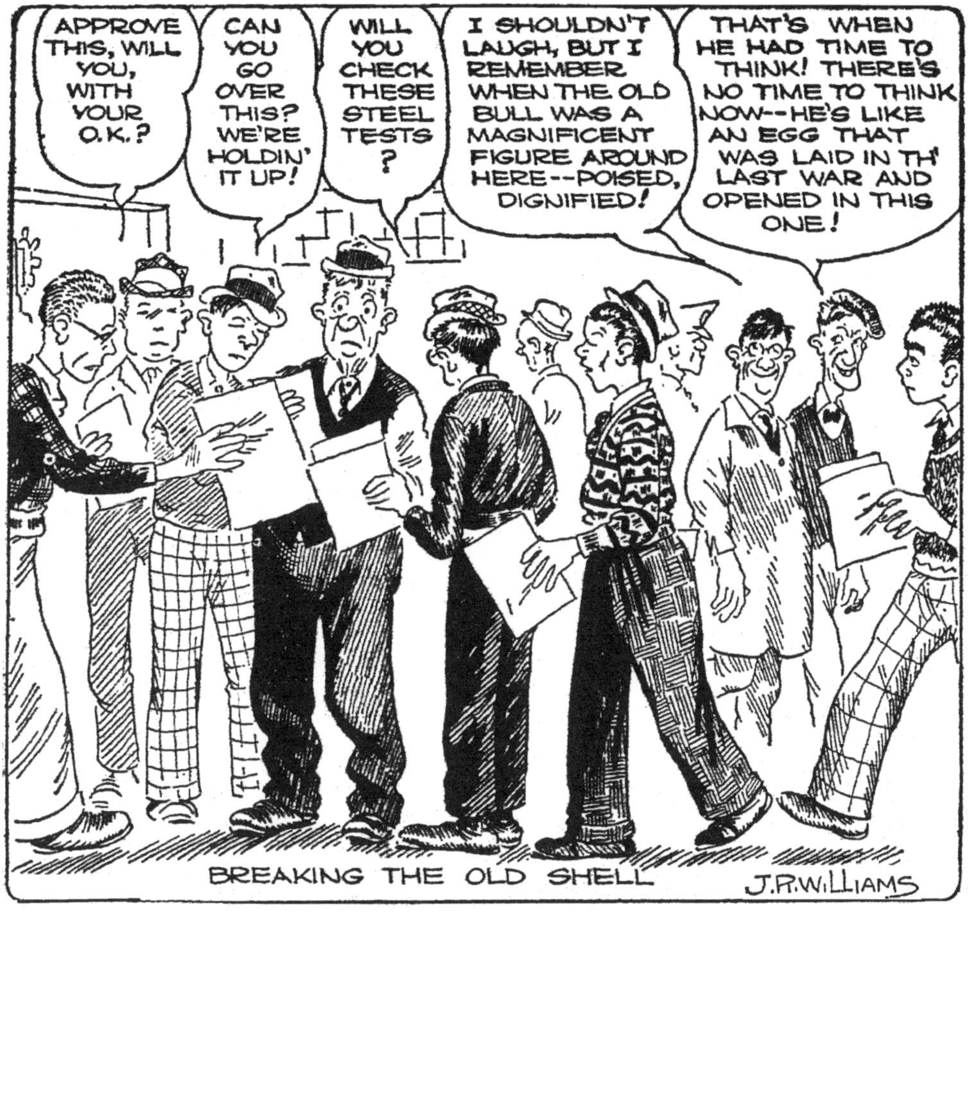
APPROVE THIS, WILL YOU, WITH YOUR O.K.?
CAN YOU GO OVER THIS? WE'RE HOLDIN' IT UP!
WILL YOU CHECK THESE STEEL TESTS?
I SHOULDN'T LAUGH, BUT I REMEMBER WHEN THE OLD BULL WAS A MAGNIFICENT FIGURE AROUND HERE--POISED, DIGNIFIED!
THAT'S WHEN HE HAD TIME TO THINK! THERE'S NO TIME TO THINK NOW--HE'S LIKE AN EGG THAT WAS LAID IN TH' LAST WAR AND OPENED IN THIS ONE!
BREAKING THE OLD SHELL
J.R. WILLIAMS

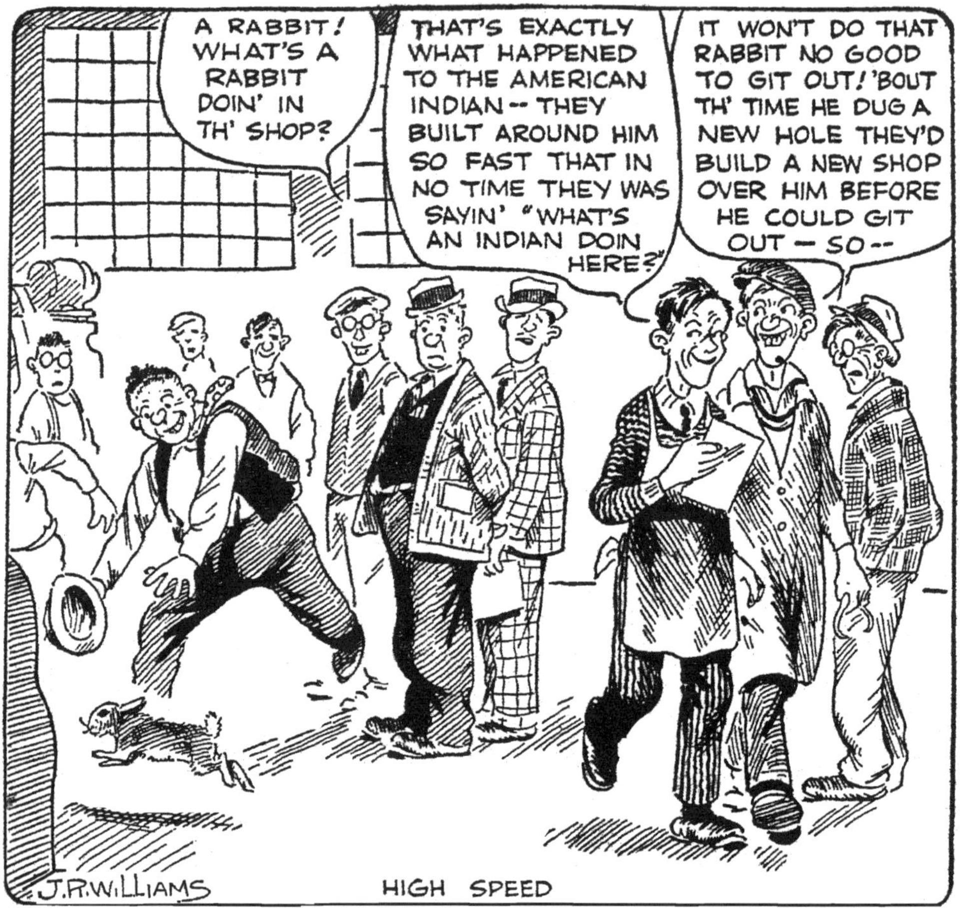
A RABBIT! WHAT'S A RABBIT DOIN' IN TH' SHOP?
THAT'S EXACTLY WHAT HAPPENED TO THE AMERICAN INDIAN -- THEY BUILT AROUND HIM SO FAST THAT IN NO TIME THEY WAS SAYIN' "WHAT'S AN INDIAN DOIN HERE?"
IT WON'T DO THAT RABBIT NO GOOD TO GIT OUT! 'BOUT TH' TIME HE DUG A NEW HOLE THEY'D BUILD A NEW SHOP OVER HIM BEFORE HE COULD GIT OUT -- SO --
J.R. WILLIAMS
HIGH SPEED

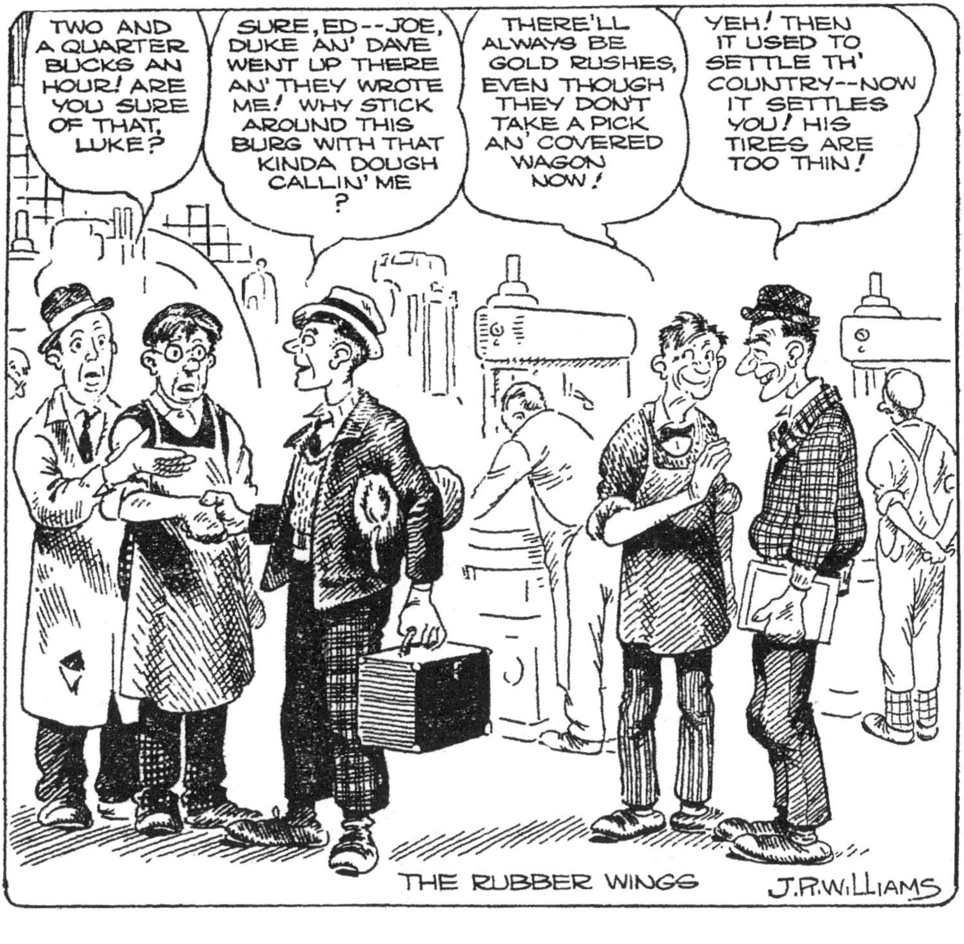
TWO AND A QUARTER BUCKS AN HOUR! ARE YOU SURE OF THAT, LUKE?
SURE, ED--JOE, DUKE AN' DAVE WENT UP THERE AN' THEY WROTE ME! WHY STICK AROUND THIS BURG WITH THAT KINDA DOUGH CALLIN' ME ?
THERE'LL ALWAYS BE GOLD RUSHES, EVEN THOUGH THEY DON'T TAKE A PICK AN' COVERED WAGON NOW!
YEH! THEN IT USED TO SETTLE TH' COUNTRY--NOW IT SETTLES YOU! HIS TIRES ARE TOO THIN!
THE RUBBER WINGS
J.R.WILLIAMS

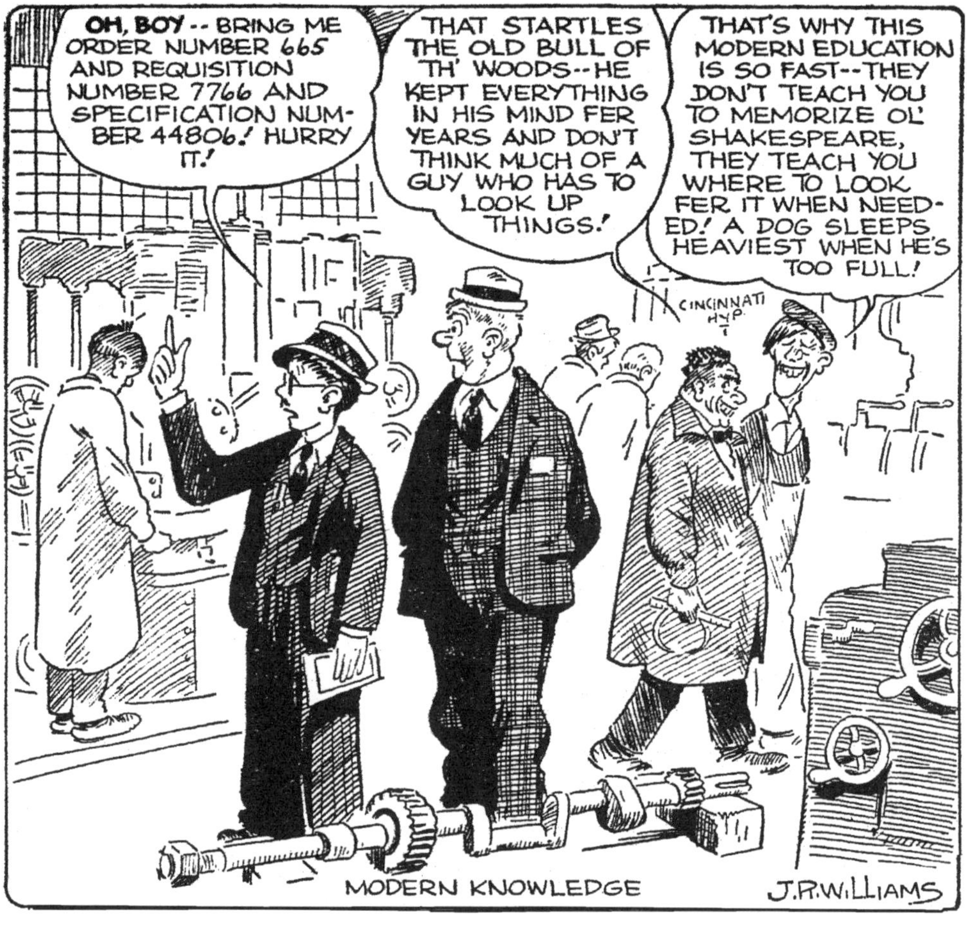
OH, BOY -- BRING ME ORDER NUMBER 665 AND REQUISITION NUMBER 7766 AND SPECIFICATION NUMBER 44806! HURRY IT!
THAT STARTLES THE OLD BULL OF TH' WOODS -- HE KEPT EVERYTHING IN HIS MIND FER YEARS AND DON'T THINK MUCH OF A GUY WHO HAS TO LOOK UP THINGS!
THAT'S WHY THIS MODERN EDUCATION IS SO FAST -- THEY DON'T TEACH YOU TO MEMORIZE OL' SHAKESPEARE, THEY TEACH YOU WHERE TO LOOK FER IT WHEN NEEDED! A DOG SLEEPS HEAVIEST WHEN HE'S TOO FULL!
CINCINNATI HYP.
MODERN KNOWLEDGE
J.R. WILLIAMS

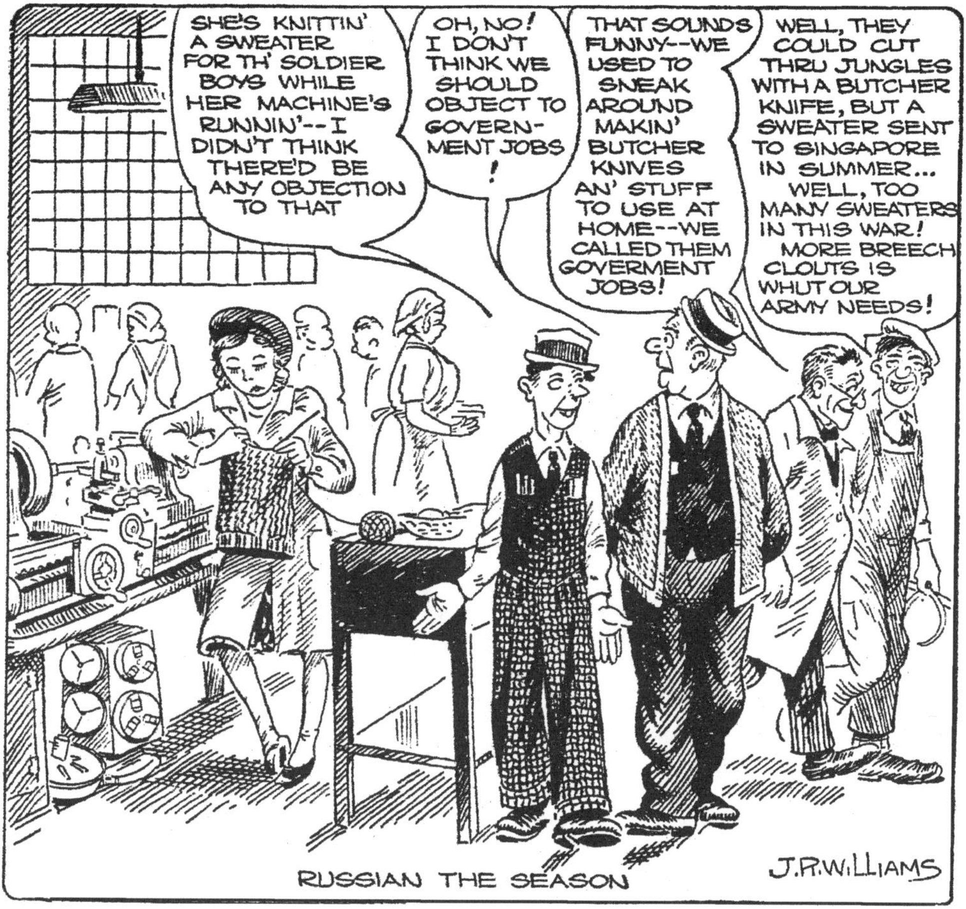
SHE'S KNITTIN' A SWEATER FOR TH' SOLDIER BOYS WHILE HER MACHINE'S RUNNIN'--I DIDN'T THINK THERE'D BE ANY OBJECTION TO THAT
OH, NO! I DON'T THINK WE SHOULD OBJECT TO GOVERN-MENT JOBS!
THAT SOUNDS FUNNY--WE USED TO SNEAK AROUND MAKIN' BUTCHER KNIVES AN' STUFF TO USE AT HOME--WE CALLED THEM GOVERMENT JOBS!
WELL, THEY COULD CUT THRU JUNGLES WITH A BUTCHER KNIFE, BUT A SWEATER SENT TO SINGAPORE IN SUMMER... WELL, TOO MANY SWEATERS IN THIS WAR! MORE BREECH CLOUTS IS WHUT OUR ARMY NEEDS!
RUSSIAN THE SEASON
J.R.WILLIAMS

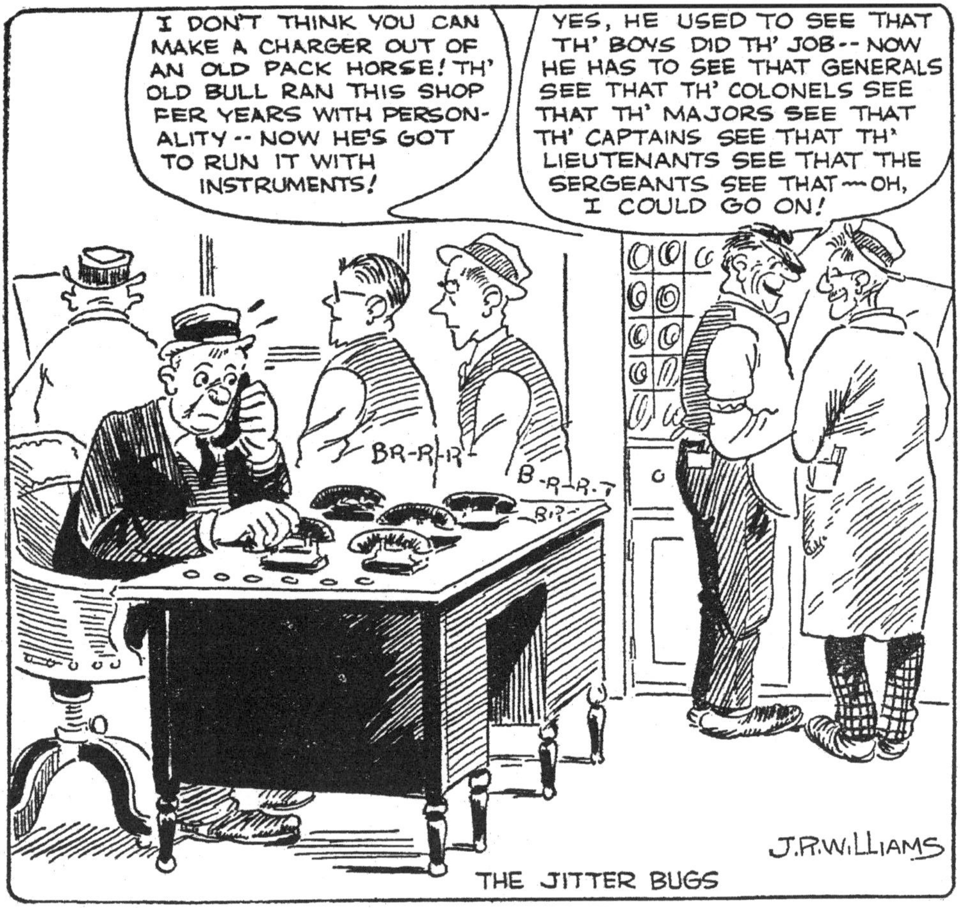
I DON'T THINK YOU CAN MAKE A CHARGER OUT OF AN OLD PACK HORSE! TH' OLD BULL RAN THIS SHOP FER YEARS WITH PERSON-ALITY -- NOW HE'S GOT TO RUN IT WITH INSTRUMENTS!
YES, HE USED TO SEE THAT TH' BOYS DID TH' JOB -- NOW HE HAS TO SEE THAT GENERALS SEE THAT TH' COLONELS SEE THAT TH' MAJORS SEE THAT TH' CAPTAINS SEE THAT TH' LIEUTENANTS SEE THAT THE SERGEANTS SEE THAT — OH, I COULD GO ON!
BR-R-R-
B-R-R-T
J.R.WILLIAMS
THE JITTER BUGS

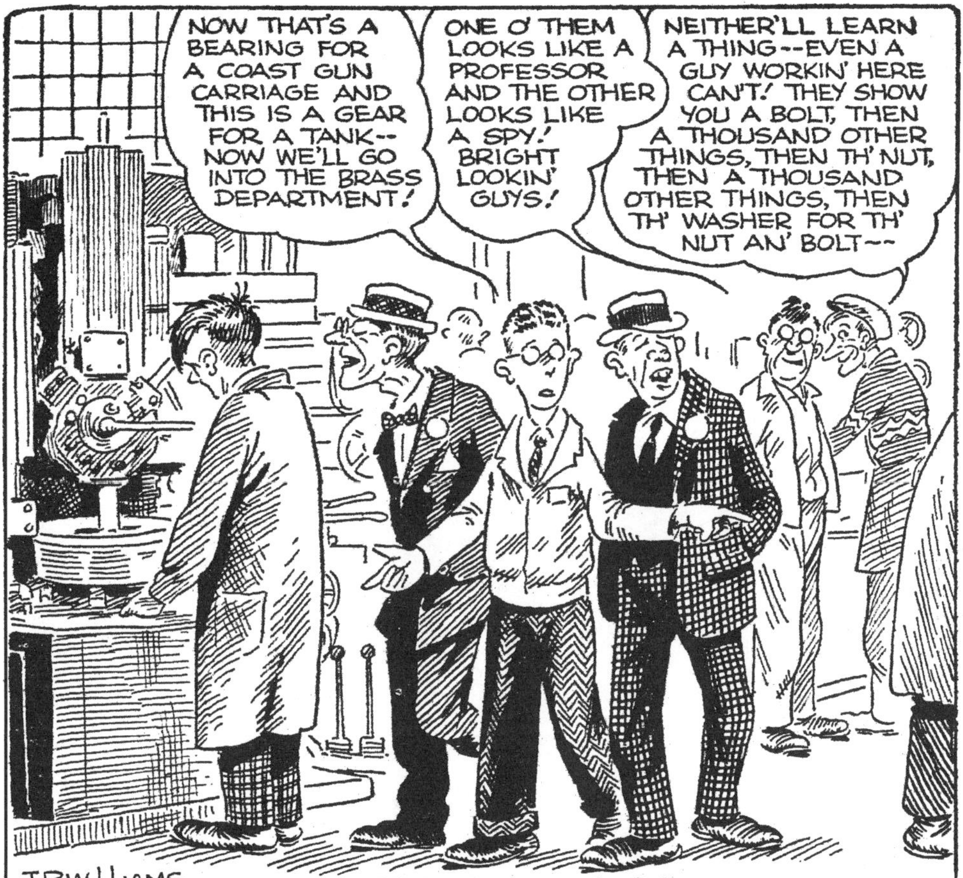
NOW THAT'S A BEARING FOR A COAST GUN CARRIAGE AND THIS IS A GEAR FOR A TANK-- NOW WE'LL GO INTO THE BRASS DEPARTMENT!
ONE O' THEM LOOKS LIKE A PROFESSOR AND THE OTHER LOOKS LIKE A SPY! BRIGHT LOOKIN' GUYS!
NEITHER'LL LEARN A THING--EVEN A GUY WORKIN' HERE CAN'T! THEY SHOW YOU A BOLT, THEN A THOUSAND OTHER THINGS, THEN TH' NUT, THEN A THOUSAND OTHER THINGS, THEN TH' WASHER FOR TH' NUT AN' BOLT--
J.R.WILLIAMS
HEROES ARE MADE, NOT BORN

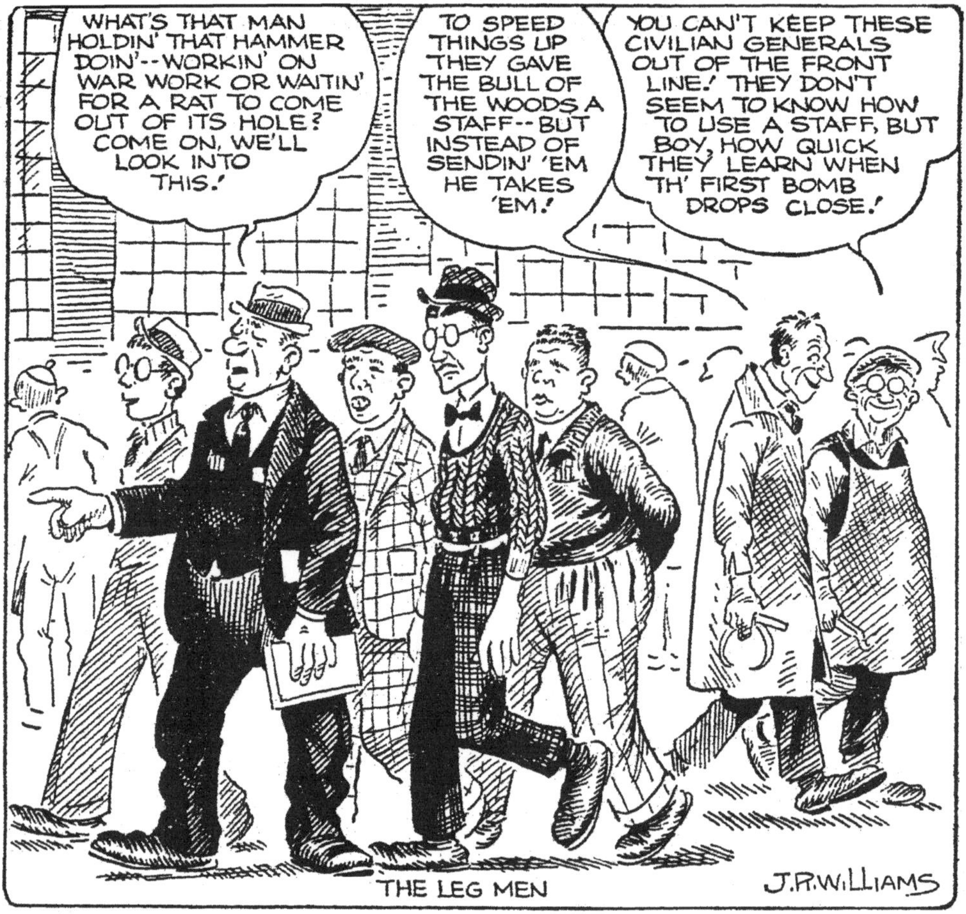
WHAT'S THAT MAN HOLDIN' THAT HAMMER DOIN'--WORKIN' ON WAR WORK OR WAITIN' FOR A RAT TO COME OUT OF ITS HOLE? COME ON, WE'LL LOOK INTO THIS!
TO SPEED THINGS UP THEY GAVE THE BULL OF THE WOODS A STAFF--BUT INSTEAD OF SENDIN' 'EM HE TAKES 'EM!
YOU CAN'T KEEP THESE CIVILIAN GENERALS OUT OF THE FRONT LINE! THEY DON'T SEEM TO KNOW HOW TO USE A STAFF, BUT BOY, HOW QUICK THEY LEARN WHEN TH' FIRST BOMB DROPS CLOSE!
THE LEG MEN
J.R.WILLIAMS

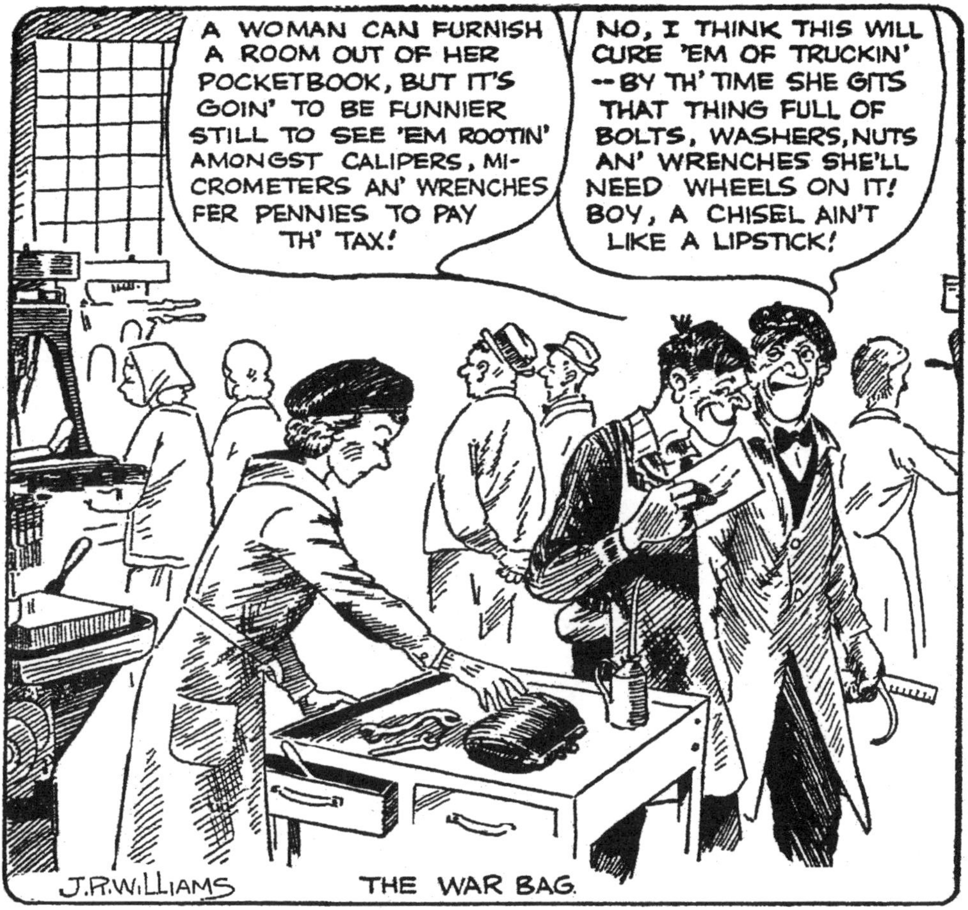
A WOMAN CAN FURNISH A ROOM OUT OF HER POCKETBOOK, BUT IT'S GOIN' TO BE FUNNIER STILL TO SEE 'EM ROOTIN' AMONGST CALIPERS, MI-CROMETERS AN' WRENCHES FER PENNIES TO PAY TH' TAX!
NO, I THINK THIS WILL CURE 'EM OF TRUCKIN' --BY TH' TIME SHE GITS THAT THING FULL OF BOLTS, WASHERS, NUTS AN' WRENCHES SHE'LL NEED WHEELS ON IT! BOY, A CHISEL AIN'T LIKE A LIPSTICK!
J.R.WILLIAMS
THE WAR BAG

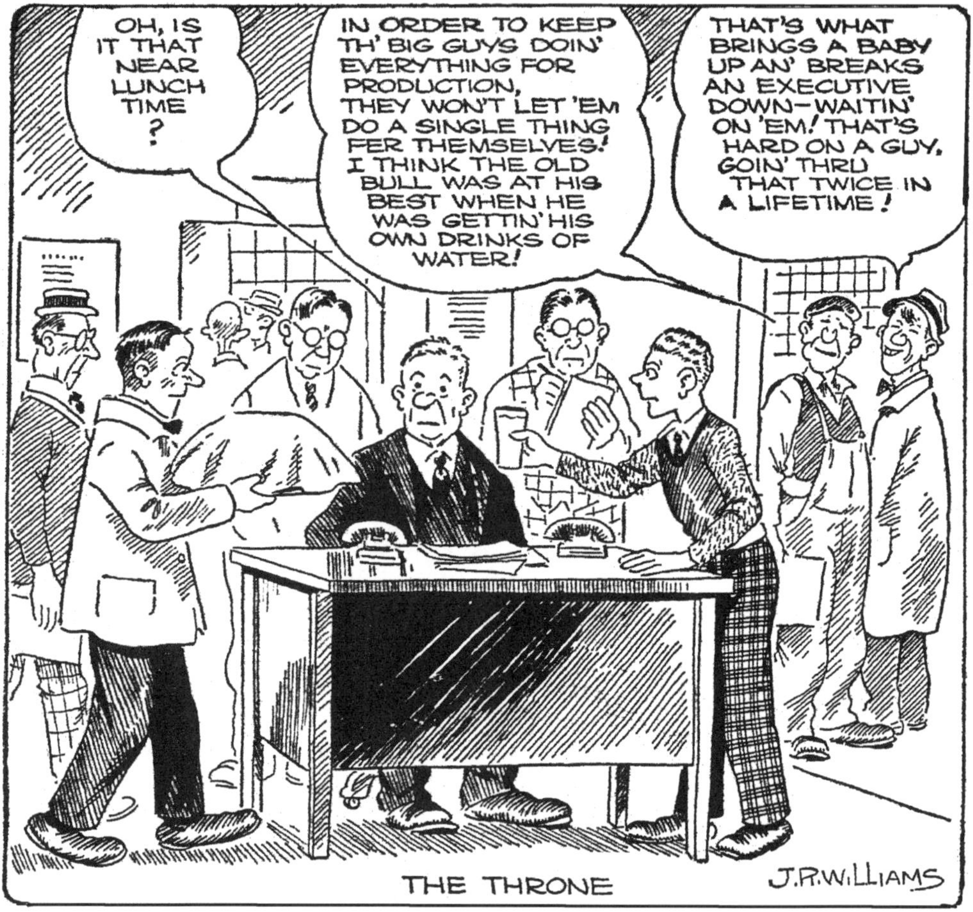
OH, IS IT THAT NEAR LUNCH TIME ?
IN ORDER TO KEEP TH' BIG GUYS DOIN' EVERYTHING FOR PRODUCTION, THEY WON'T LET 'EM DO A SINGLE THING FER THEMSELVES! I THINK THE OLD BULL WAS AT HIS BEST WHEN HE WAS GETTIN' HIS OWN DRINKS OF WATER!
THAT'S WHAT BRINGS A BABY UP AN' BREAKS AN EXECUTIVE DOWN—WAITIN' ON 'EM! THAT'S HARD ON A GUY, GOIN' THRU THAT TWICE IN A LIFETIME!
THE THRONE
J.R.WILLIAMS

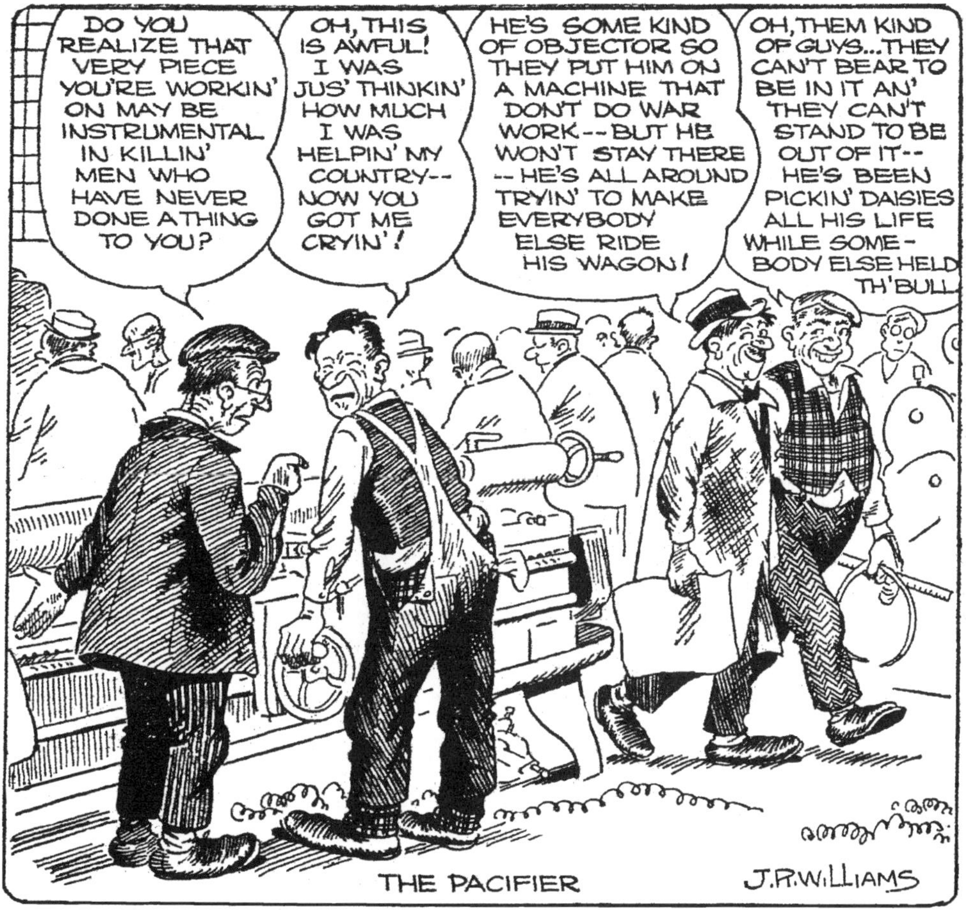
DO YOU REALIZE THAT VERY PIECE YOU'RE WORKIN' ON MAY BE INSTRUMENTAL IN KILLIN' MEN WHO HAVE NEVER DONE A THING TO YOU?
OH, THIS IS AWFUL! I WAS JUS' THINKIN' HOW MUCH I WAS HELPIN' MY COUNTRY-- NOW YOU GOT ME CRYIN'!
HE'S SOME KIND OF OBJECTOR SO THEY PUT HIM ON A MACHINE THAT DON'T DO WAR WORK--BUT HE WON'T STAY THERE --HE'S ALL AROUND TRYIN' TO MAKE EVERYBODY ELSE RIDE HIS WAGON!
OH, THEM KIND OF GUYS...THEY CAN'T BEAR TO BE IN IT AN' THEY CAN'T STAND TO BE OUT OF IT-- HE'S BEEN PICKIN' DAISIES ALL HIS LIFE WHILE SOME-BODY ELSE HELD TH' BULL
THE PACIFIER
J.R. WILLIAMS

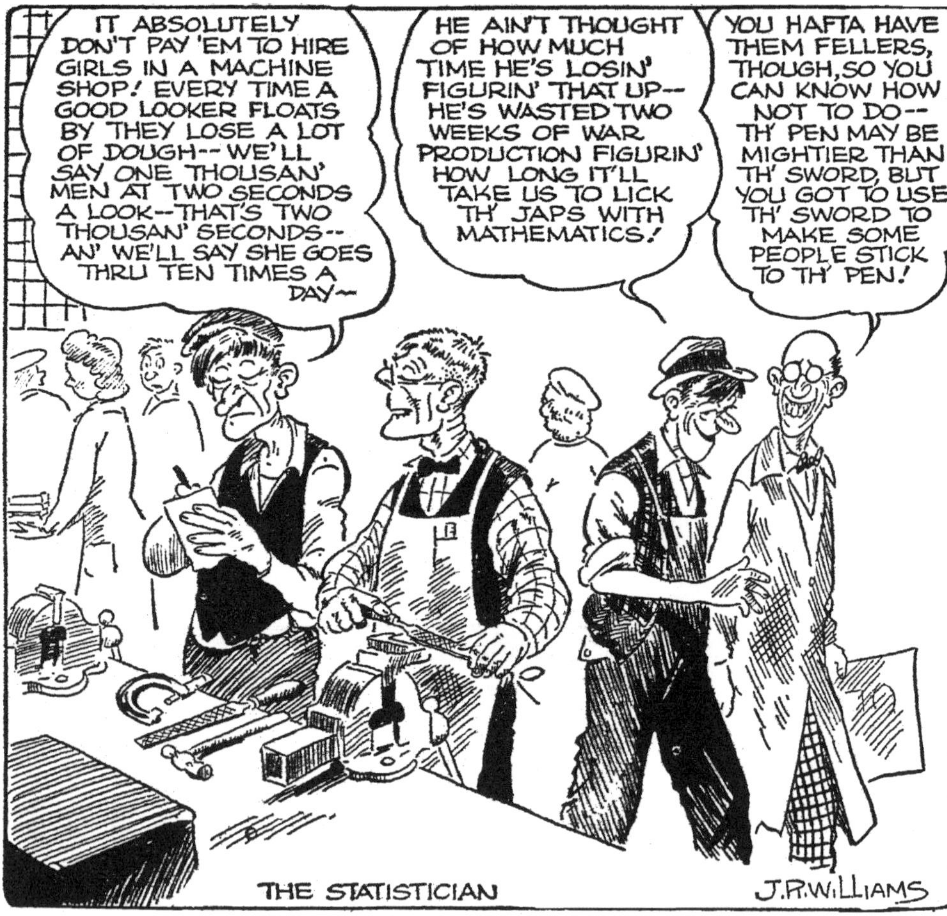
IT ABSOLUTELY DON'T PAY 'EM TO HIRE GIRLS IN A MACHINE SHOP! EVERY TIME A GOOD LOOKER FLOATS BY THEY LOSE A LOT OF DOUGH-- WE'LL SAY ONE THOUSAN' MEN AT TWO SECONDS A LOOK--THAT'S TWO THOUSAN' SECONDS-- AN' WE'LL SAY SHE GOES THRU TEN TIMES A DAY--
HE AIN'T THOUGHT OF HOW MUCH TIME HE'S LOSIN' FIGURIN' THAT UP-- HE'S WASTED TWO WEEKS OF WAR PRODUCTION FIGURIN' HOW LONG IT'LL TAKE US TO LICK TH' JAPS WITH MATHEMATICS!
YOU HAFTA HAVE THEM FELLERS, THOUGH, SO YOU CAN KNOW HOW NOT TO DO-- TH' PEN MAY BE MIGHTIER THAN TH' SWORD, BUT YOU GOT TO USE TH' SWORD TO MAKE SOME PEOPLE STICK TO TH' PEN!
THE STATISTICIAN
J.R.WILLIAMS

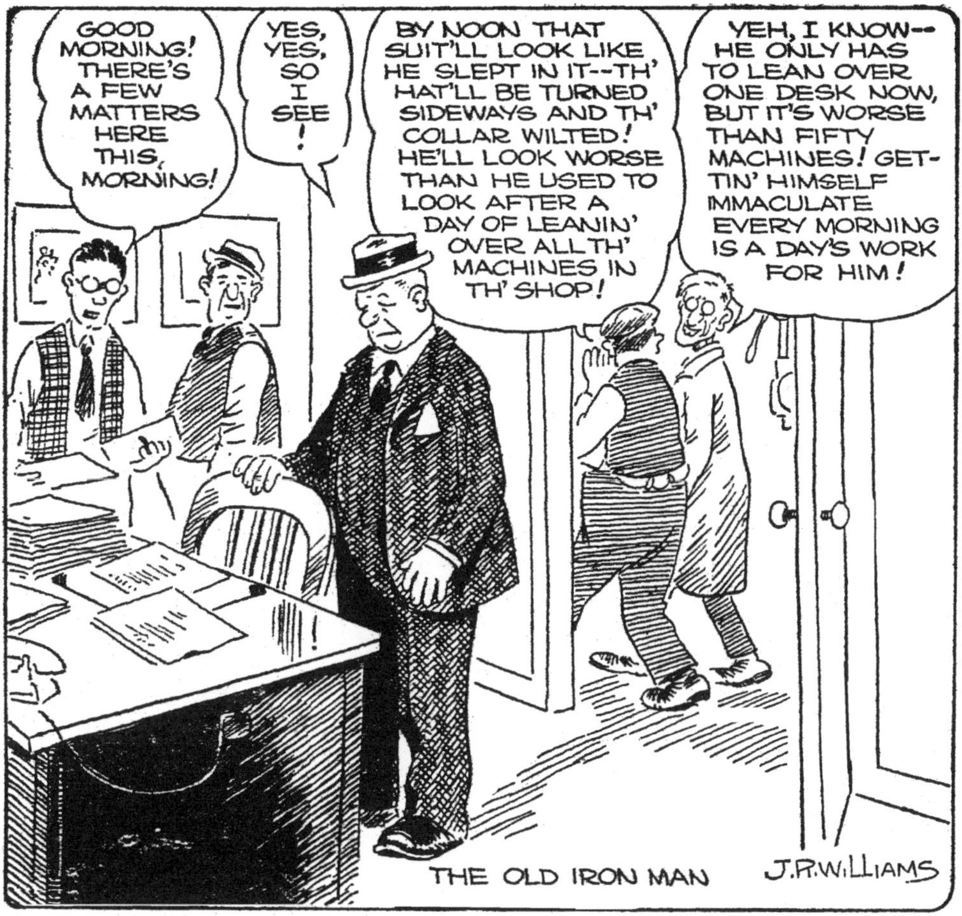
GOOD MORNING! THERE'S A FEW MATTERS HERE THIS, MORNING!
YES, YES, SO I SEE!
BY NOON THAT SUIT'LL LOOK LIKE HE SLEPT IN IT--TH' HAT'LL BE TURNED SIDEWAYS AND TH' COLLAR WILTED! HE'LL LOOK WORSE THAN HE USED TO LOOK AFTER A DAY OF LEANIN' OVER ALL TH' MACHINES IN TH' SHOP!
YEH, I KNOW-- HE ONLY HAS TO LEAN OVER ONE DESK NOW, BUT IT'S WORSE THAN FIFTY MACHINES! GET-TIN' HIMSELF IMMACULATE EVERY MORNING IS A DAY'S WORK FOR HIM!
THE OLD IRON MAN
J.R.WILLIAMS

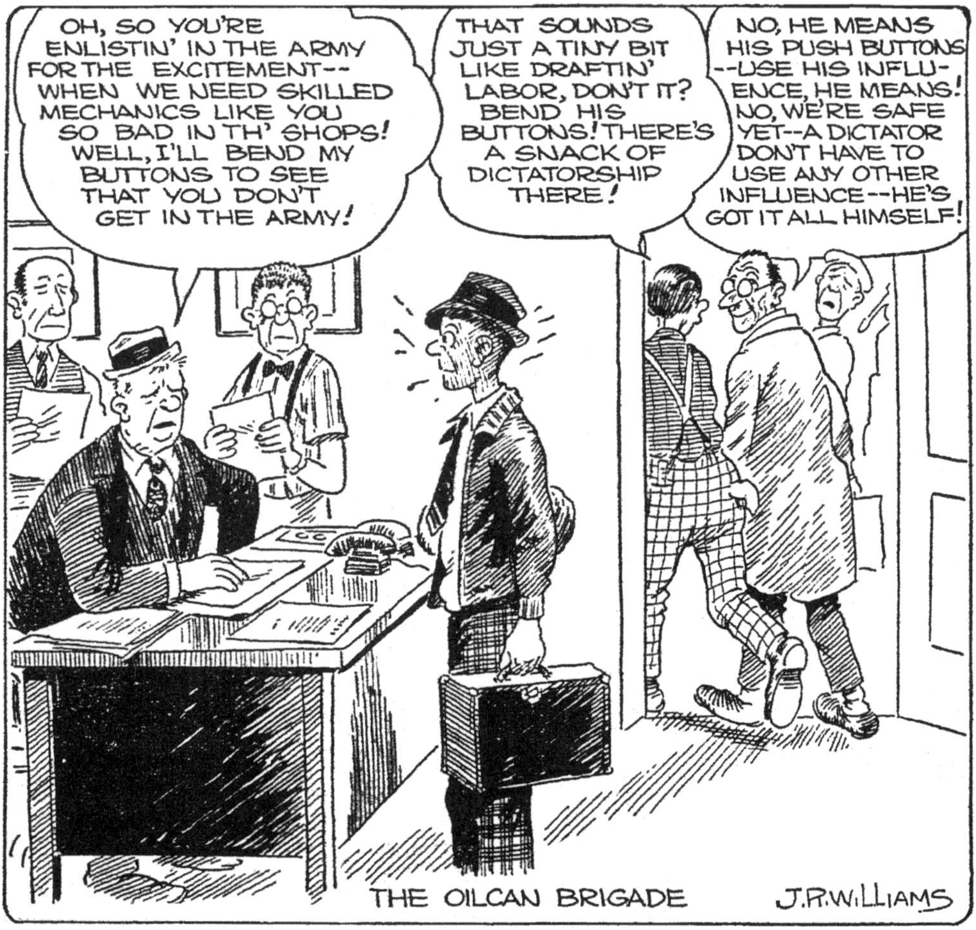

OH, SO YOU'RE ENLISTIN' IN THE ARMY FOR THE EXCITEMENT-- WHEN WE NEED SKILLED MECHANICS LIKE YOU SO BAD IN TH' SHOPS! WELL, I'LL BEND MY BUTTONS TO SEE THAT YOU DON'T GET IN THE ARMY!
THAT SOUNDS JUST A TINY BIT LIKE DRAFTIN' LABOR, DON'T IT? BEND HIS BUTTONS! THERE'S A SNACK OF DICTATORSHIP THERE!
NO, HE MEANS HIS PUSH BUTTONS --USE HIS INFLU-ENCE, HE MEANS! NO, WE'RE SAFE YET--A DICTATOR DON'T HAVE TO USE ANY OTHER INFLUENCE--HE'S GOT IT ALL HIMSELF!
THE OILCAN BRIGADE
J.R.WILLIAMS

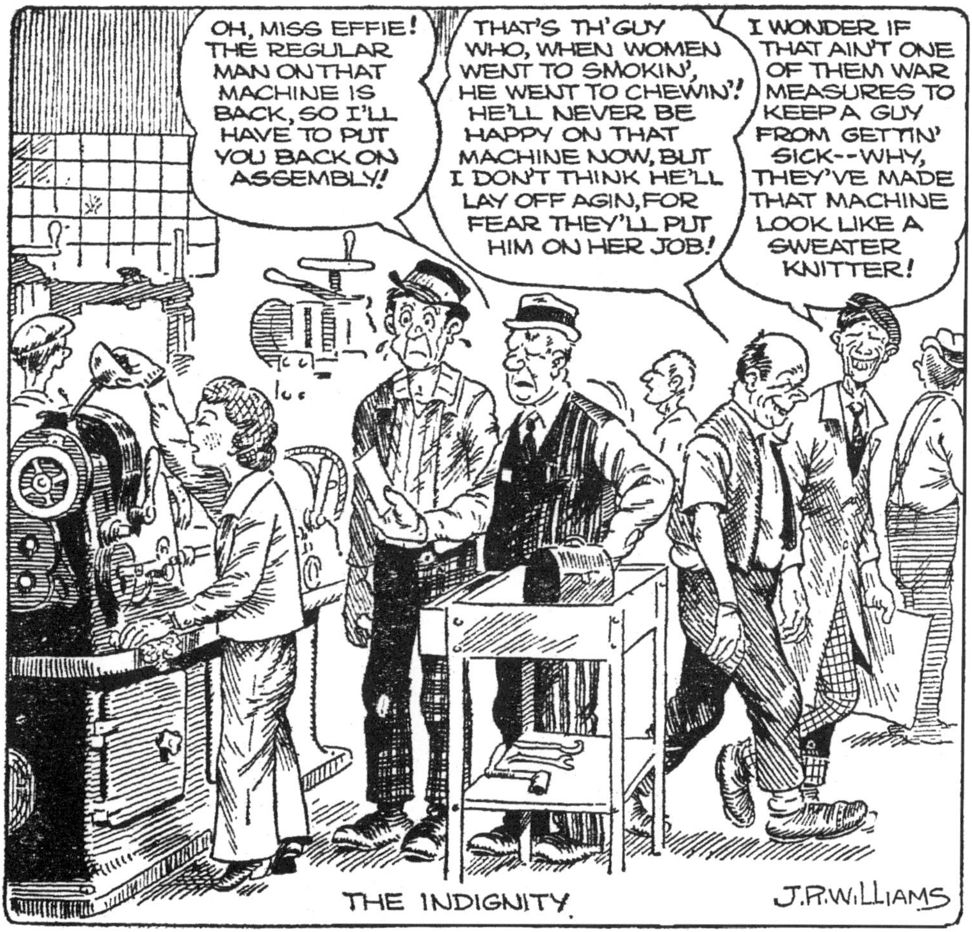
OH, MISS EFFIE! THE REGULAR MAN ON THAT MACHINE IS BACK, SO I'LL HAVE TO PUT YOU BACK ON ASSEMBLY!
THAT'S TH' GUY WHO, WHEN WOMEN WENT TO SMOKIN', HE WENT TO CHEWIN'! HE'LL NEVER BE HAPPY ON THAT MACHINE NOW, BUT I DON'T THINK HE'LL LAY OFF AGIN, FOR FEAR THEY'LL PUT HIM ON HER JOB!
I WONDER IF THAT AIN'T ONE OF THEM WAR MEASURES TO KEEP A GUY FROM GETTIN' SICK--WHY, THEY'VE MADE THAT MACHINE LOOK LIKE A SWEATER KNITTER!
THE INDIGNITY
J.R. WILLIAMS

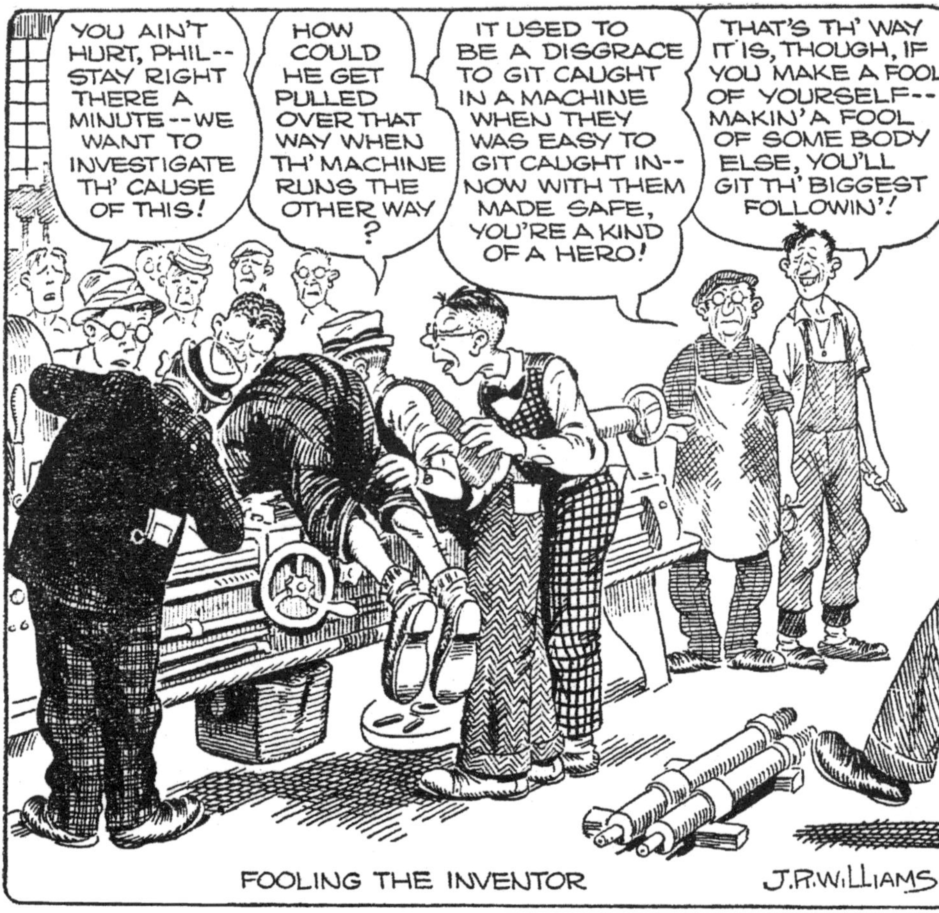

YOU AIN'T HURT, PHIL-- STAY RIGHT THERE A MINUTE--WE WANT TO INVESTIGATE TH' CAUSE OF THIS!
HOW COULD HE GET PULLED OVER THAT WAY WHEN TH' MACHINE RUNS THE OTHER WAY?
IT USED TO BE A DISGRACE TO GIT CAUGHT IN A MACHINE WHEN THEY WAS EASY TO GIT CAUGHT IN-- NOW WITH THEM MADE SAFE, YOU'RE A KIND OF A HERO!
THAT'S TH' WAY IT IS, THOUGH, IF YOU MAKE A FOOL OF YOURSELF-- MAKIN' A FOOL OF SOME BODY ELSE, YOU'LL GIT TH' BIGGEST FOLLOWIN'!
FOOLING THE INVENTOR
J.R.WILLIAMS

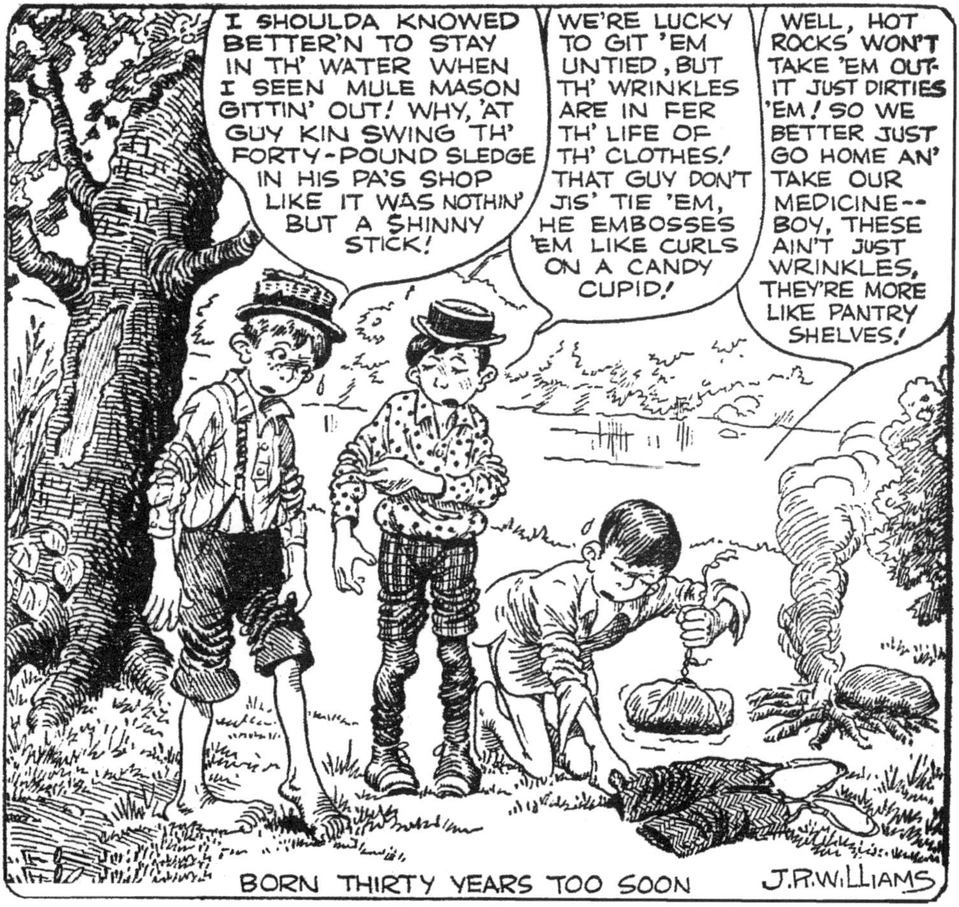
I SHOULDA KNOWED BETTER'N TO STAY IN TH' WATER WHEN I SEEN MULE MASON GITTIN' OUT! WHY, 'AT GUY KIN SWING TH' FORTY-POUND SLEDGE IN HIS PA'S SHOP LIKE IT WAS NOTHIN' BUT A $HINNY STICK!
WE'RE LUCKY TO GIT 'EM UNTIED, BUT TH' WRINKLES ARE IN FER TH' LIFE OF TH' CLOTHES! THAT GUY DON'T JIS' TIE 'EM, HE EMBOSSES 'EM LIKE CURLS ON A CANDY CUPID!
WELL, HOT ROCKS WON'T TAKE 'EM OUT- IT JUST DIRTIES 'EM! SO WE BETTER JUST GO HOME AN' TAKE OUR MEDICINE-- BOY, THESE AIN'T JUST WRINKLES, THEY'RE MORE LIKE PANTRY SHELVES!
BORN THIRTY YEARS TOO SOON
J.R.WILLIAMS

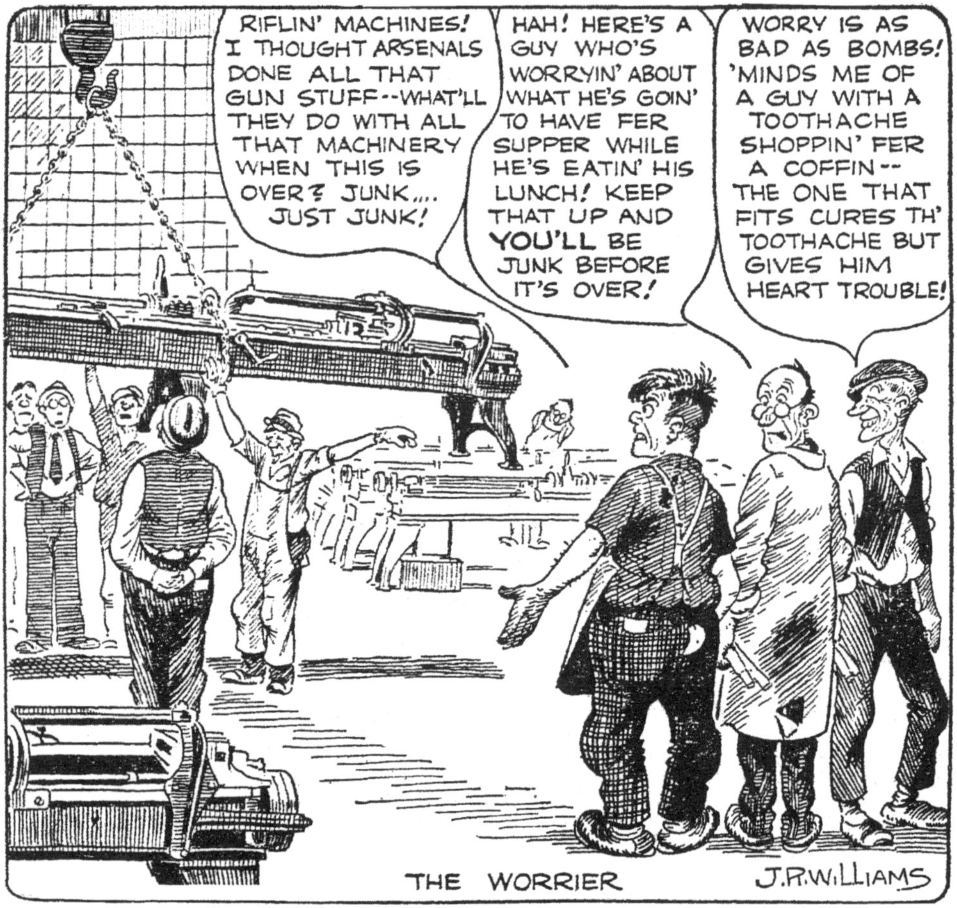
RIFLIN' MACHINES! I THOUGHT ARSENALS DONE ALL THAT GUN STUFF--WHAT'LL THEY DO WITH ALL THAT MACHINERY WHEN THIS IS OVER? JUNK,... JUST JUNK!
HAH! HERE'S A GUY WHO'S WORRYIN' ABOUT WHAT HE'S GOIN' TO HAVE FER SUPPER WHILE HE'S EATIN' HIS LUNCH! KEEP THAT UP AND YOU'LL BE JUNK BEFORE IT'S OVER!
WORRY IS AS BAD AS BOMBS! 'MINDS ME OF A GUY WITH A TOOTHACHE SHOPPIN' FER A COFFIN-- THE ONE THAT FITS CURES TH' TOOTHACHE BUT GIVES HIM HEART TROUBLE!
THE WORRIER
J.R.WILLIAMS

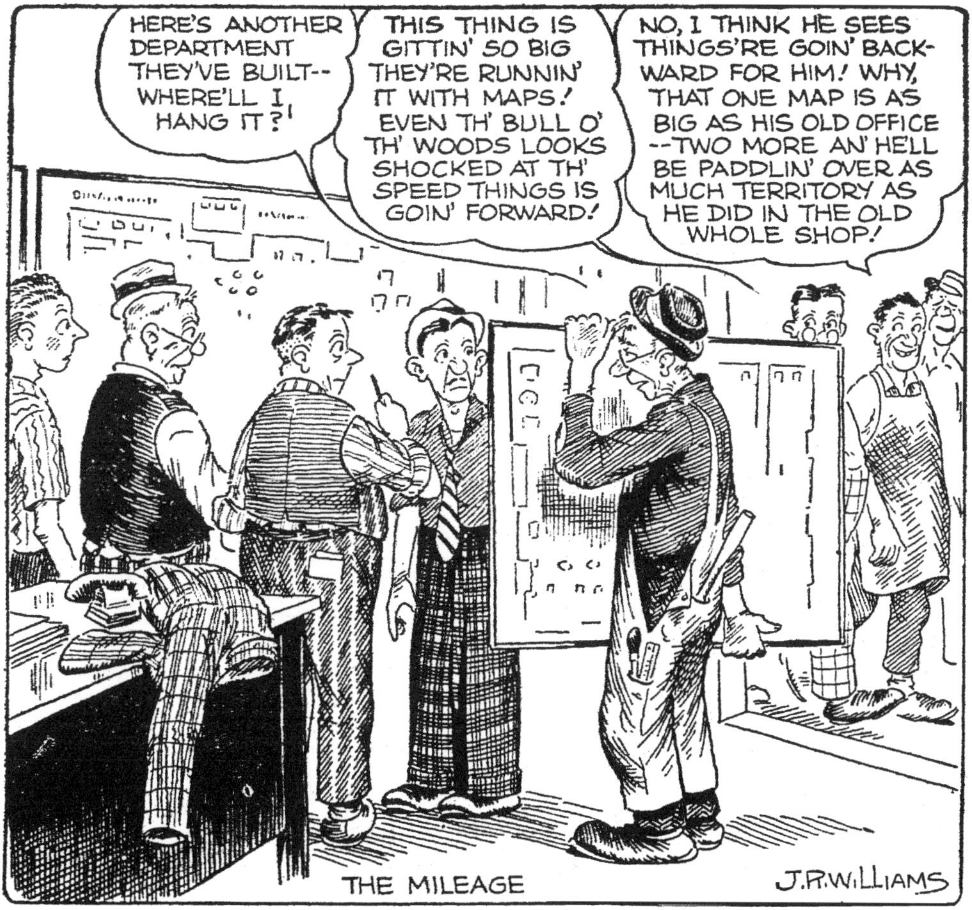
HERE'S ANOTHER DEPARTMENT THEY'VE BUILT-- WHERE'LL I HANG IT?
THIS THING IS GITTIN' SO BIG THEY'RE RUNNIN' IT WITH MAPS! EVEN TH' BULL O' TH' WOODS LOOKS SHOCKED AT TH' SPEED THINGS IS GOIN' FORWARD!
NO, I THINK HE SEES THINGS'RE GOIN' BACKWARD FOR HIM! WHY, THAT ONE MAP IS AS BIG AS HIS OLD OFFICE --TWO MORE AN' HE'LL BE PADDLIN' OVER AS MUCH TERRITORY AS HE DID IN THE OLD WHOLE SHOP!
THE MILEAGE
J.R.WILLIAMS

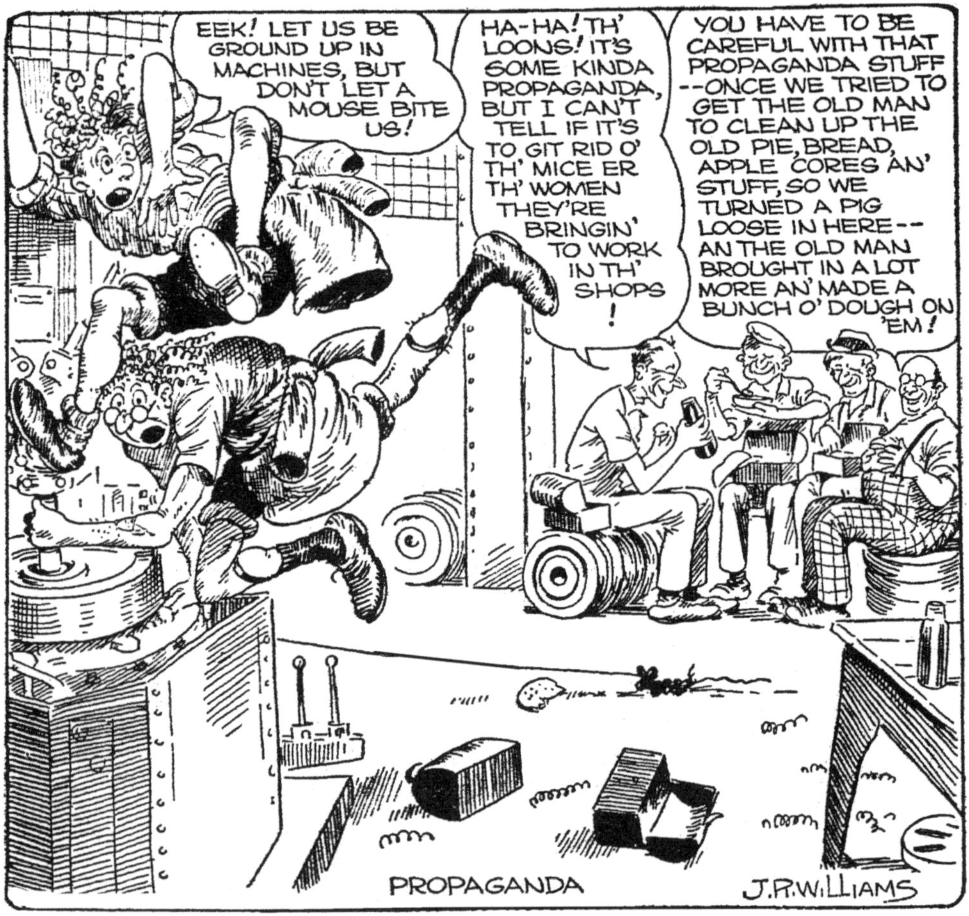
EEK! LET US BE GROUND UP IN MACHINES, BUT DON'T LET A MOUSE BITE US!
HA-HA! TH' LOONS! IT'S SOME KINDA PROPAGANDA, BUT I CAN'T TELL IF IT'S TO GIT RID O' TH' MICE ER TH' WOMEN THEY'RE BRINGIN' TO WORK IN TH' SHOPS!
YOU HAVE TO BE CAREFUL WITH THAT PROPAGANDA STUFF --ONCE WE TRIED TO GET THE OLD MAN TO CLEAN UP THE OLD PIE, BREAD, APPLE CORES AN' STUFF, SO WE TURNED A PIG LOOSE IN HERE-- AN THE OLD MAN BROUGHT IN A LOT MORE AN' MADE A BUNCH O' DOUGH ON 'EM!
PROPAGANDA
J.R.WILLIAMS

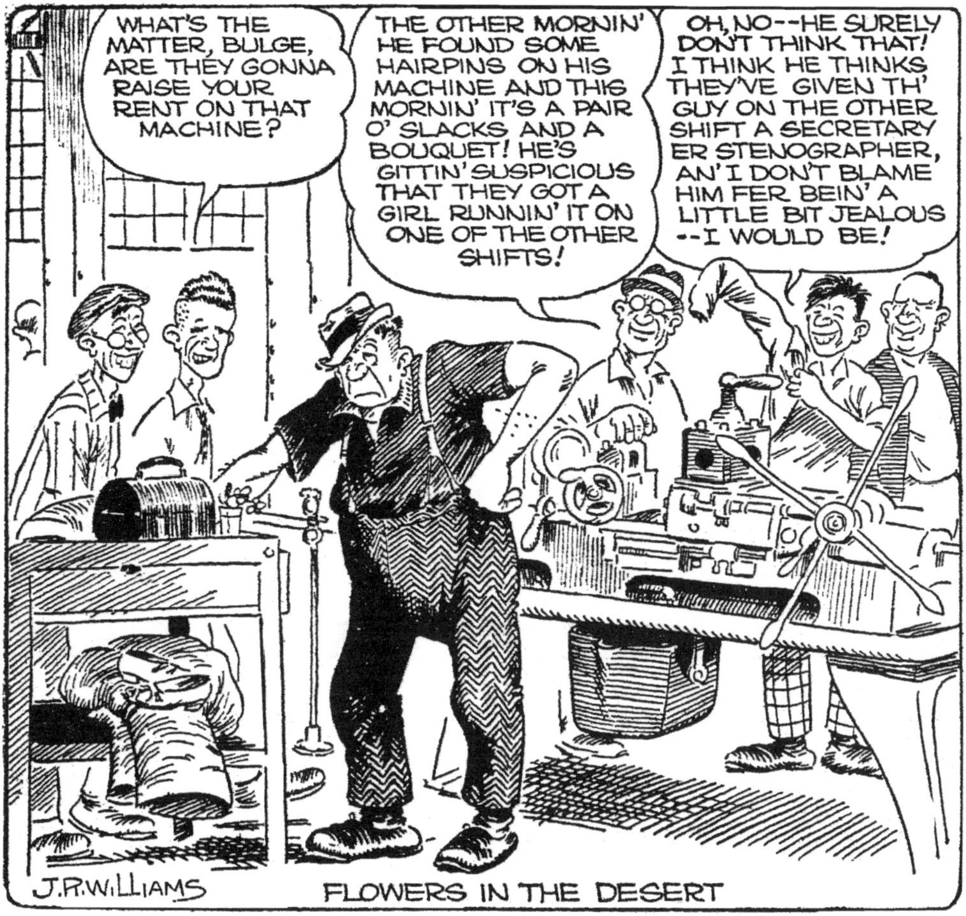
WHAT'S THE MATTER, BULGE, ARE THEY GONNA RAISE YOUR RENT ON THAT MACHINE?
THE OTHER MORNIN' HE FOUND SOME HAIRPINS ON HIS MACHINE AND THIS MORNIN' IT'S A PAIR O' SLACKS AND A BOUQUET! HE'S GITTIN' SUSPICIOUS THAT THEY GOT A GIRL RUNNIN' IT ON ONE OF THE OTHER SHIFTS!
OH, NO--HE SURELY DON'T THINK THAT! I THINK HE THINKS THEY'VE GIVEN TH' GUY ON THE OTHER SHIFT A SECRETARY ER STENOGRAPHER, AN' I DON'T BLAME HIM FER BEIN' A LITTLE BIT JEALOUS --I WOULD BE!
J.R.WILLIAMS
FLOWERS IN THE DESERT

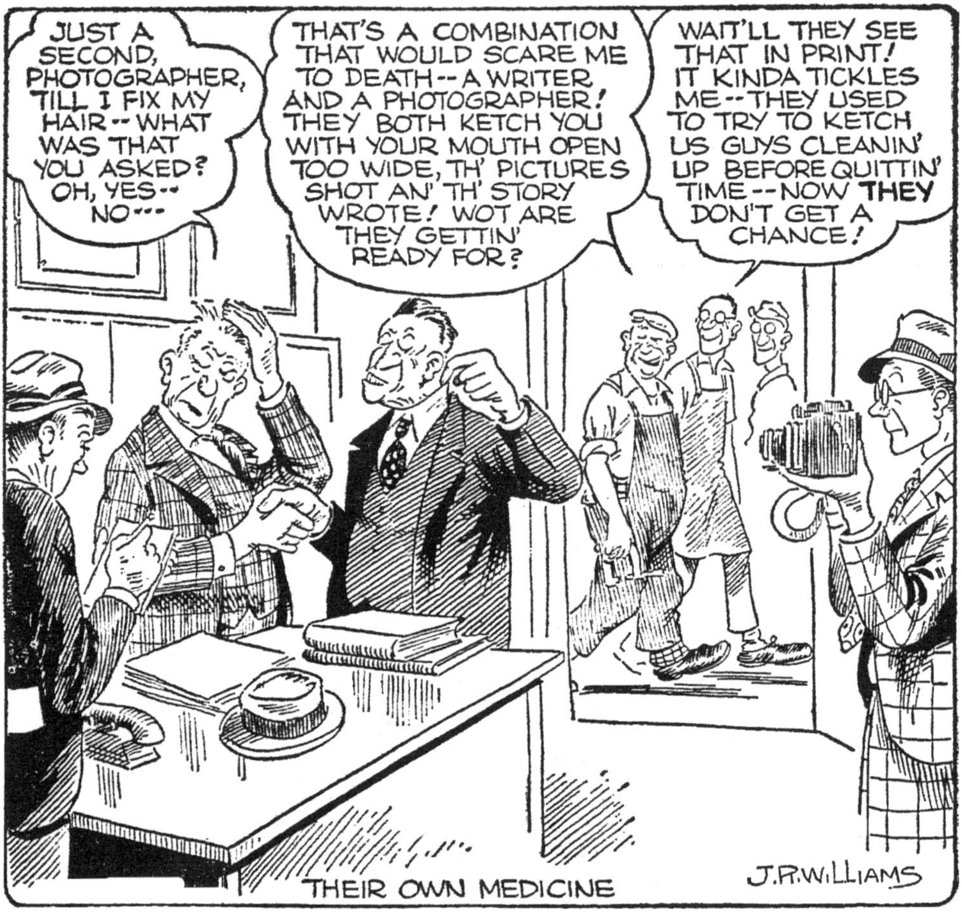
JUST A SECOND, PHOTOGRAPHER, TILL I FIX MY HAIR -- WHAT WAS THAT YOU ASKED? OH, YES-- NO---
THAT'S A COMBINATION THAT WOULD SCARE ME TO DEATH -- A WRITER AND A PHOTOGRAPHER! THEY BOTH KETCH YOU WITH YOUR MOUTH OPEN TOO WIDE, TH' PICTURES SHOT AN' TH' STORY WROTE! WOT ARE THEY GETTIN' READY FOR?
WAIT'LL THEY SEE THAT IN PRINT! IT KINDA TICKLES ME -- THEY USED TO TRY TO KETCH US GUYS CLEANIN' UP BEFORE QUITTIN' TIME -- NOW THEY DON'T GET A CHANCE!
THEIR OWN MEDICINE
J.R.WILLIAMS

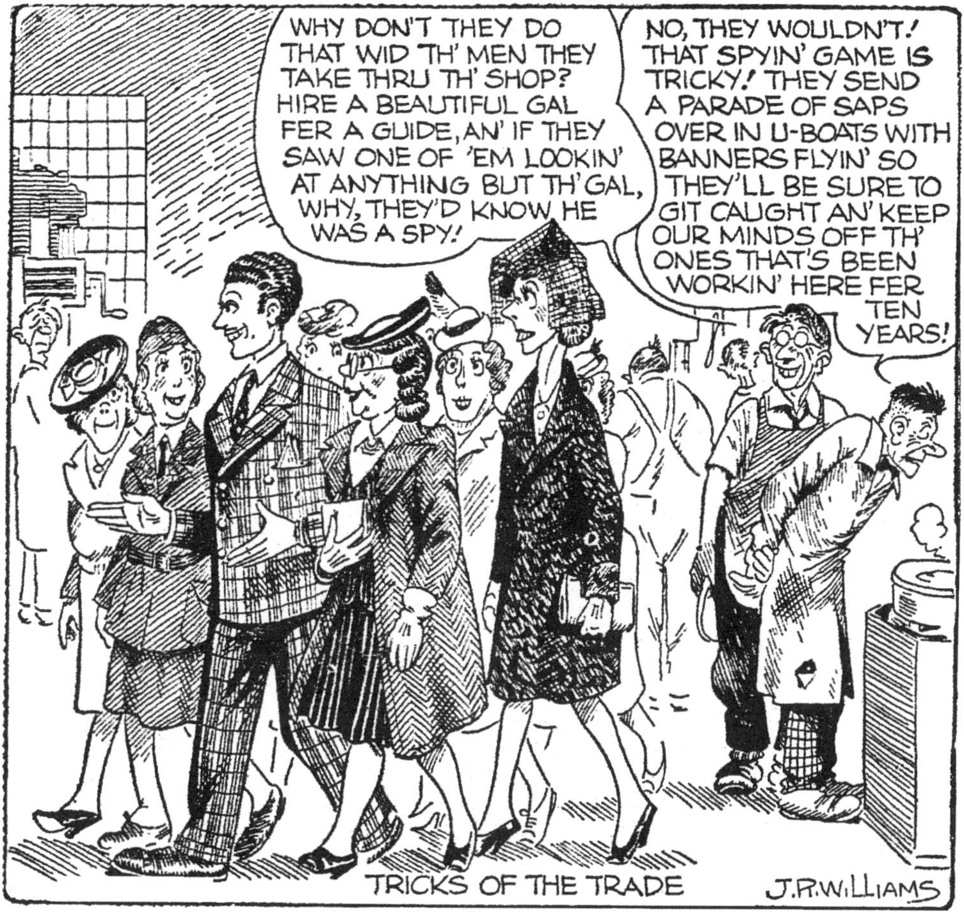
WHY DON'T THEY DO THAT WID TH' MEN THEY TAKE THRU TH' SHOP? HIRE A BEAUTIFUL GAL FER A GUIDE, AN' IF THEY SAW ONE OF 'EM LOOKIN' AT ANYTHING BUT TH' GAL, WHY, THEY'D KNOW HE WAS A SPY!
NO, THEY WOULDN'T! THAT SPYIN' GAME IS TRICKY! THEY SEND A PARADE OF SAPS OVER IN U-BOATS WITH BANNERS FLYIN' SO THEY'LL BE SURE TO GIT CAUGHT AN' KEEP OUR MINDS OFF TH' ONES THAT'S BEEN WORKIN' HERE FER TEN YEARS!
TRICKS OF THE TRADE
J.R.WILLIAMS

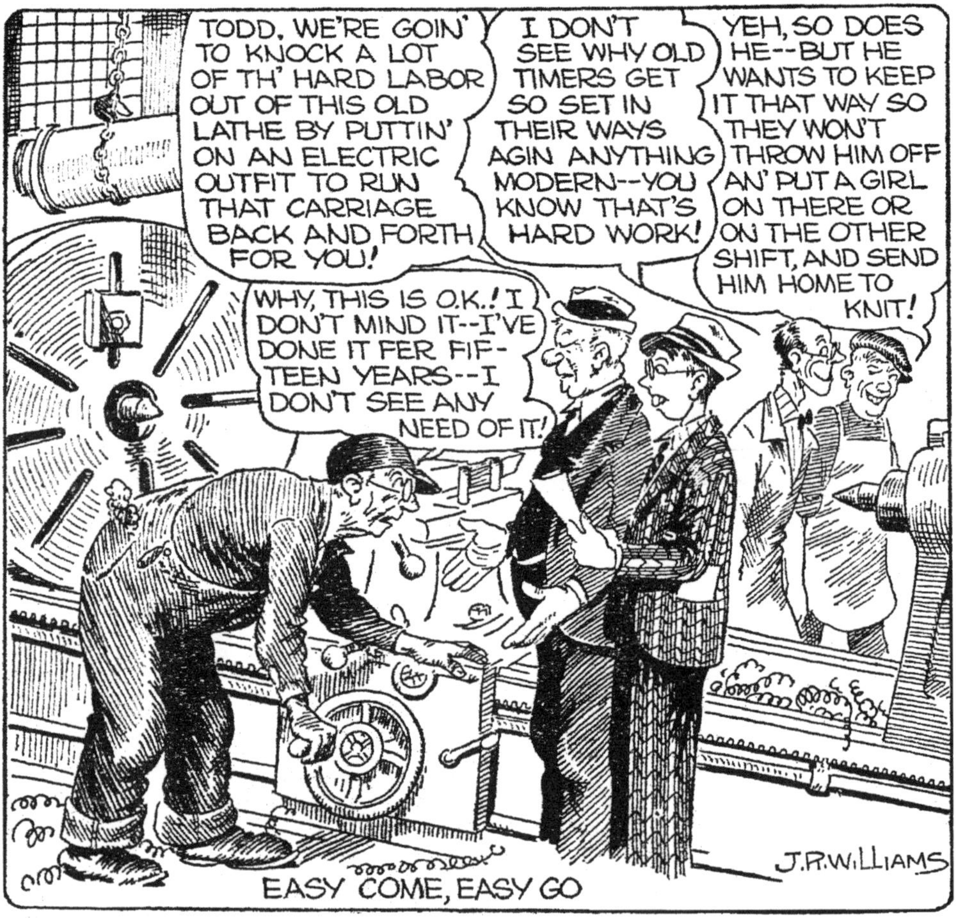
TODD, WE'RE GOIN' TO KNOCK A LOT OF TH' HARD LABOR OUT OF THIS OLD LATHE BY PUTTIN' ON AN ELECTRIC OUTFIT TO RUN THAT CARRIAGE BACK AND FORTH FOR YOU!
I DON'T SEE WHY OLD TIMERS GET SO SET IN THEIR WAYS AGIN ANYTHING MODERN--YOU KNOW THAT'S HARD WORK!
YEH, SO DOES HE--BUT HE WANTS TO KEEP IT THAT WAY SO THEY WON'T THROW HIM OFF AN' PUT A GIRL ON THERE OR ON THE OTHER SHIFT, AND SEND HIM HOME TO KNIT!
WHY, THIS IS O.K.! I DON'T MIND IT--I'VE DONE IT FER FIFTEEN YEARS--I DON'T SEE ANY NEED OF IT!
J.R.WILLIAMS
EASY COME, EASY GO

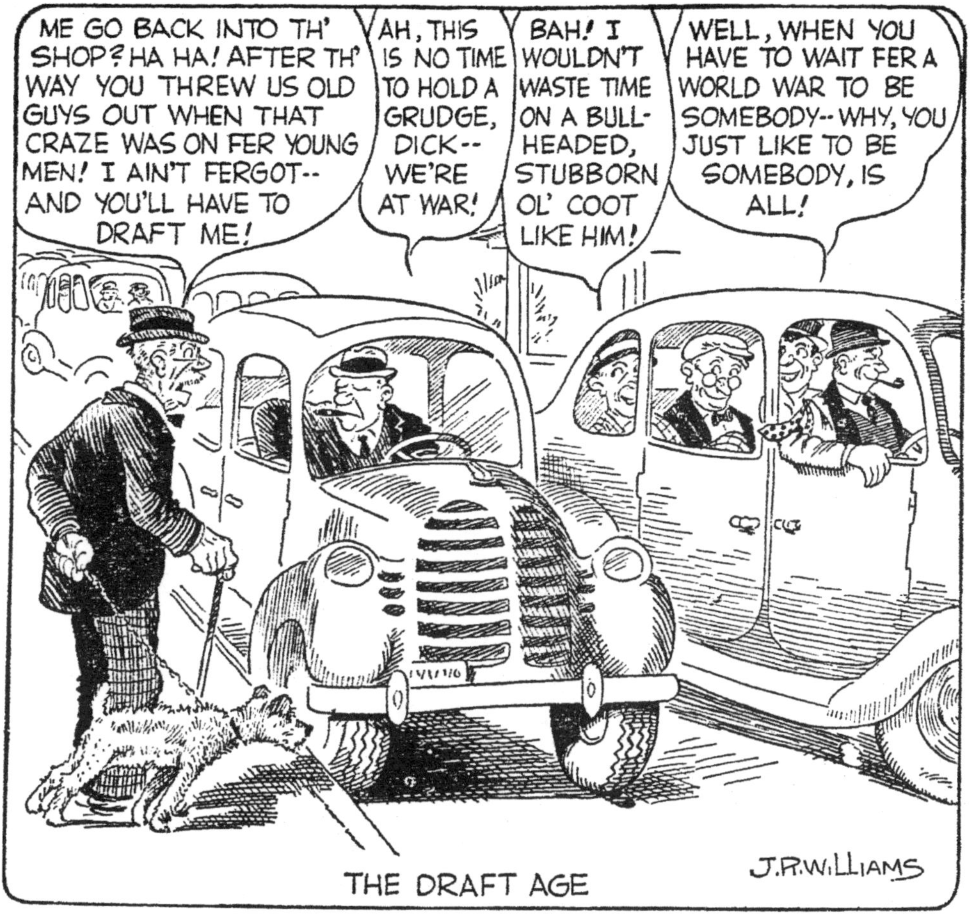
ME GO BACK INTO TH' SHOP? HA HA! AFTER TH' WAY YOU THREW US OLD GUYS OUT WHEN THAT CRAZE WAS ON FER YOUNG MEN! I AIN'T FERGOT-- AND YOU'LL HAVE TO DRAFT ME!
AH, THIS IS NO TIME TO HOLD A GRUDGE, DICK-- WE'RE AT WAR!
BAH! I WOULDN'T WASTE TIME ON A BULL-HEADED, STUBBORN OL' COOT LIKE HIM!
WELL, WHEN YOU HAVE TO WAIT FER A WORLD WAR TO BE SOMEBODY--WHY, YOU JUST LIKE TO BE SOMEBODY, IS ALL!
J.R.WILLIAMS
THE DRAFT AGE

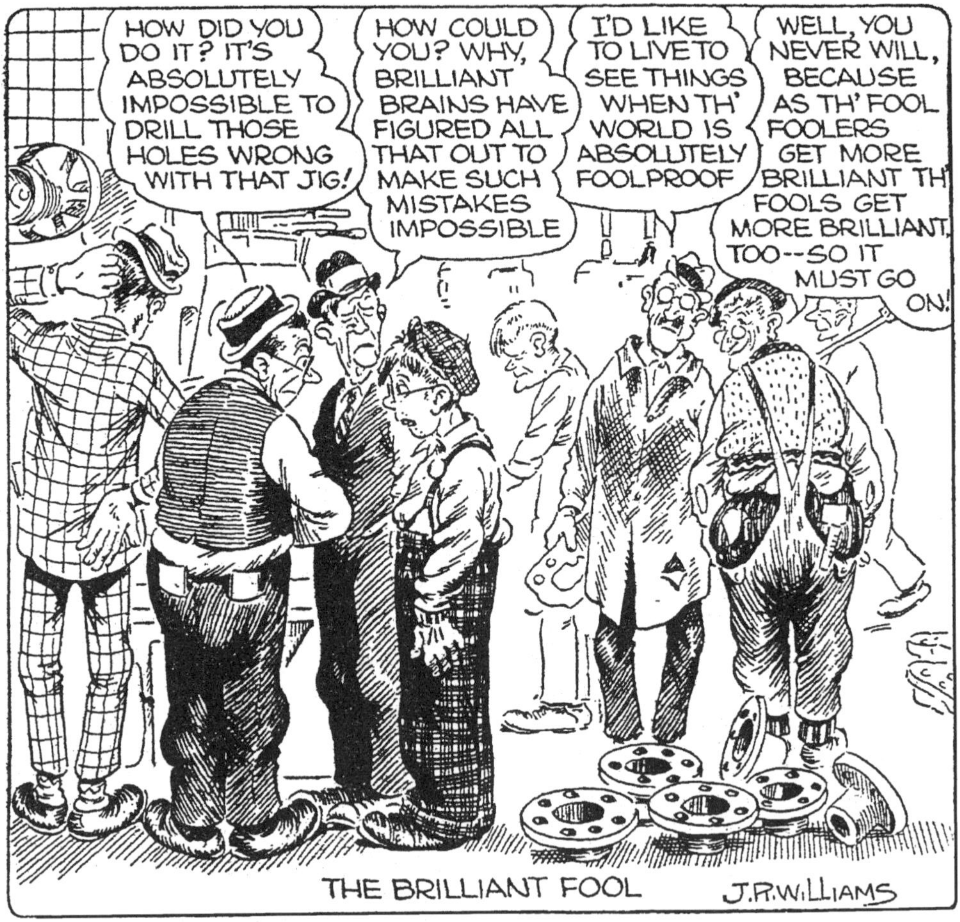
HOW DID YOU DO IT? IT'S ABSOLUTELY IMPOSSIBLE TO DRILL THOSE HOLES WRONG WITH THAT JIG!
HOW COULD YOU? WHY, BRILLIANT BRAINS HAVE FIGURED ALL THAT OUT TO MAKE SUCH MISTAKES IMPOSSIBLE
I'D LIKE TO LIVE TO SEE THINGS WHEN TH' WORLD IS ABSOLUTELY FOOLPROOF
WELL, YOU NEVER WILL, BECAUSE AS TH' FOOL FOOLERS GET MORE BRILLIANT TH' FOOLS GET MORE BRILLIANT, TOO--SO IT MUST GO ON!
THE BRILLIANT FOOL
J.R.WILLIAMS

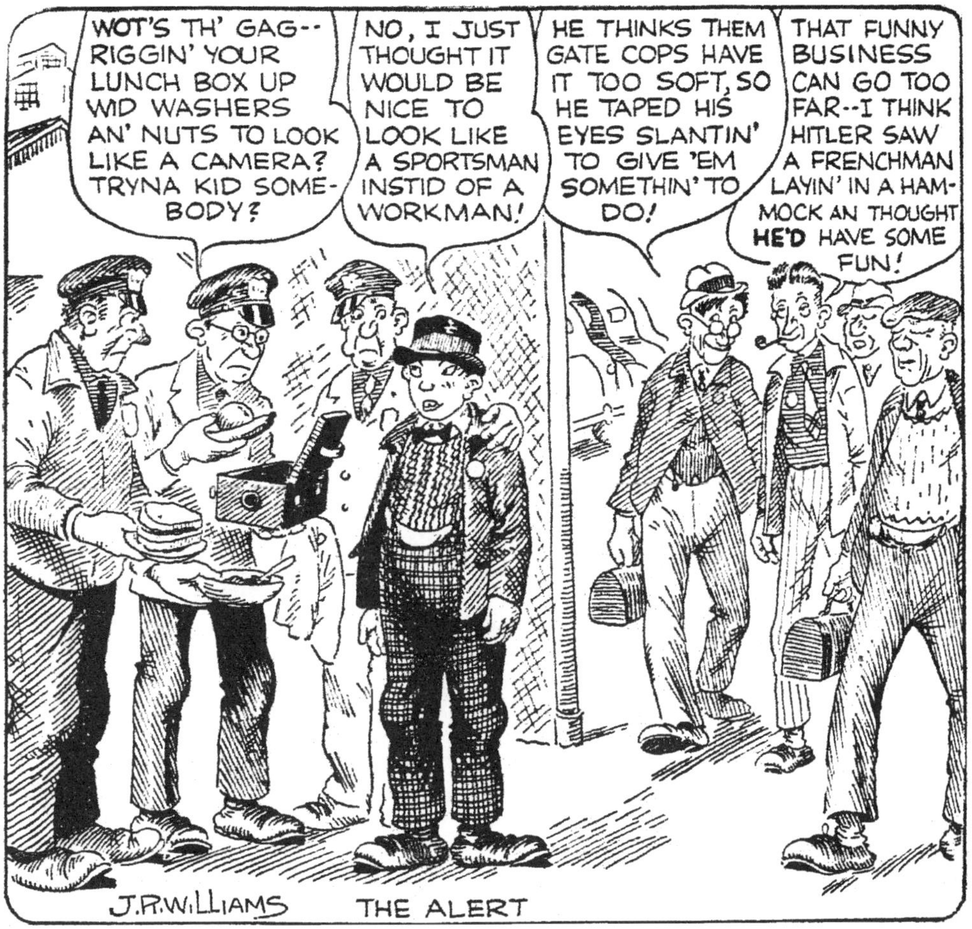
WOT'S TH' GAG--RIGGIN' YOUR LUNCH BOX UP WID WASHERS AN' NUTS TO LOOK LIKE A CAMERA? TRYNA KID SOMEBODY?
NO, I JUST THOUGHT IT WOULD BE NICE TO LOOK LIKE A SPORTSMAN INSTID OF A WORKMAN!
HE THINKS THEM GATE COPS HAVE IT TOO SOFT, SO HE TAPED HIS EYES SLANTIN' TO GIVE 'EM SOMETHIN' TO DO!
THAT FUNNY BUSINESS CAN GO TOO FAR--I THINK HITLER SAW A FRENCHMAN LAYIN' IN A HAMMOCK AN THOUGHT HE'D HAVE SOME FUN!
J.R.WILLIAMS
THE ALERT

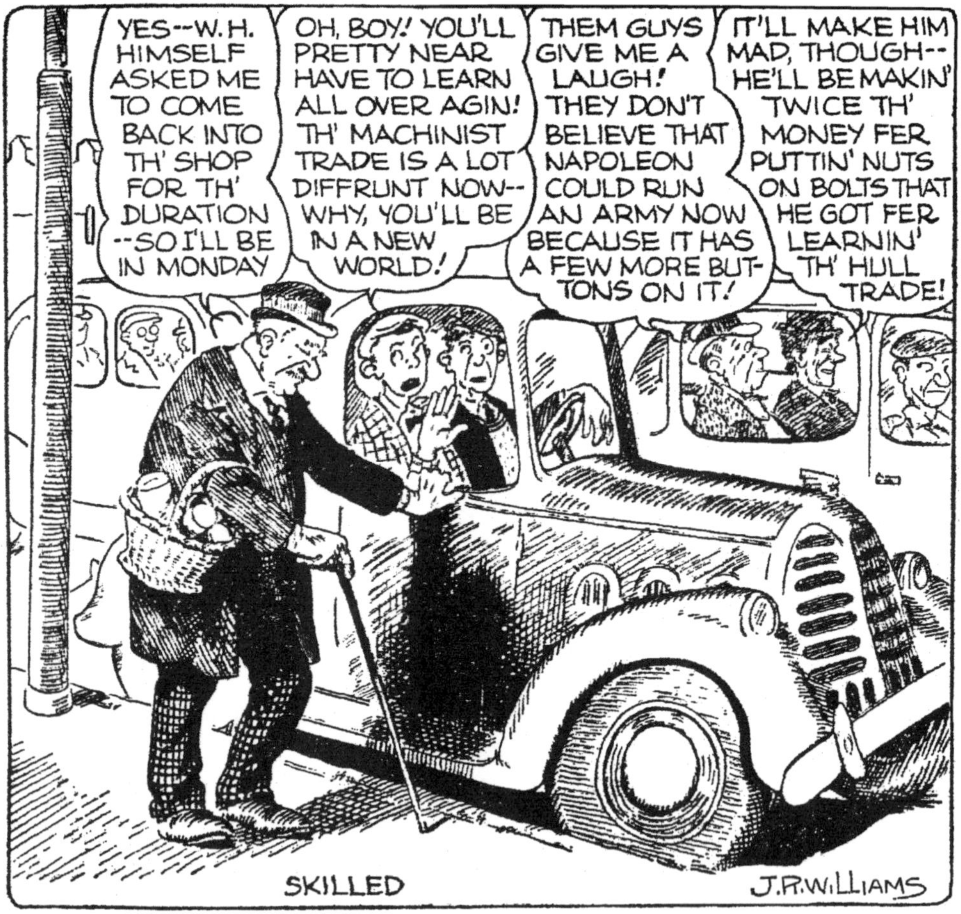
YES--W.H. HIMSELF ASKED ME TO COME BACK INTO TH' SHOP FOR TH' DURATION --SO I'LL BE IN MONDAY
OH, BOY! YOU'LL PRETTY NEAR HAVE TO LEARN ALL OVER AGIN! TH' MACHINIST TRADE IS A LOT DIFFRUNT NOW--WHY, YOU'LL BE IN A NEW WORLD!
THEM GUYS GIVE ME A LAUGH! THEY DON'T BELIEVE THAT NAPOLEON COULD RUN AN ARMY NOW BECAUSE IT HAS A FEW MORE BUT-TONS ON IT!
IT'LL MAKE HIM MAD, THOUGH--HE'LL BE MAKIN' TWICE TH' MONEY FER PUTTIN' NUTS ON BOLTS THAT HE GOT FER LEARNIN' TH' HULL TRADE!
SKILLED
J.R.WILLIAMS

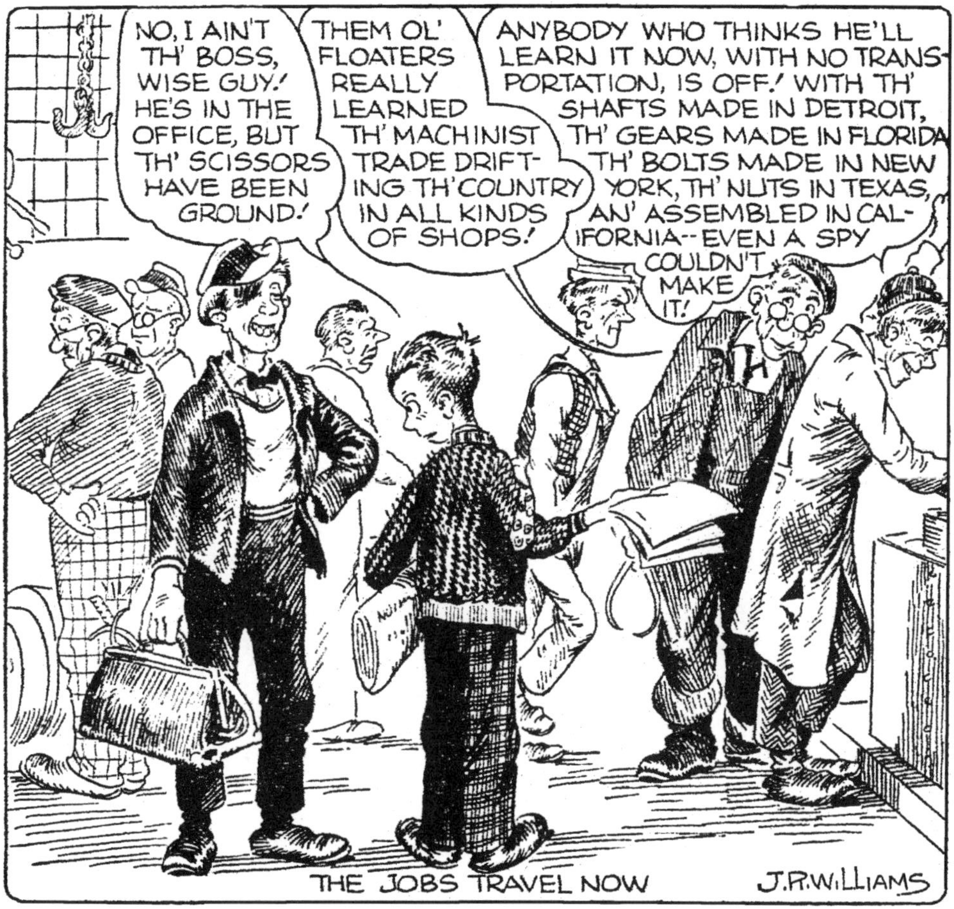
NO, I AIN'T TH' BOSS, WISE GUY! HE'S IN THE OFFICE, BUT TH' SCISSORS HAVE BEEN GROUND!
THEM OL' FLOATERS REALLY LEARNED TH' MACHINIST TRADE DRIFTING TH' COUNTRY IN ALL KINDS OF SHOPS!
ANYBODY WHO THINKS HE'LL LEARN IT NOW, WITH NO TRANSPORTATION, IS OFF! WITH TH' SHAFTS MADE IN DETROIT, TH' GEARS MADE IN FLORIDA, TH' BOLTS MADE IN NEW YORK, TH' NUTS IN TEXAS, AN' ASSEMBLED IN CALIFORNIA--EVEN A SPY COULDN'T MAKE IT!
THE JOBS TRAVEL NOW
J.R. WILLIAMS

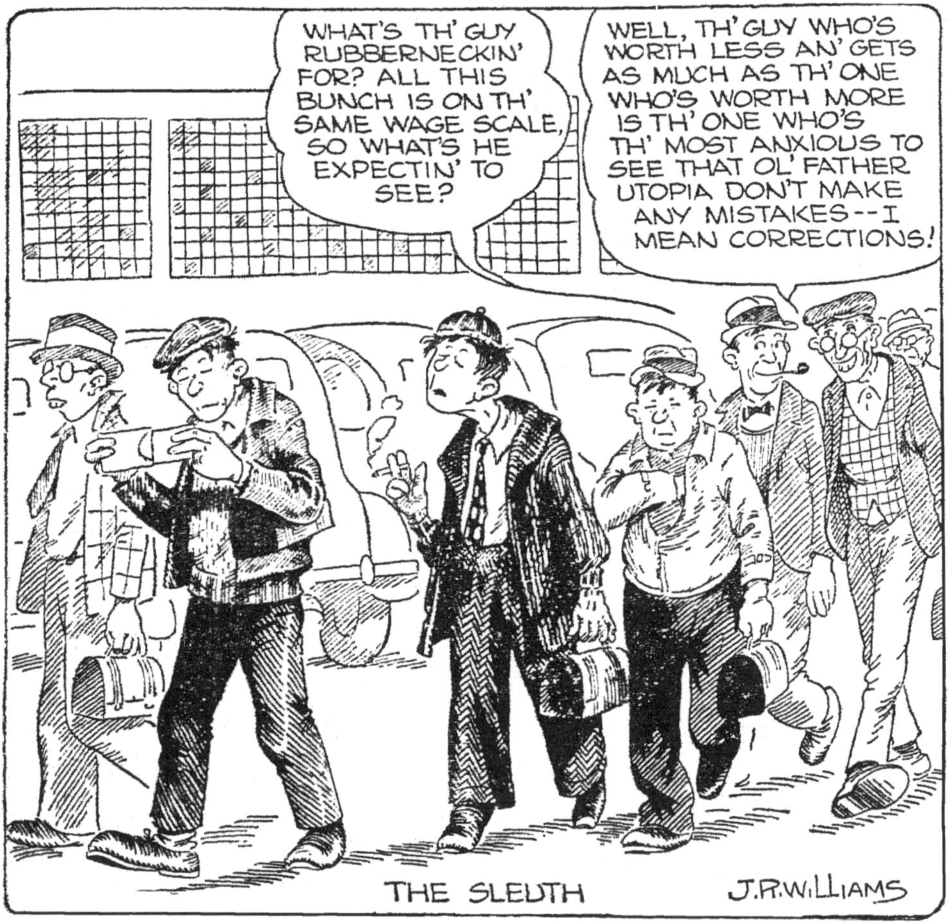
WHAT'S TH' GUY RUBBERNECKIN' FOR? ALL THIS BUNCH IS ON TH' SAME WAGE SCALE, SO WHAT'S HE EXPECTIN' TO SEE?
WELL, TH' GUY WHO'S WORTH LESS AN' GETS AS MUCH AS TH' ONE WHO'S WORTH MORE IS TH' ONE WHO'S TH' MOST ANXIOUS TO SEE THAT OL' FATHER UTOPIA DON'T MAKE ANY MISTAKES--I MEAN CORRECTIONS!
THE SLEUTH
J.R.WILLIAMS

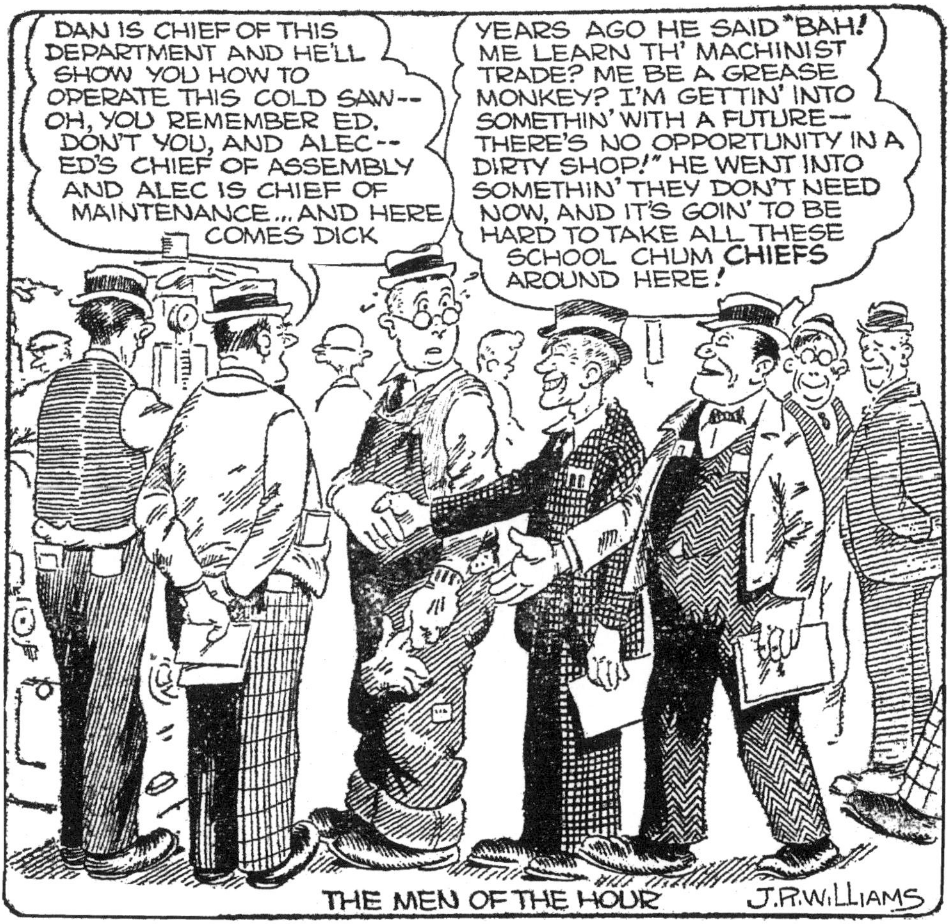
DAN IS CHIEF OF THIS DEPARTMENT AND HE'LL SHOW YOU HOW TO OPERATE THIS COLD SAW-- OH, YOU REMEMBER ED. DON'T YOU, AND ALEC-- ED'S CHIEF OF ASSEMBLY AND ALEC IS CHIEF OF MAINTENANCE... AND HERE COMES DICK
YEARS AGO HE SAID "BAH! ME LEARN TH' MACHINIST TRADE? ME BE A GREASE MONKEY? I'M GETTIN' INTO SOMETHIN' WITH A FUTURE— THERE'S NO OPPORTUNITY IN A DIRTY SHOP!" HE WENT INTO SOMETHIN' THEY DON'T NEED NOW, AND IT'S GOIN' TO BE HARD TO TAKE ALL THESE SCHOOL CHUM **CHIEFS** AROUND HERE!
THE MEN OF THE HOUR
J.R.WILLIAMS

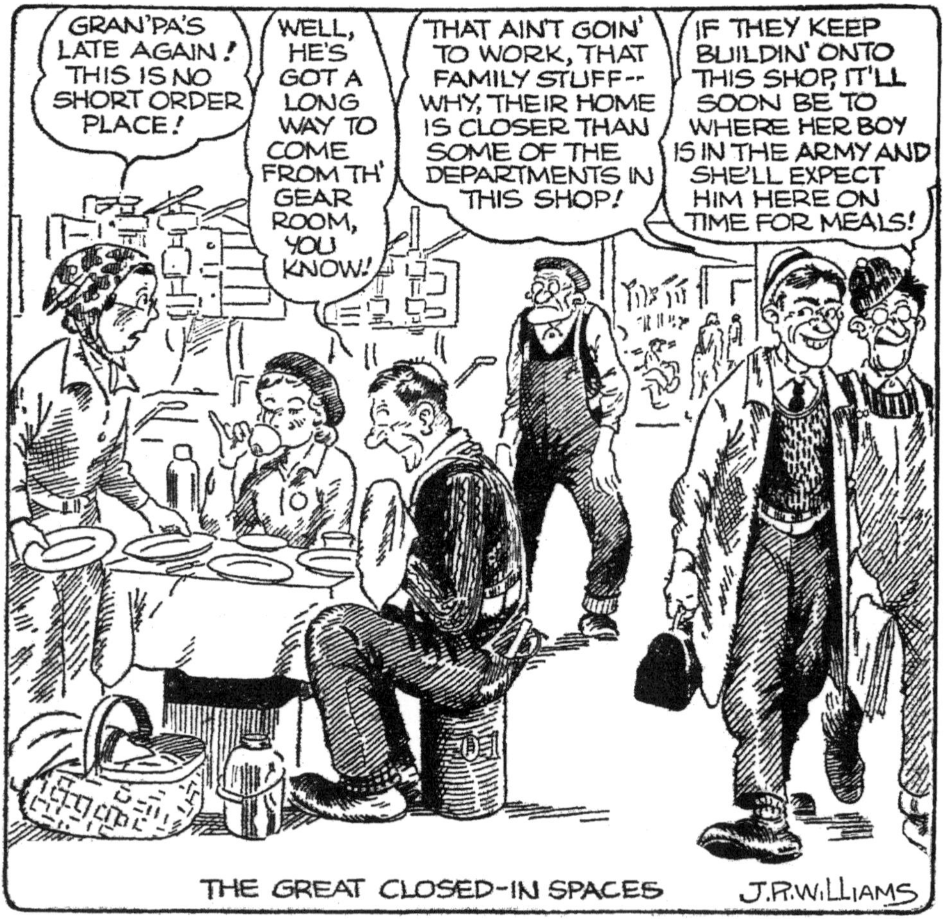
GRAN'PA'S LATE AGAIN! THIS IS NO SHORT ORDER PLACE!
WELL, HE'S GOT A LONG WAY TO COME FROM TH' GEAR ROOM, YOU KNOW!
THAT AIN'T GOIN' TO WORK, THAT FAMILY STUFF-- WHY, THEIR HOME IS CLOSER THAN SOME OF THE DEPARTMENTS IN THIS SHOP!
IF THEY KEEP BUILDIN' ONTO THIS SHOP, IT'LL SOON BE TO WHERE HER BOY IS IN THE ARMY AND SHE'LL EXPECT HIM HERE ON TIME FOR MEALS!
THE GREAT CLOSED-IN SPACES
J.R. WILLIAMS

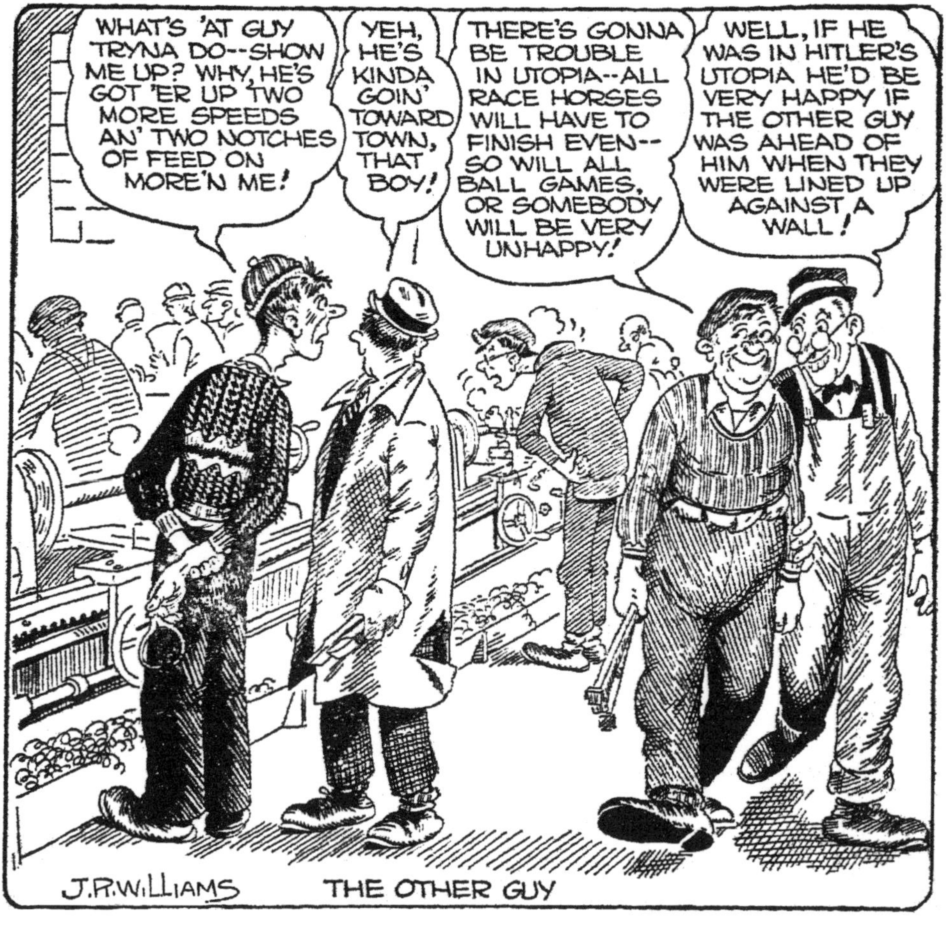
WHAT'S 'AT GUY TRYNA DO--SHOW ME UP? WHY, HE'S GOT 'ER UP TWO MORE SPEEDS AN' TWO NOTCHES OF FEED ON MORE'N ME!
YEH, HE'S KINDA GOIN' TOWARD TOWN, THAT BOY!
THERE'S GONNA BE TROUBLE IN UTOPIA--ALL RACE HORSES WILL HAVE TO FINISH EVEN--SO WILL ALL BALL GAMES, OR SOMEBODY WILL BE VERY UNHAPPY!
WELL, IF HE WAS IN HITLER'S UTOPIA HE'D BE VERY HAPPY IF THE OTHER GUY WAS AHEAD OF HIM WHEN THEY WERE LINED UP AGAINST A WALL!
J.R.WILLIAMS
THE OTHER GUY

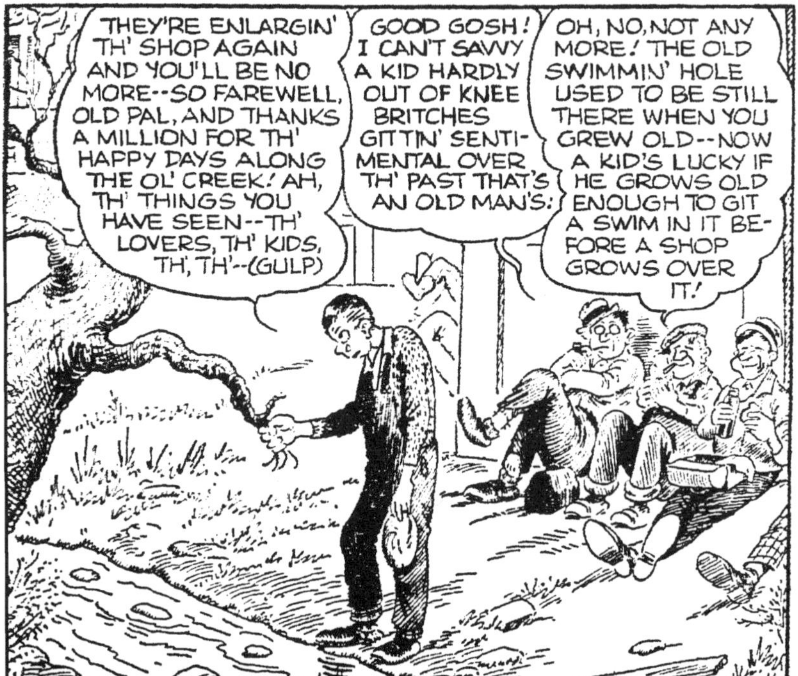
THEY'RE ENLARGIN' TH' SHOP AGAIN AND YOU'LL BE NO MORE--SO FAREWELL, OLD PAL, AND THANKS A MILLION FOR TH' HAPPY DAYS ALONG THE OL' CREEK! AH, TH' THINGS YOU HAVE SEEN--TH' LOVERS, TH' KIDS, TH', TH'--(GULP)
GOOD GOSH! I CAN'T SAVVY A KID HARDLY OUT OF KNEE BRITCHES GITTIN' SENTI-MENTAL OVER TH' PAST THAT'S AN OLD MAN'S!
OH, NO, NOT ANY MORE! THE OLD SWIMMIN' HOLE USED TO BE STILL THERE WHEN YOU GREW OLD--NOW A KID'S LUCKY IF HE GROWS OLD ENOUGH TO GIT A SWIM IN IT BE-FORE A SHOP GROWS OVER IT!
YESTERDAY'S SUBURBS
J.R. WILLIAMS

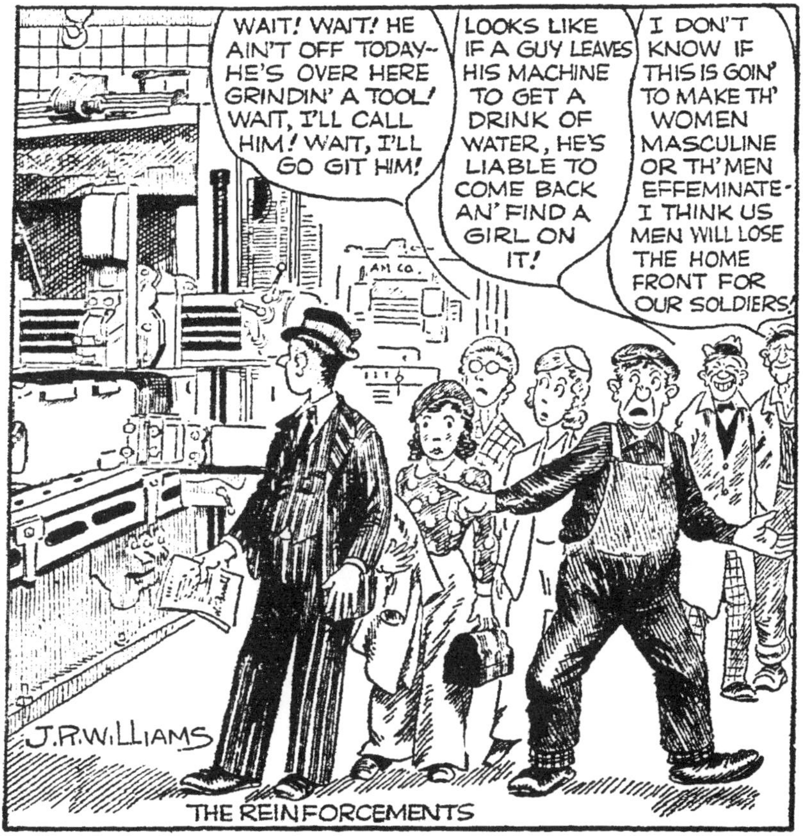
WAIT! WAIT! HE AIN'T OFF TODAY-- HE'S OVER HERE GRINDIN' A TOOL! WAIT, I'LL CALL HIM! WAIT, I'LL GO GIT HIM!
LOOKS LIKE IF A GUY LEAVES HIS MACHINE TO GET A DRINK OF WATER, HE'S LIABLE TO COME BACK AN' FIND A GIRL ON IT!
I DON'T KNOW IF THIS IS GOIN' TO MAKE TH' WOMEN MASCULINE OR TH' MEN EFFEMINATE- I THINK US MEN WILL LOSE THE HOME FRONT FOR OUR SOLDIERS!
J.R. WILLIAMS
THE REINFORCEMENTS

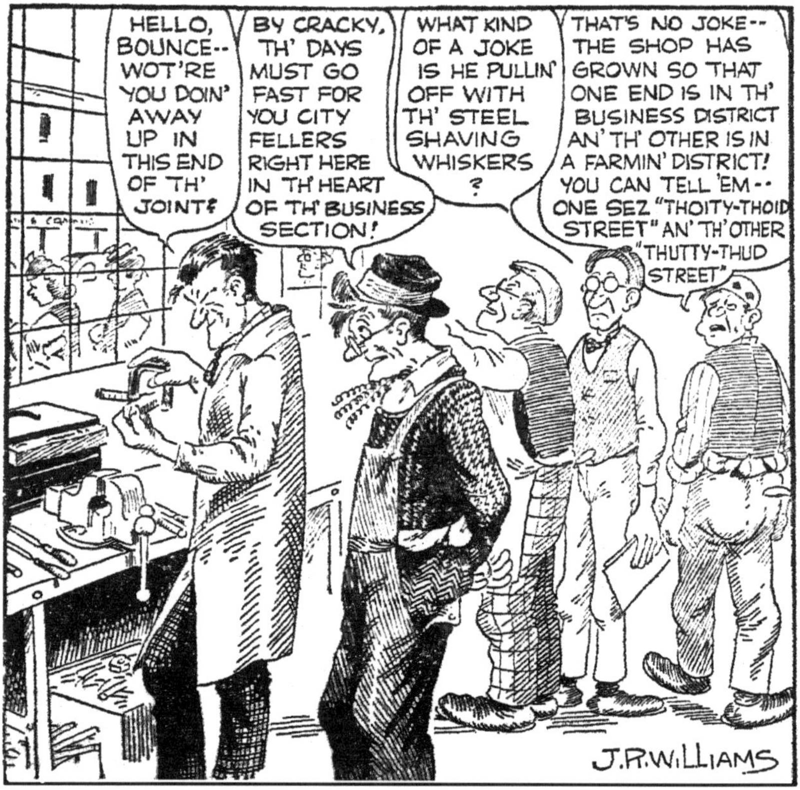
HELLO, BOUNCE-- WOT'RE YOU DOIN' AWAY UP IN THIS END OF TH' JOINT?
BY CRACKY, TH' DAYS MUST GO FAST FOR YOU CITY FELLERS RIGHT HERE IN TH' HEART OF TH' BUSINESS SECTION!
WHAT KIND OF A JOKE IS HE PULLIN' OFF WITH TH' STEEL SHAVING WHISKERS ?
THAT'S NO JOKE-- THE SHOP HAS GROWN SO THAT ONE END IS IN TH' BUSINESS DISTRICT AN' TH' OTHER IS IN A FARMIN' DISTRICT! YOU CAN TELL 'EM-- ONE SEZ "THOITY-THOID STREET" AN' TH' OTHER "THUTTY-THUD STREET"
J.R.WILLIAMS

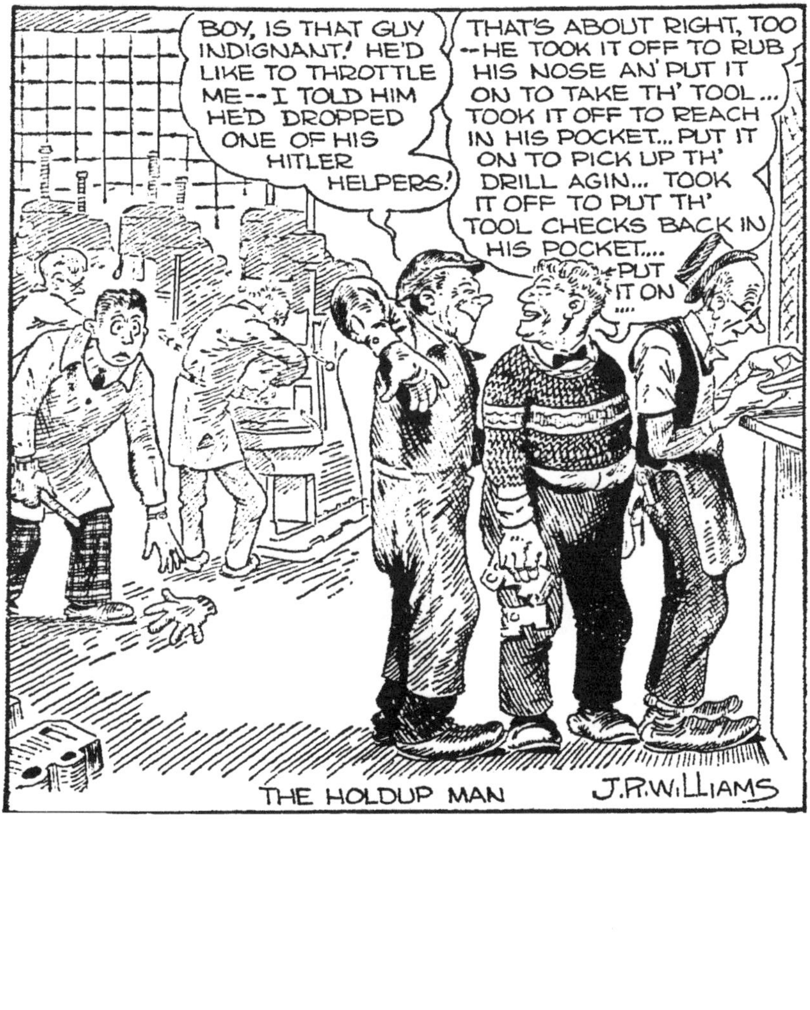
BOY, IS THAT GUY INDIGNANT! HE'D LIKE TO THROTTLE ME--I TOLD HIM HE'D DROPPED ONE OF HIS HITLER HELPERS!
THAT'S ABOUT RIGHT, TOO --HE TOOK IT OFF TO RUB HIS NOSE AN' PUT IT ON TO TAKE TH' TOOL... TOOK IT OFF TO REACH IN HIS POCKET... PUT IT ON TO PICK UP TH' DRILL AGIN... TOOK IT OFF TO PUT TH' TOOL CHECKS BACK IN HIS POCKET.... PUT IT ON ....
THE HOLDUP MAN
J.R. WILLIAMS

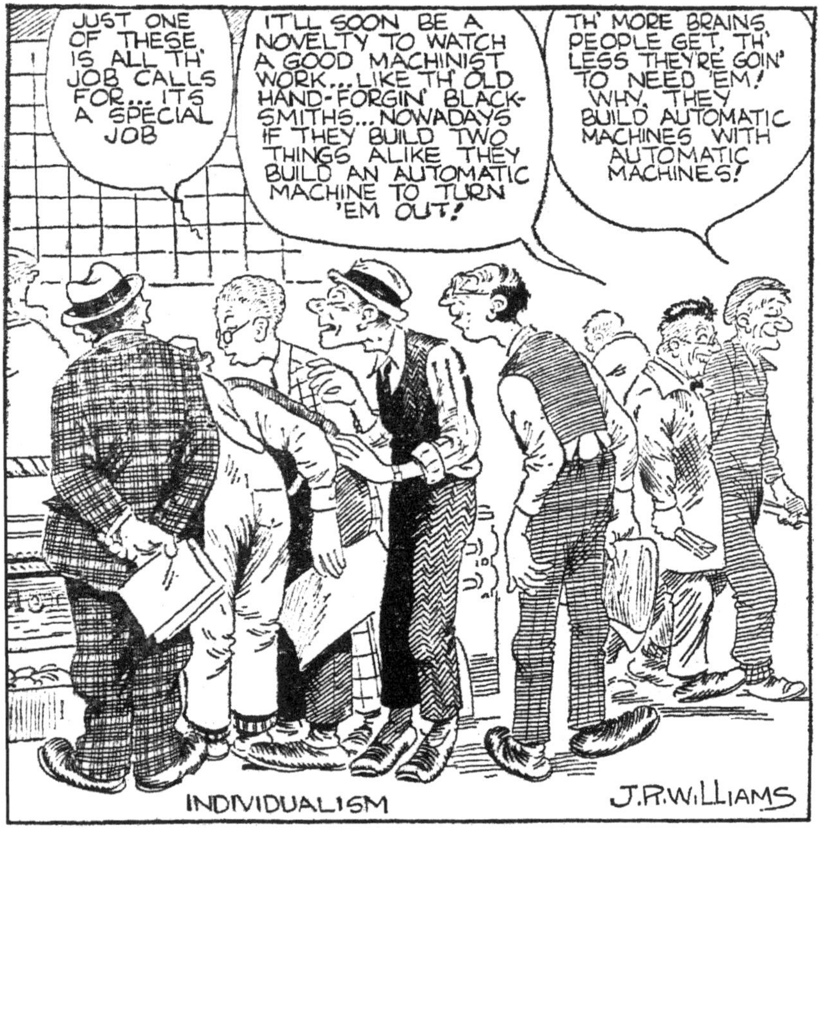
JUST ONE OF THESE IS ALL TH' JOB CALLS FOR... ITS A SPECIAL JOB
IT'LL SOON BE A NOVELTY TO WATCH A GOOD MACHINIST WORK... LIKE TH' OLD HAND-FORGIN' BLACK-SMITHS... NOWADAYS IF THEY BUILD TWO THINGS ALIKE THEY BUILD AN AUTOMATIC MACHINE TO TURN 'EM OUT!
TH' MORE BRAINS PEOPLE GET, TH' LESS THEY'RE GOIN' TO NEED 'EM! WHY, THEY BUILD AUTOMATIC MACHINES WITH AUTOMATIC MACHINES!
INDIVIDUALISM
J.R.WILLIAMS

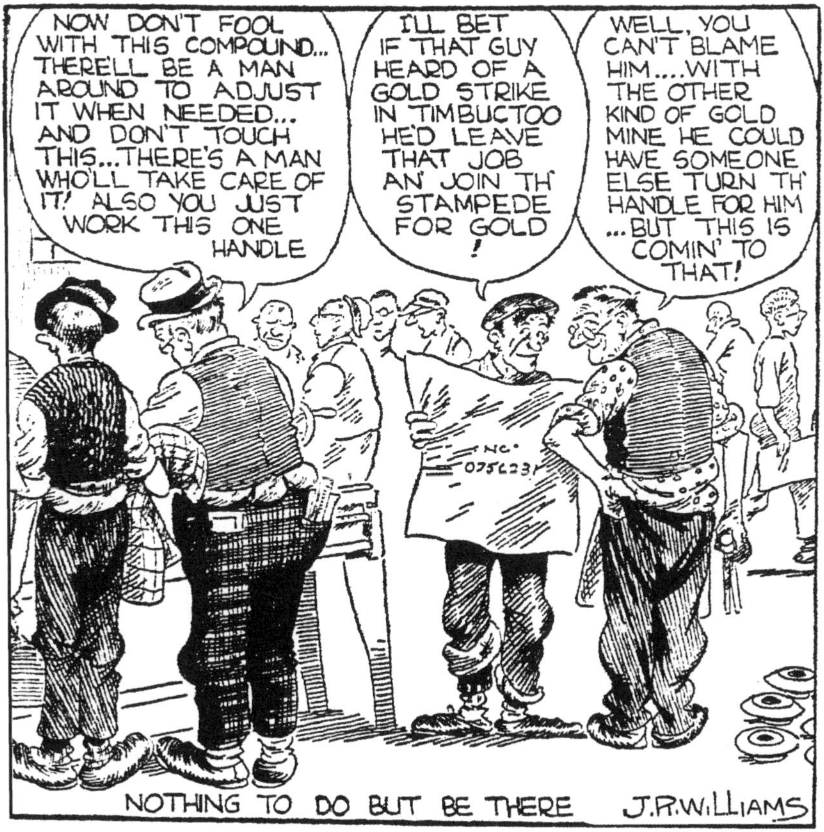
NOW DON'T FOOL WITH THIS COMPOUND... THERE'LL BE A MAN AROUND TO ADJUST IT WHEN NEEDED... AND DON'T TOUCH THIS...THERE'S A MAN WHO'LL TAKE CARE OF IT! ALSO YOU JUST WORK THIS ONE HANDLE
I'LL BET IF THAT GUY HEARD OF A GOLD STRIKE IN TIMBUCTOO HE'D LEAVE THAT JOB AN' JOIN TH' STAMPEDE FOR GOLD!
WELL, YOU CAN'T BLAME HIM....WITH THE OTHER KIND OF GOLD MINE HE COULD HAVE SOMEONE ELSE TURN TH' HANDLE FOR HIM ...BUT THIS IS COMIN' TO THAT!
NO. 0756231
NOTHING TO DO BUT BE THERE
J.R.WILLIAMS

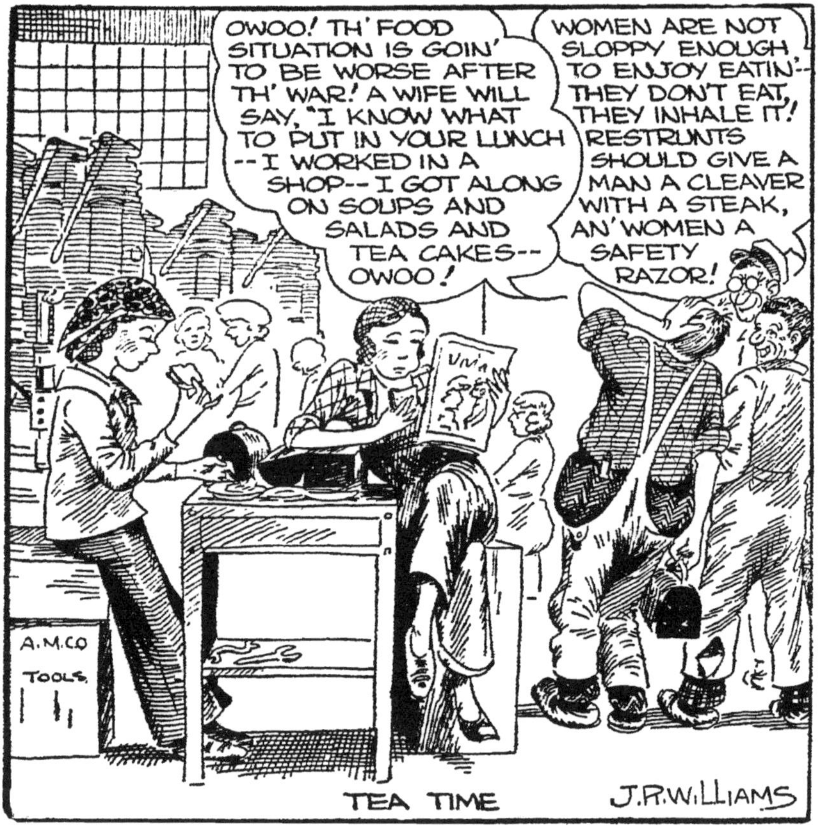
OWOO! TH' FOOD SITUATION IS GOIN' TO BE WORSE AFTER TH' WAR! A WIFE WILL SAY, "I KNOW WHAT TO PUT IN YOUR LUNCH --I WORKED IN A SHOP-- I GOT ALONG ON SOUPS AND SALADS AND TEA CAKES-- OWOO!
WOMEN ARE NOT SLOPPY ENOUGH TO ENJOY EATIN'-- THEY DON'T EAT, THEY INHALE IT! RESTRUNTS SHOULD GIVE A MAN A CLEAVER WITH A STEAK, AN' WOMEN A SAFETY RAZOR!
A.M.CO TOOLS
TEA TIME
J.R.WILLIAMS

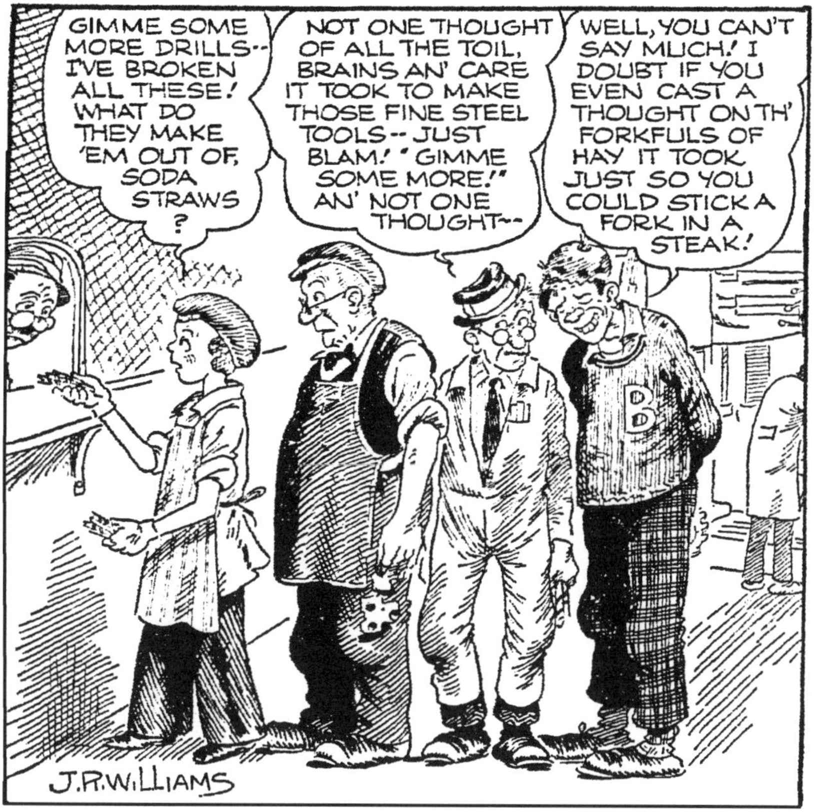
GIMME SOME MORE DRILLS-- I'VE BROKEN ALL THESE! WHAT DO THEY MAKE 'EM OUT OF, SODA STRAWS?
NOT ONE THOUGHT OF ALL THE TOIL, BRAINS AN' CARE IT TOOK TO MAKE THOSE FINE STEEL TOOLS-- JUST BLAM! "GIMME SOME MORE!" AN' NOT ONE THOUGHT--
WELL, YOU CAN'T SAY MUCH! I DOUBT IF YOU EVEN CAST A THOUGHT ON TH' FORKFULS OF HAY IT TOOK JUST SO YOU COULD STICK A FORK IN A STEAK!
J.R. WILLIAMS

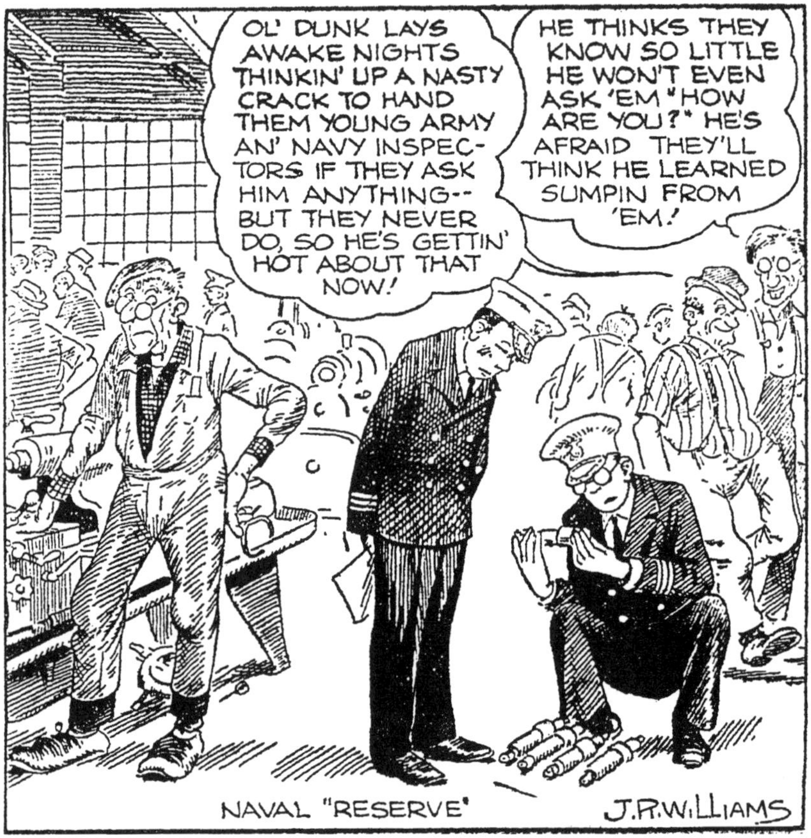
OL' DUNK LAYS AWAKE NIGHTS THINKIN' UP A NASTY CRACK TO HAND THEM YOUNG ARMY AN' NAVY INSPECTORS IF THEY ASK HIM ANYTHING-- BUT THEY NEVER DO, SO HE'S GETTIN' HOT ABOUT THAT NOW!
HE THINKS THEY KNOW SO LITTLE HE WON'T EVEN ASK 'EM "HOW ARE YOU?" HE'S AFRAID THEY'LL THINK HE LEARNED SUMPIN FROM 'EM!
NAVAL "RESERVE"
J.R.WILLIAMS

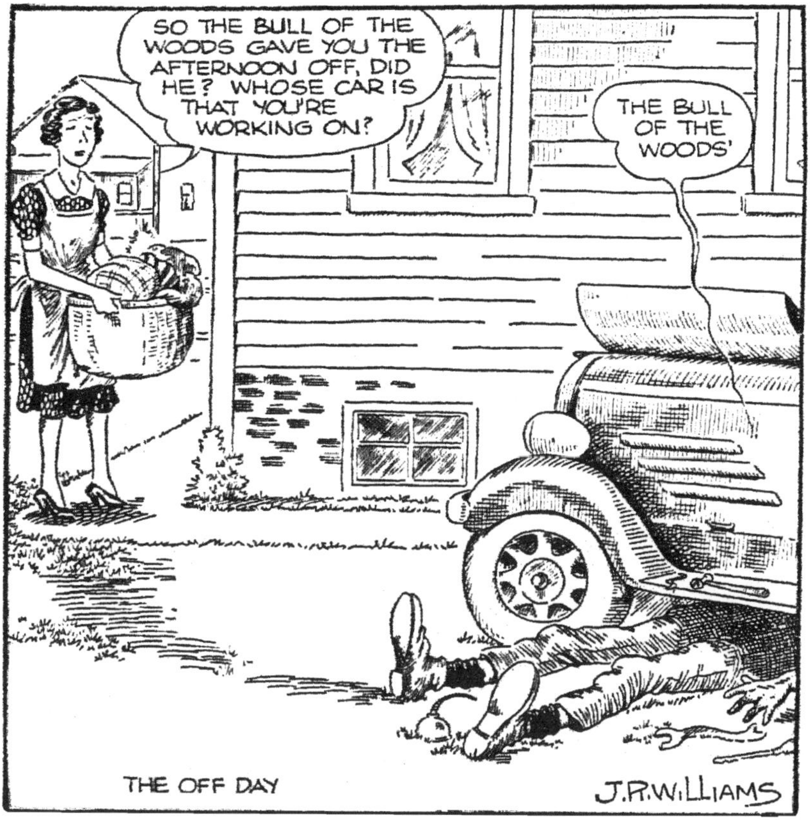
SO THE BULL OF THE WOODS GAVE YOU THE AFTERNOON OFF, DID HE? WHOSE CAR IS THAT YOU'RE WORKING ON?
THE BULL OF THE WOODS'
THE OFF DAY
J.R.WILLIAMS

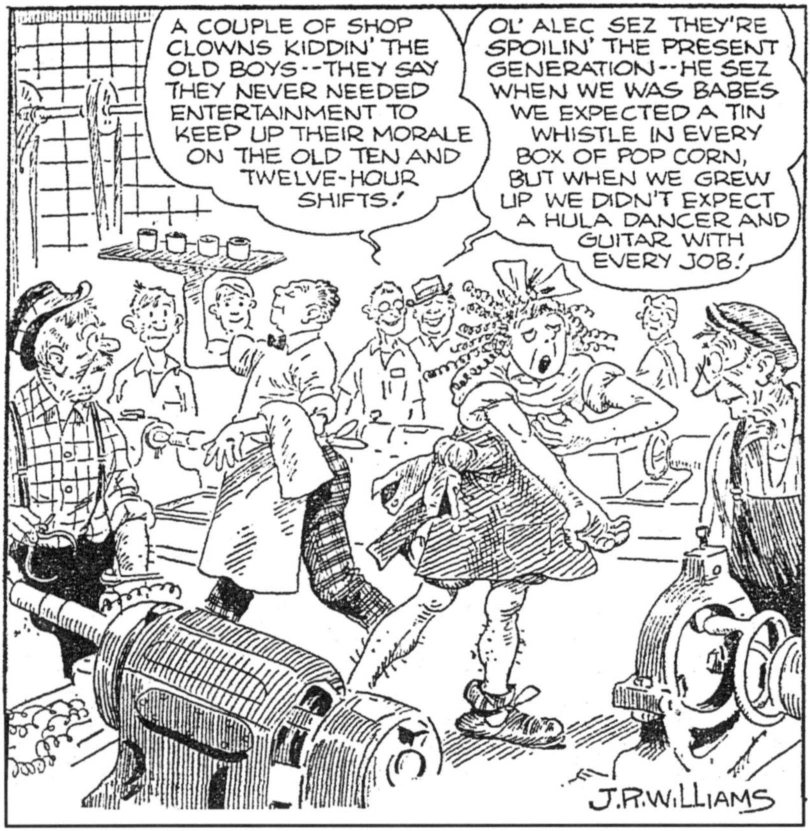
A COUPLE OF SHOP CLOWNS KIDDIN' THE OLD BOYS--THEY SAY THEY NEVER NEEDED ENTERTAINMENT TO KEEP UP THEIR MORALE ON THE OLD TEN AND TWELVE-HOUR SHIFTS!
OL' ALEC SEZ THEY'RE SPOILIN' THE PRESENT GENERATION--HE SEZ WHEN WE WAS BABES WE EXPECTED A TIN WHISTLE IN EVERY BOX OF POP CORN, BUT WHEN WE GREW UP WE DIDN'T EXPECT A HULA DANCER AND GUITAR WITH EVERY JOB!
J.R. WILLIAMS

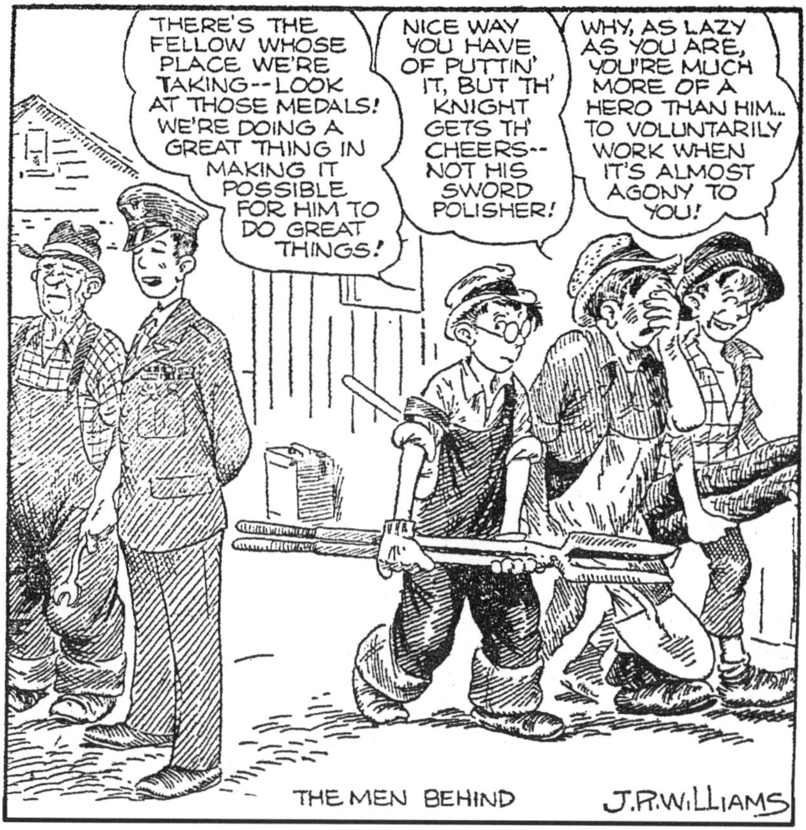
THERE'S THE FELLOW WHOSE PLACE WE'RE TAKING--LOOK AT THOSE MEDALS! WE'RE DOING A GREAT THING IN MAKING IT POSSIBLE FOR HIM TO DO GREAT THINGS!
NICE WAY YOU HAVE OF PUTTIN' IT, BUT TH' KNIGHT GETS TH' CHEERS--NOT HIS SWORD POLISHER!
WHY, AS LAZY AS YOU ARE, YOU'RE MUCH MORE OF A HERO THAN HIM... TO VOLUNTARILY WORK WHEN IT'S ALMOST AGONY TO YOU!
THE MEN BEHIND
J.R.WILLIAMS

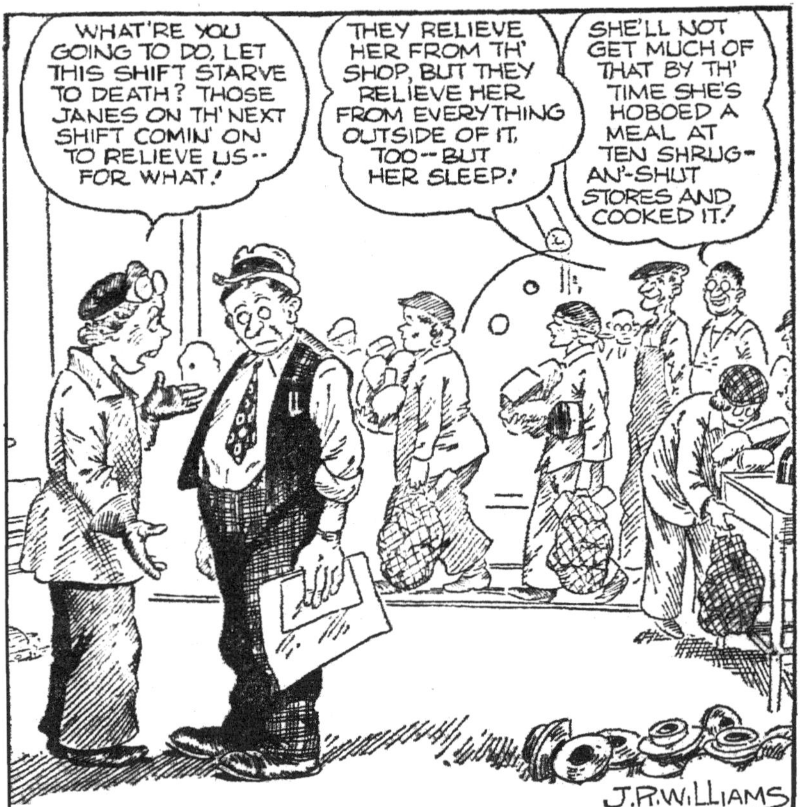
WHAT'RE YOU GOING TO DO, LET THIS SHIFT STARVE TO DEATH? THOSE JANES ON TH' NEXT SHIFT COMIN' ON TO RELIEVE US-- FOR WHAT!
THEY RELIEVE HER FROM TH' SHOP, BUT THEY RELIEVE HER FROM EVERYTHING OUTSIDE OF IT, TOO--BUT HER SLEEP!
SHE'LL NOT GET MUCH OF THAT BY TH' TIME SHE'S HOBOED A MEAL AT TEN SHRUG-AN'-SHUT STORES AND COOKED IT!
J.R.WILLIAMS

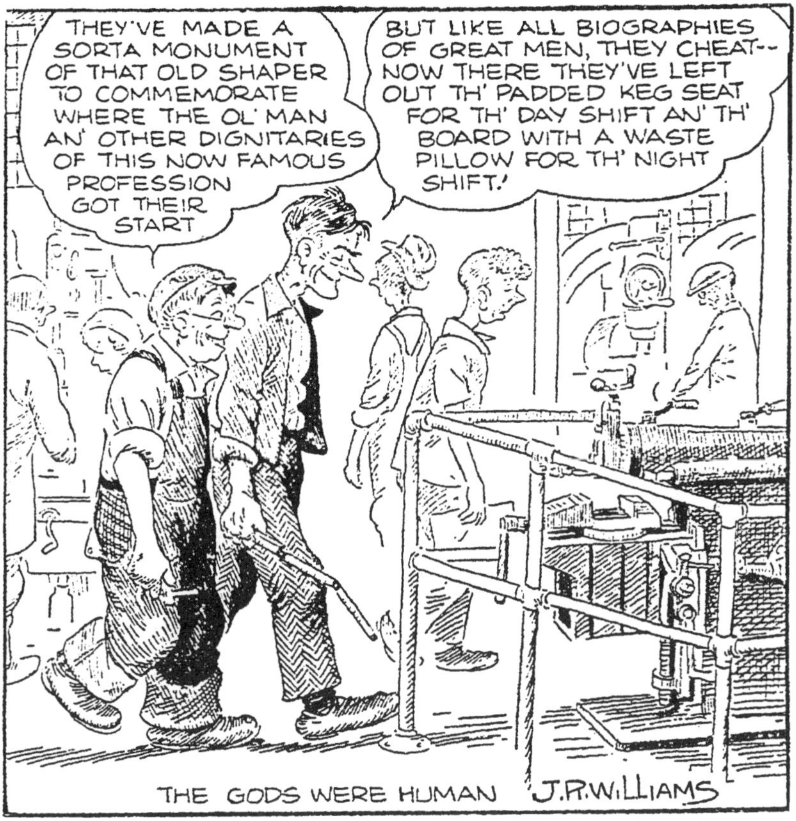
THEY'VE MADE A SORTA MONUMENT OF THAT OLD SHAPER TO COMMEMORATE WHERE THE OL' MAN AN' OTHER DIGNITARIES OF THIS NOW FAMOUS PROFESSION GOT THEIR START
BUT LIKE ALL BIOGRAPHIES OF GREAT MEN, THEY CHEAT-- NOW THERE THEY'VE LEFT OUT TH' PADDED KEG SEAT FOR TH' DAY SHIFT AN' TH' BOARD WITH A WASTE PILLOW FOR TH' NIGHT SHIFT!
THE GODS WERE HUMAN
J.R.WILLIAMS

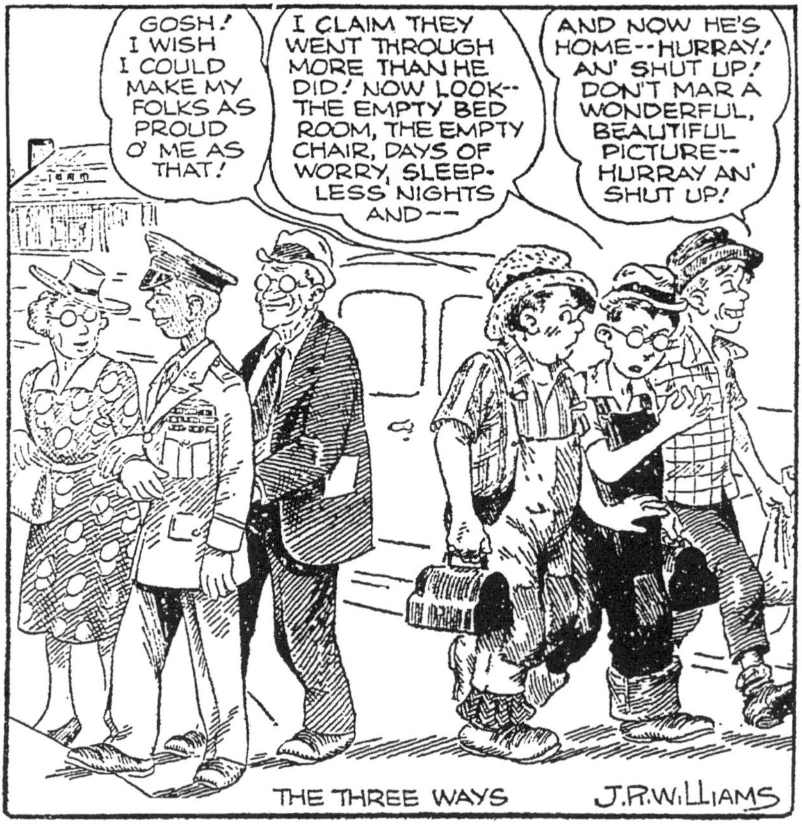
GOSH! I WISH I COULD MAKE MY FOLKS AS PROUD O' ME AS THAT!
I CLAIM THEY WENT THROUGH MORE THAN HE DID! NOW LOOK-- THE EMPTY BED ROOM, THE EMPTY CHAIR, DAYS OF WORRY, SLEEP-LESS NIGHTS AND--
AND NOW HE'S HOME--HURRAY! AN' SHUT UP! DON'T MAR A WONDERFUL, BEAUTIFUL PICTURE-- HURRAY AN' SHUT UP!
THE THREE WAYS
J.R.WILLIAMS

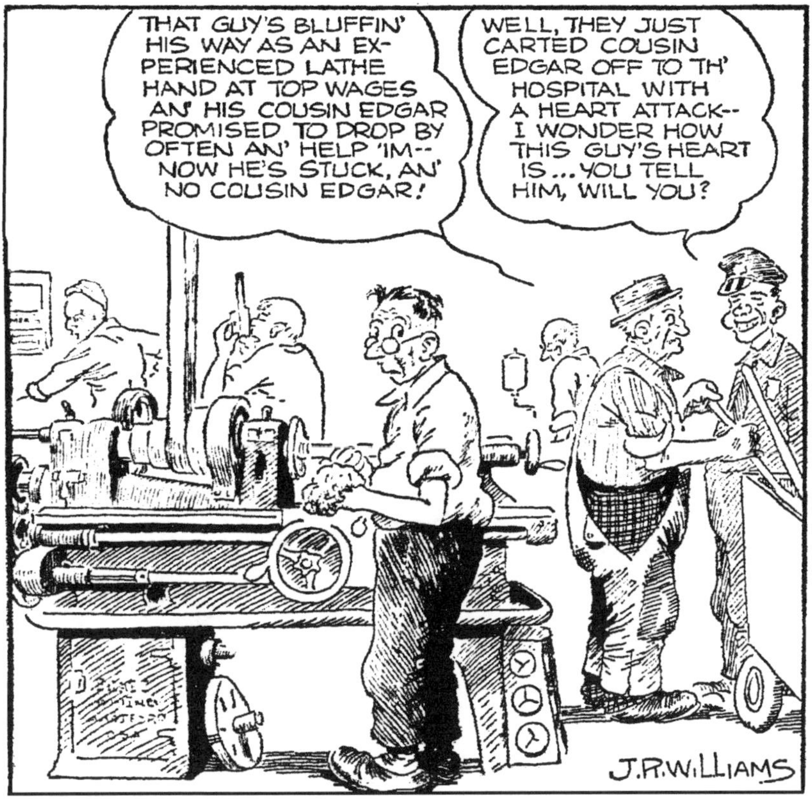
THAT GUY'S BLUFFIN' HIS WAY AS AN EX-PERIENCED LATHE HAND AT TOP WAGES AN' HIS COUSIN EDGAR PROMISED TO DROP BY OFTEN AN' HELP 'IM-- NOW HE'S STUCK, AN' NO COUSIN EDGAR!
WELL, THEY JUST CARTED COUSIN EDGAR OFF TO TH' HOSPITAL WITH A HEART ATTACK-- I WONDER HOW THIS GUY'S HEART IS... YOU TELL HIM, WILL YOU?
J.R.WILLIAMS

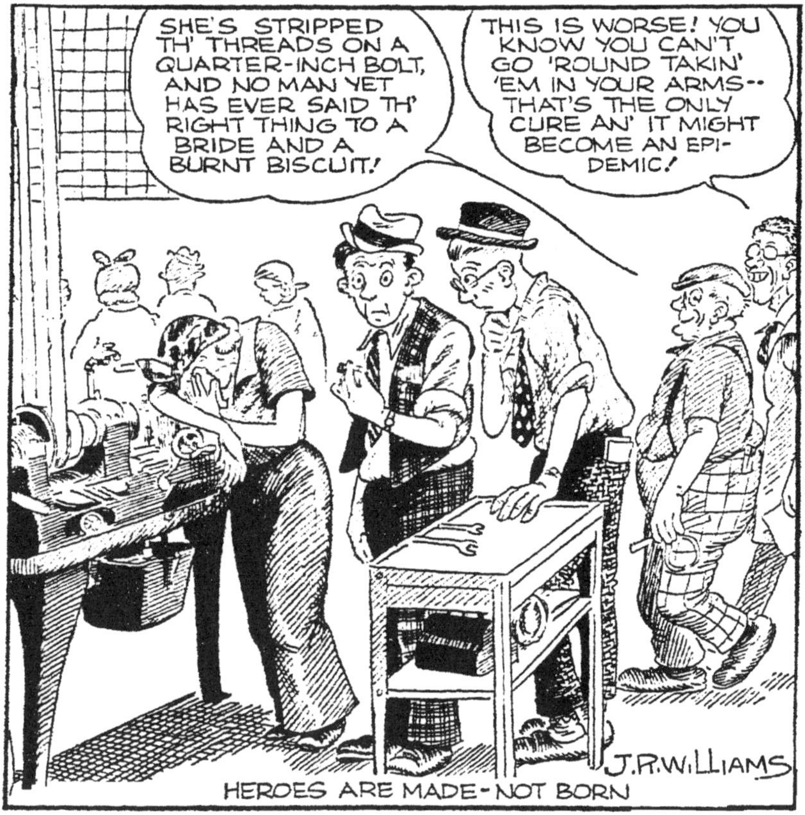
SHE'S STRIPPED TH' THREADS ON A QUARTER-INCH BOLT, AND NO MAN YET HAS EVER SAID TH' RIGHT THING TO A BRIDE AND A BURNT BISCUIT!
THIS IS WORSE! YOU KNOW YOU CAN'T GO 'ROUND TAKIN' 'EM IN YOUR ARMS-- THAT'S THE ONLY CURE AN' IT MIGHT BECOME AN EPI-DEMIC!
J.R.WILLIAMS
HEROES ARE MADE-NOT BORN

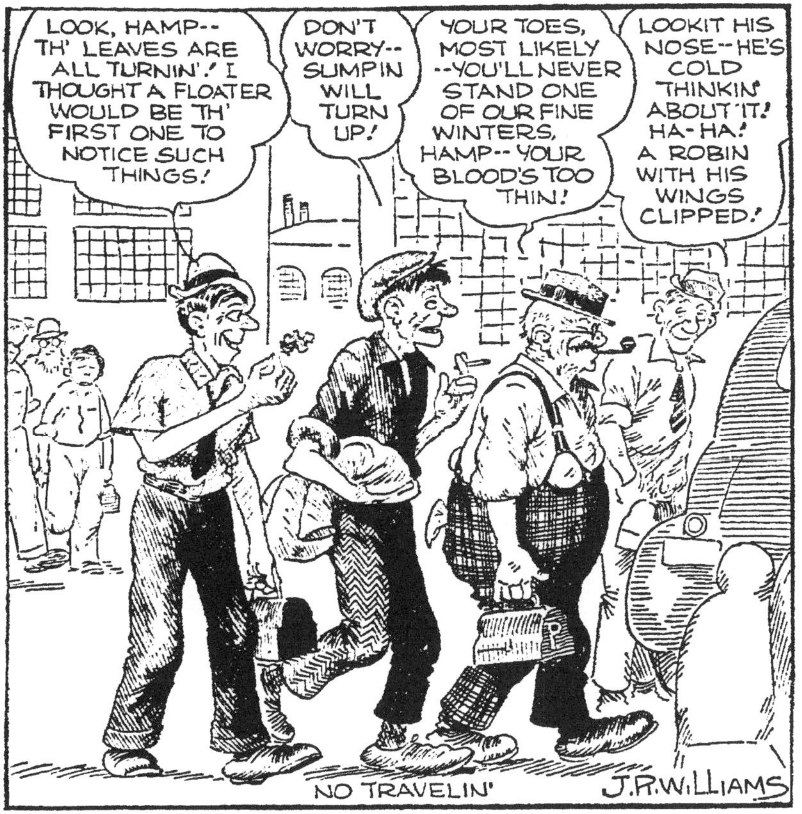
LOOK, HAMP-- TH' LEAVES ARE ALL TURNIN'! I THOUGHT A FLOATER WOULD BE TH' FIRST ONE TO NOTICE SUCH THINGS!
DON'T WORRY-- SUMPIN WILL TURN UP!
YOUR TOES, MOST LIKELY --YOU'LL NEVER STAND ONE OF OUR FINE WINTERS, HAMP-- YOUR BLOOD'S TOO THIN!
LOOKIT HIS NOSE--HE'S COLD THINKIN' ABOUT IT! HA-HA! A ROBIN WITH HIS WINGS CLIPPED!
NO TRAVELIN'
J.R.WILLIAMS

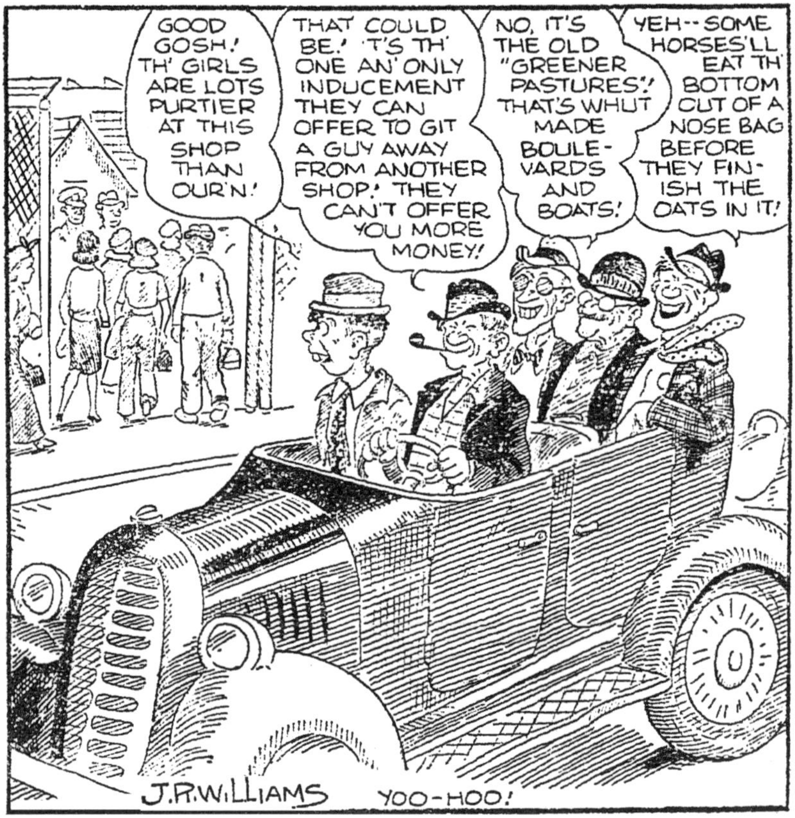
GOOD GOSH! TH' GIRLS ARE LOTS PURTIER AT THIS SHOP THAN OUR'N!
THAT COULD BE! 'T'S TH' ONE AN' ONLY INDUCEMENT THEY CAN OFFER TO GIT A GUY AWAY FROM ANOTHER SHOP! THEY CAN'T OFFER YOU MORE MONEY!
NO, IT'S THE OLD "GREENER PASTURES"! THAT'S WHUT MADE BOULE-VARDS AND BOATS!
YEH--SOME HORSES'LL EAT TH' BOTTOM OUT OF A NOSE BAG BEFORE THEY FIN-ISH THE OATS IN IT!
J.R.WILLIAMS
YOO-HOO!

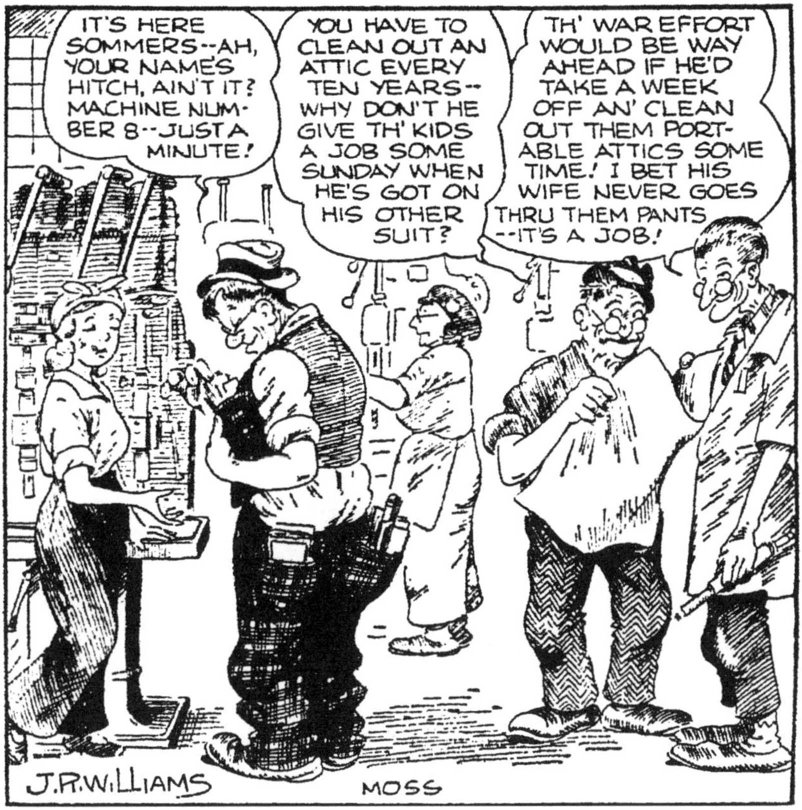
IT'S HERE SOMMERS--AH, YOUR NAME'S HITCH, AIN'T IT? MACHINE NUMBER 8--JUST A MINUTE!
YOU HAVE TO CLEAN OUT AN ATTIC EVERY TEN YEARS--WHY DON'T HE GIVE TH' KIDS A JOB SOME SUNDAY WHEN HE'S GOT ON HIS OTHER SUIT?
TH' WAR EFFORT WOULD BE WAY AHEAD IF HE'D TAKE A WEEK OFF AN' CLEAN OUT THEM PORTABLE ATTICS SOME TIME! I BET HIS WIFE NEVER GOES THRU THEM PANTS--IT'S A JOB!
J.R.WILLIAMS
MOSS

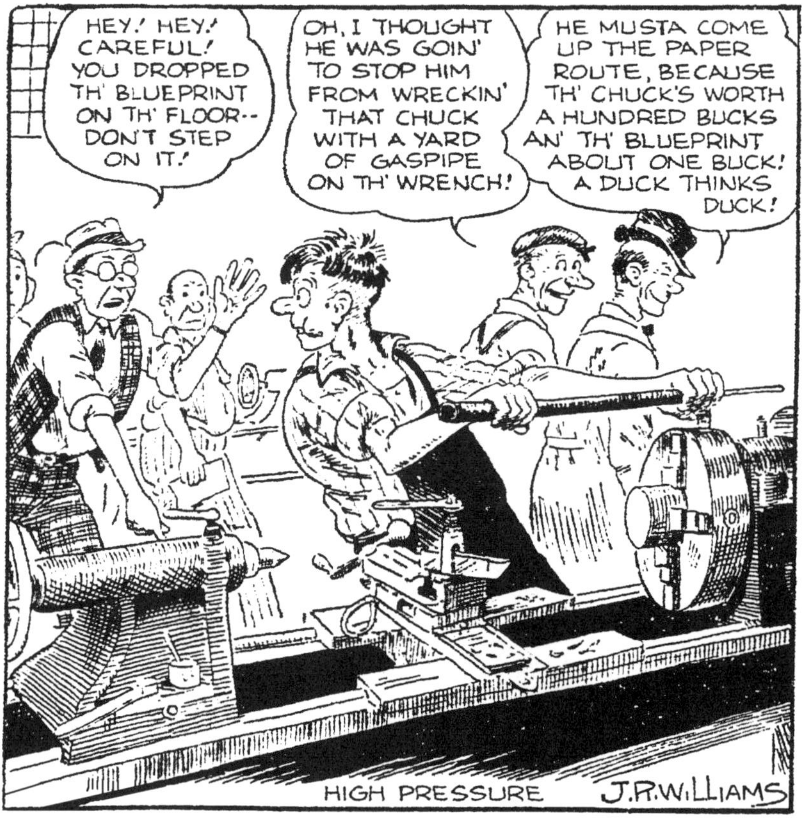
HEY! HEY! CAREFUL! YOU DROPPED TH' BLUEPRINT ON TH' FLOOR-- DON'T STEP ON IT!
OH, I THOUGHT HE WAS GOIN' TO STOP HIM FROM WRECKIN' THAT CHUCK WITH A YARD OF GASPIPE ON TH' WRENCH!
HE MUSTA COME UP THE PAPER ROUTE, BECAUSE TH' CHUCK'S WORTH A HUNDRED BUCKS AN' TH' BLUEPRINT ABOUT ONE BUCK! A DUCK THINKS DUCK!
HIGH PRESSURE
J.R.WILLIAMS

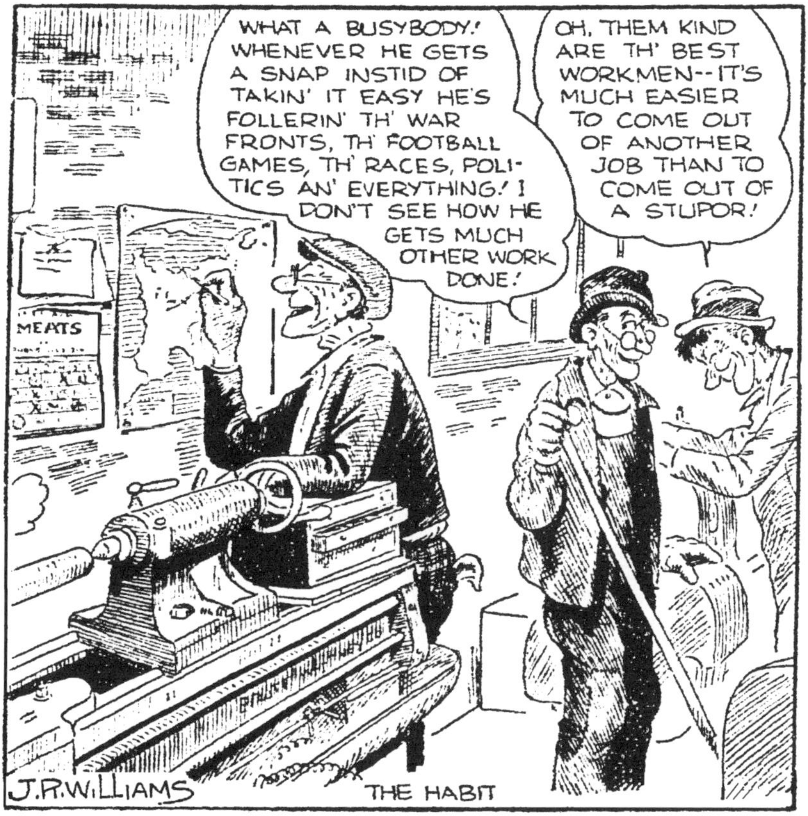
WHAT A BUSYBODY! WHENEVER HE GETS A SNAP INSTID OF TAKIN' IT EASY HE'S FOLLERIN' TH' WAR FRONTS, TH' FOOTBALL GAMES, TH' RACES, POLITICS AN' EVERYTHING! I DON'T SEE HOW HE GETS MUCH OTHER WORK DONE!
OH, THEM KIND ARE TH' BEST WORKMEN--IT'S MUCH EASIER TO COME OUT OF ANOTHER JOB THAN TO COME OUT OF A STUPOR!
MEATS
J.R.WILLIAMS
THE HABIT

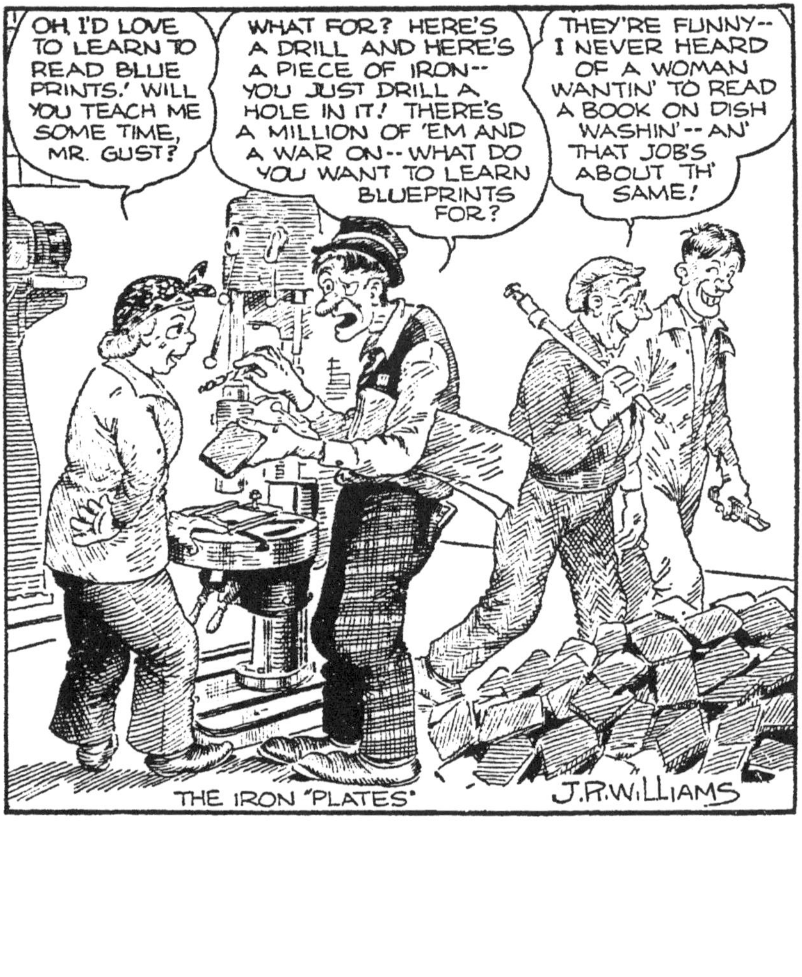
OH, I'D LOVE TO LEARN TO READ BLUE PRINTS! WILL YOU TEACH ME SOME TIME, MR. GUST?
WHAT FOR? HERE'S A DRILL AND HERE'S A PIECE OF IRON-- YOU JUST DRILL A HOLE IN IT! THERE'S A MILLION OF 'EM AND A WAR ON-- WHAT DO YOU WANT TO LEARN BLUEPRINTS FOR?
THEY'RE FUNNY-- I NEVER HEARD OF A WOMAN WANTIN' TO READ A BOOK ON DISH WASHIN'-- AN' THAT JOB'S ABOUT TH' SAME!
J.R.WILLIAMS
THE IRON "PLATES"

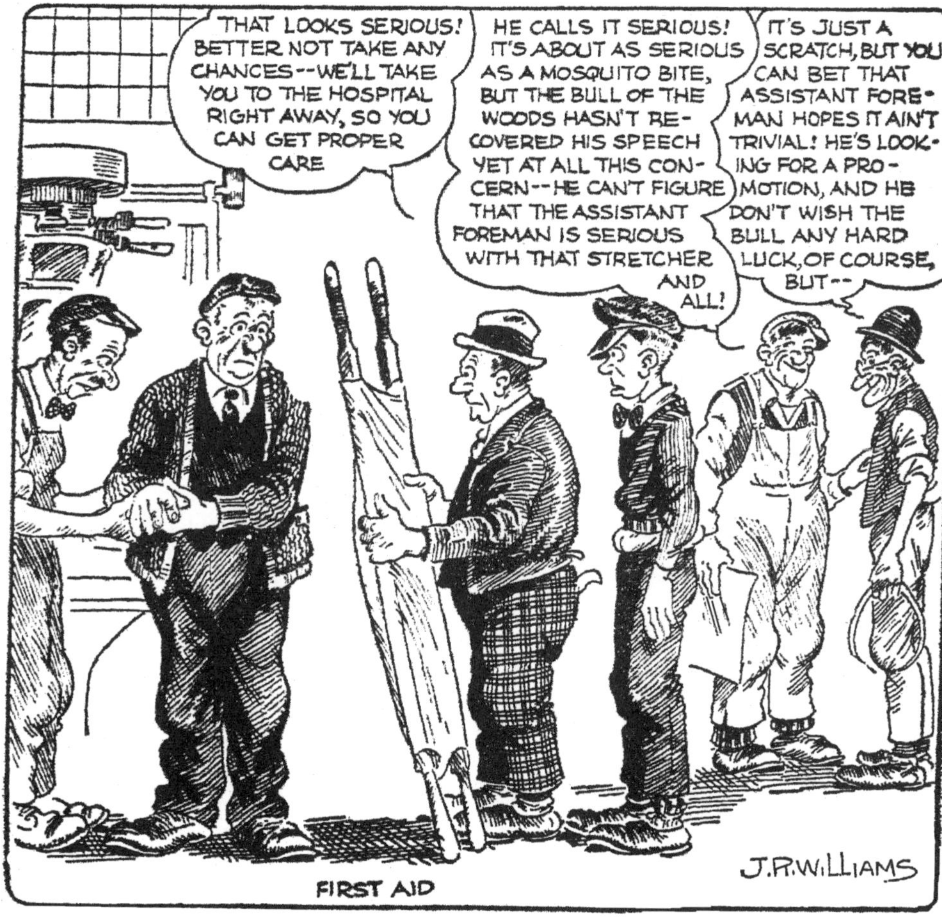
THAT LOOKS SERIOUS! BETTER NOT TAKE ANY CHANCES--WE'LL TAKE YOU TO THE HOSPITAL RIGHT AWAY, SO YOU CAN GET PROPER CARE
HE CALLS IT SERIOUS! IT'S ABOUT AS SERIOUS AS A MOSQUITO BITE, BUT THE BULL OF THE WOODS HASN'T RE-COVERED HIS SPEECH YET AT ALL THIS CON-CERN--HE CAN'T FIGURE THAT THE ASSISTANT FOREMAN IS SERIOUS WITH THAT STRETCHER AND ALL!
IT'S JUST A SCRATCH, BUT YOU CAN BET THAT ASSISTANT FORE-MAN HOPES IT AIN'T TRIVIAL! HE'S LOOK-ING FOR A PRO-MOTION, AND HE DON'T WISH THE BULL ANY HARD LUCK, OF COURSE, BUT--
J.R. WILLIAMS
FIRST AID

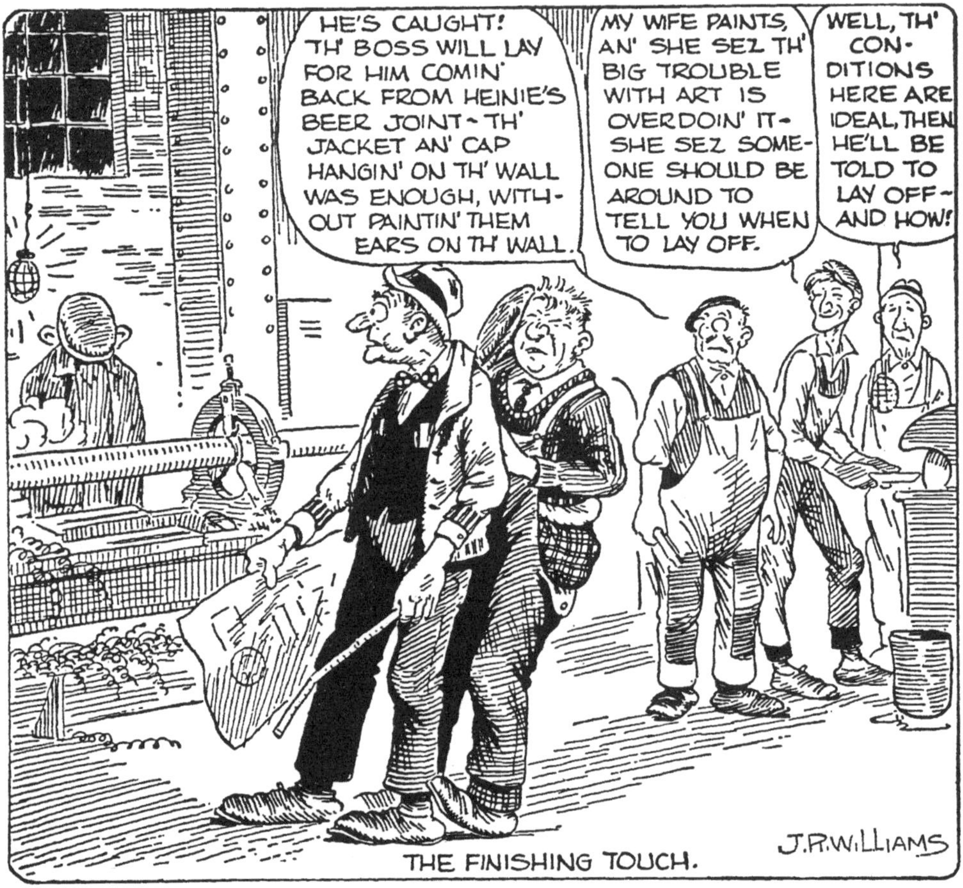
HE'S CAUGHT! TH' BOSS WILL LAY FOR HIM COMIN' BACK FROM HEINIE'S BEER JOINT - TH' JACKET AN' CAP HANGIN' ON TH' WALL WAS ENOUGH, WITHOUT PAINTIN' THEM EARS ON TH' WALL.
MY WIFE PAINTS, AN' SHE SEZ TH' BIG TROUBLE WITH ART IS OVERDOIN' IT - SHE SEZ SOMEONE SHOULD BE AROUND TO TELL YOU WHEN TO LAY OFF.
WELL, TH' CONDITIONS HERE ARE IDEAL, THEN HE'LL BE TOLD TO LAY OFF - AND HOW!
J.R.WILLIAMS
THE FINISHING TOUCH.

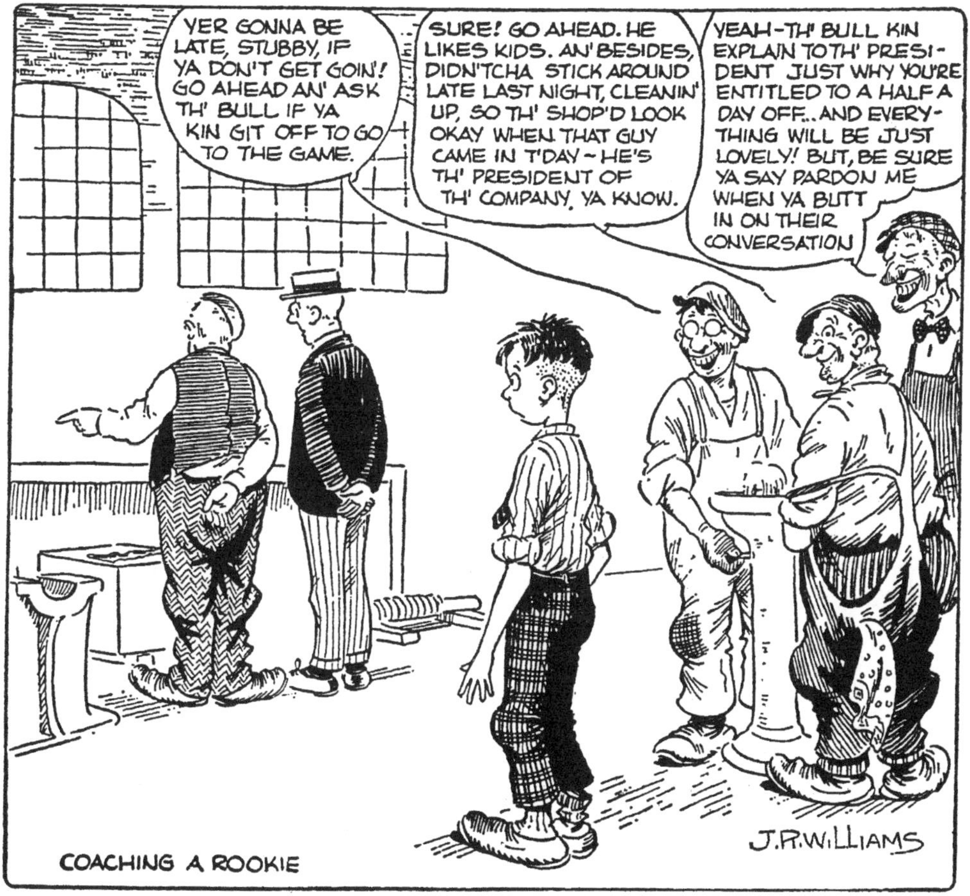
YER GONNA BE LATE, STUBBY, IF YA DON'T GET GOIN'! GO AHEAD AN' ASK TH' BULL IF YA KIN GIT OFF TO GO TO THE GAME.
SURE! GO AHEAD. HE LIKES KIDS. AN' BESIDES, DIDN'TCHA STICK AROUND LATE LAST NIGHT, CLEANIN' UP, SO TH' SHOP'D LOOK OKAY WHEN THAT GUY CAME IN T'DAY ~ HE'S TH' PRESIDENT OF TH' COMPANY, YA KNOW.
YEAH-TH' BULL KIN EXPLAIN TO TH' PRESI-DENT JUST WHY YOU'RE ENTITLED TO A HALF A DAY OFF... AND EVERY-THING WILL BE JUST LOVELY! BUT, BE SURE YA SAY PARDON ME WHEN YA BUTT IN ON THEIR CONVERSATION
J.R. WILLIAMS
COACHING A ROOKIE

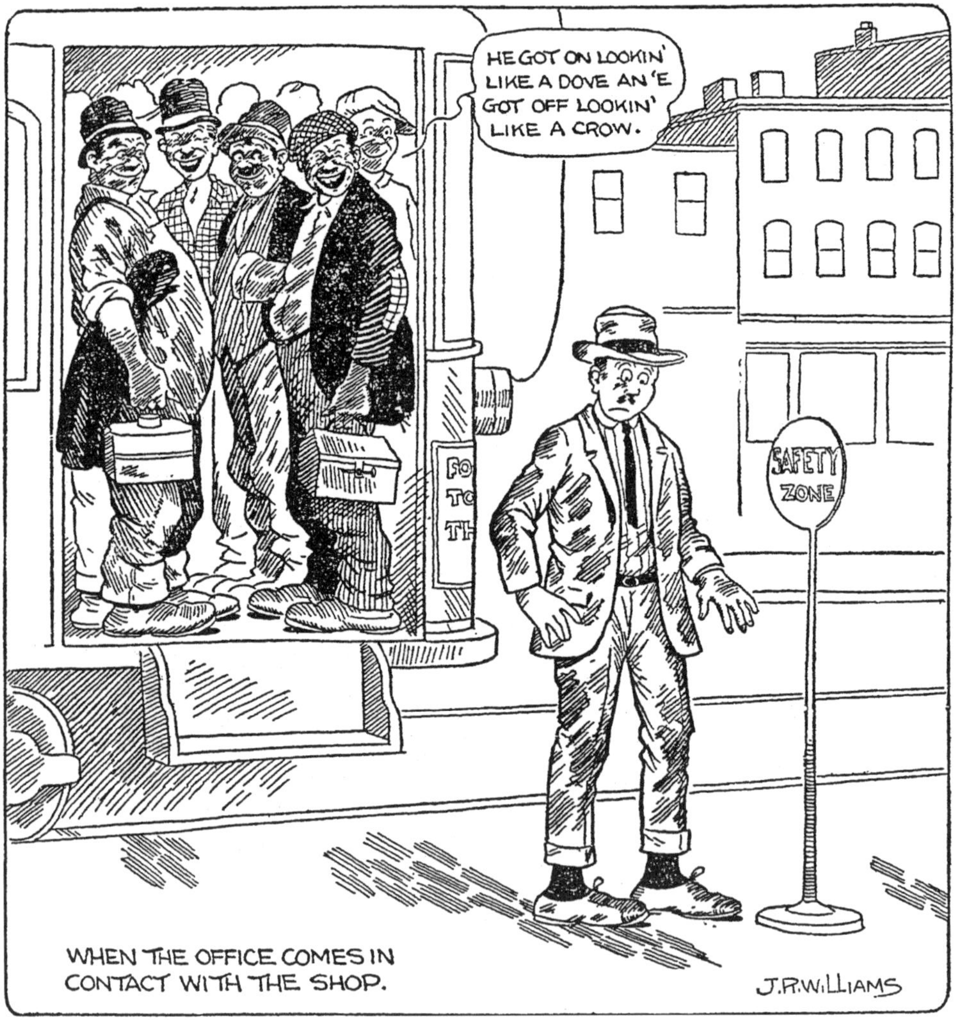
HE GOT ON LOOKIN' LIKE A DOVE AN 'E GOT OFF LOOKIN' LIKE A CROW.
SAFETY ZONE
J.R.WILLIAMS
WHEN THE OFFICE COMES IN CONTACT WITH THE SHOP.

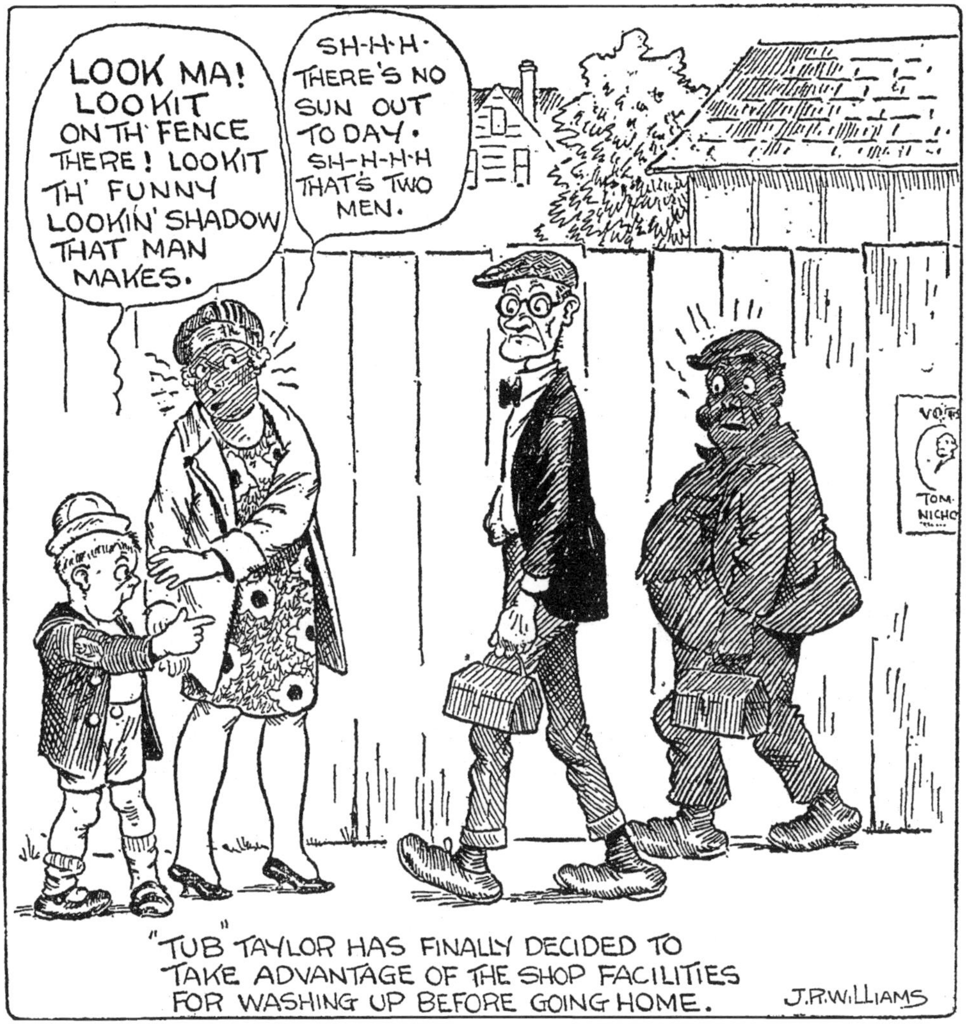
LOOK MA! LOOKIT ON TH' FENCE THERE! LOOKIT TH' FUNNY LOOKIN' SHADOW THAT MAN MAKES.
SH-H-H. THERE'S NO SUN OUT TO DAY. SH-H-H-H THAT'S TWO MEN.
"TUB" TAYLOR HAS FINALLY DECIDED TO TAKE ADVANTAGE OF THE SHOP FACILITIES FOR WASHING UP BEFORE GOING HOME.
J.R.WILLIAMS

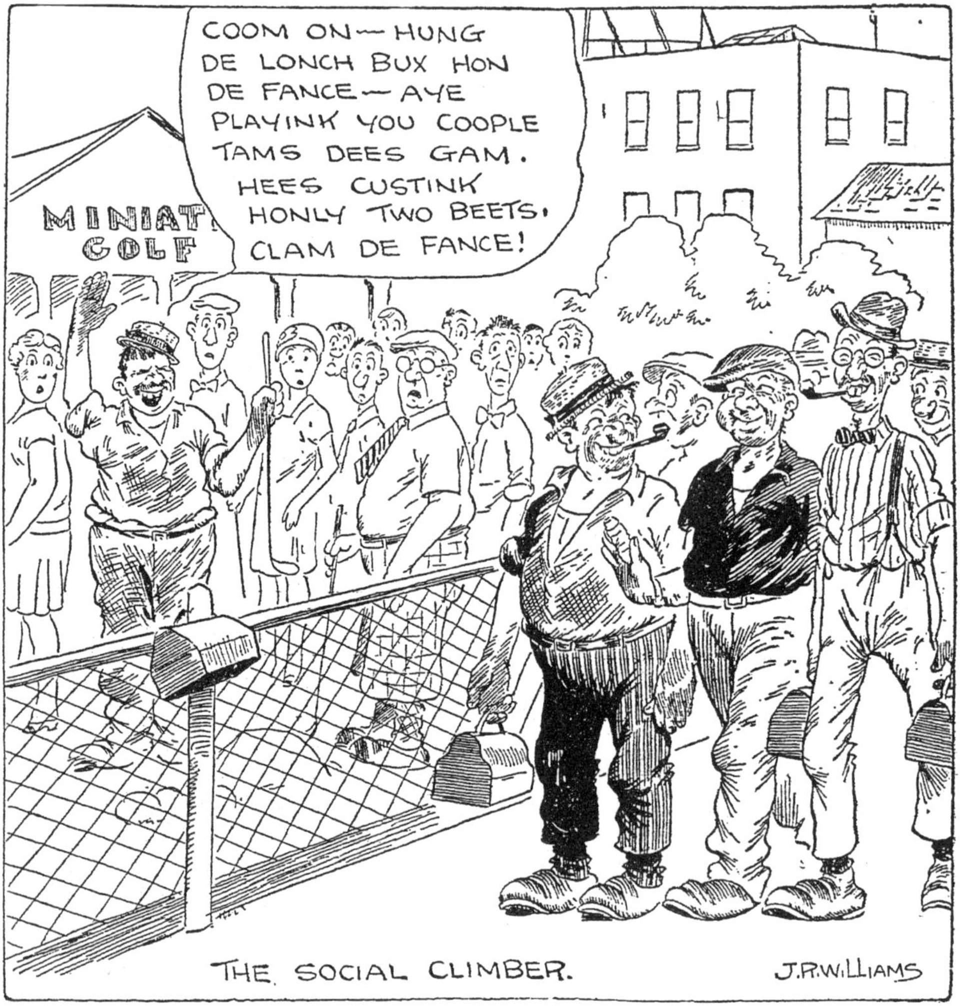
COOM ON—HUNG DE LONCH BUX HON DE FANCE—AYE PLAYINK YOU COOPLE TAMS DEES GAM. HEES CUSTINK HONLY TWO BEETS. CLAM DE FANCE!
MINIAT
GOLF
THE SOCIAL CLIMBER.
J.R. WILLIAMS

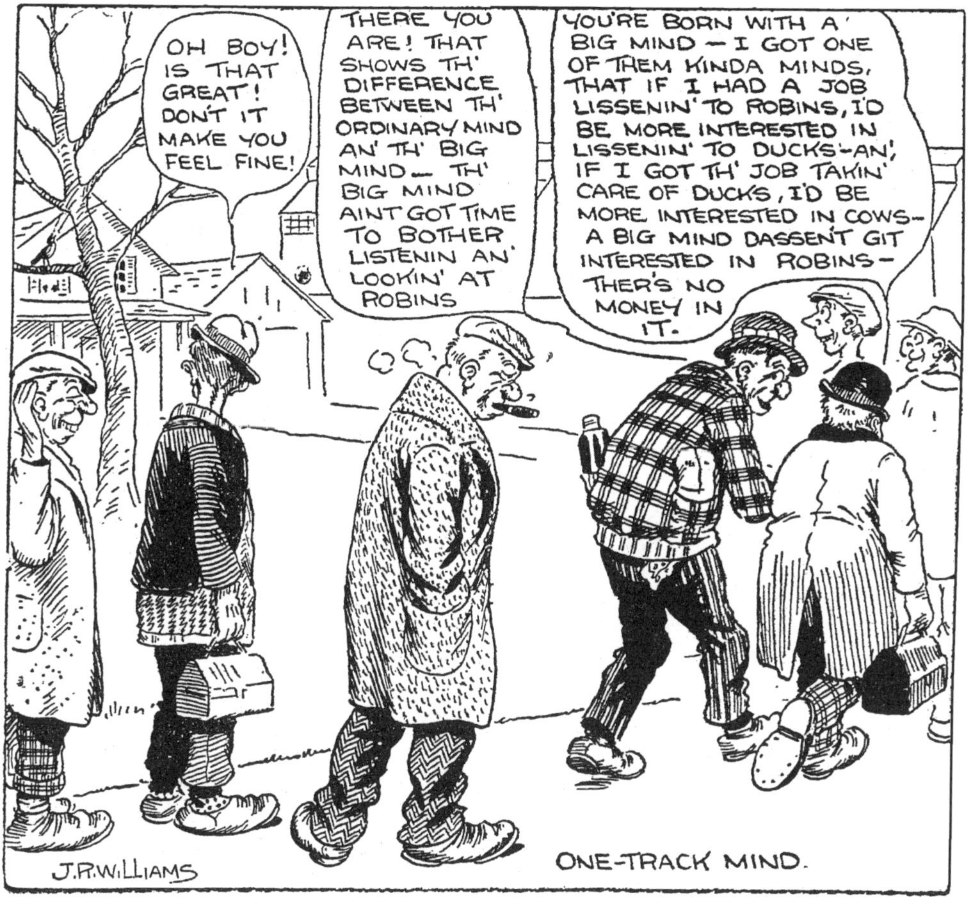
OH BOY! IS THAT GREAT! DON'T IT MAKE YOU FEEL FINE!
THERE YOU ARE! THAT SHOWS TH' DIFFERENCE BETWEEN TH' ORDINARY MIND AN' TH' BIG MIND — TH' BIG MIND AINT GOT TIME TO BOTHER LISTENIN AN' LOOKIN' AT ROBINS
YOU'RE BORN WITH A BIG MIND — I GOT ONE OF THEM KINDA MINDS, THAT IF I HAD A JOB LISSENIN' TO ROBINS, I'D BE MORE INTERESTED IN LISSENIN' TO DUCKS — AN', IF I GOT TH' JOB TAKIN' CARE OF DUCKS, I'D BE MORE INTERESTED IN COWS — A BIG MIND DASSEN'T GIT INTERESTED IN ROBINS — THER'S NO MONEY IN IT.
J.R.WILLIAMS
ONE-TRACK MIND.

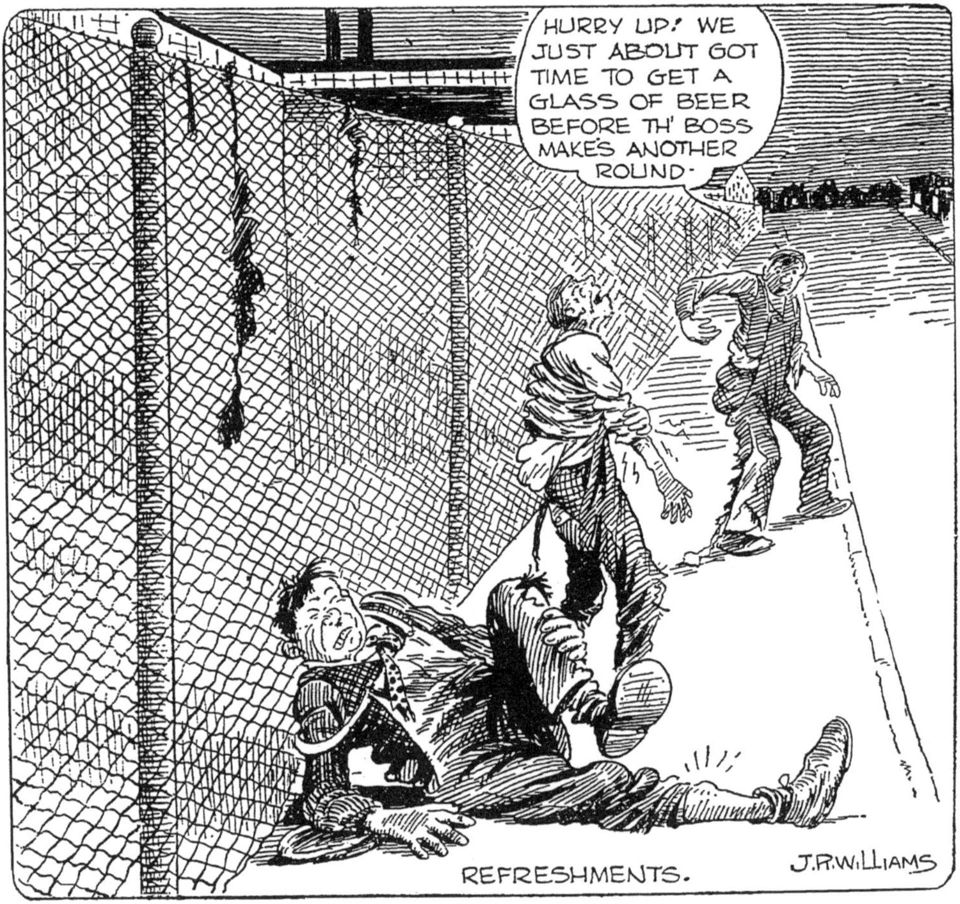
HURRY UP! WE JUST ABOUT GOT TIME TO GET A GLASS OF BEER BEFORE TH' BOSS MAKES ANOTHER ROUND-
REFRESHMENTS.
J.R.WILLIAMS

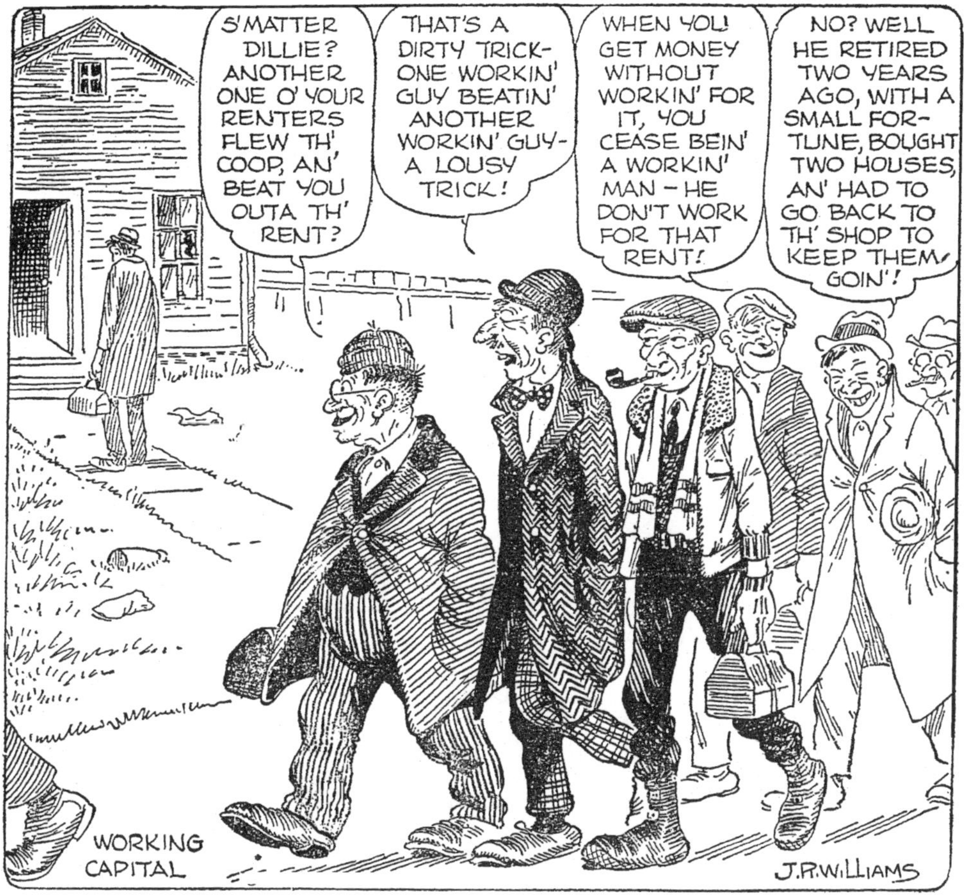
S'MATTER DILLIE? ANOTHER ONE O' YOUR RENTERS FLEW TH' COOP, AN' BEAT YOU OUTA TH' RENT?
THAT'S A DIRTY TRICK- ONE WORKIN' GUY BEATIN' ANOTHER WORKIN' GUY- A LOUSY TRICK!
WHEN YOU GET MONEY WITHOUT WORKIN' FOR IT, YOU CEASE BEIN' A WORKIN' MAN - HE DON'T WORK FOR THAT RENT!
NO? WELL HE RETIRED TWO YEARS AGO, WITH A SMALL FOR-TUNE, BOUGHT TWO HOUSES, AN' HAD TO GO BACK TO TH' SHOP TO KEEP THEM GOIN'!
WORKING CAPITAL
J.R. WILLIAMS

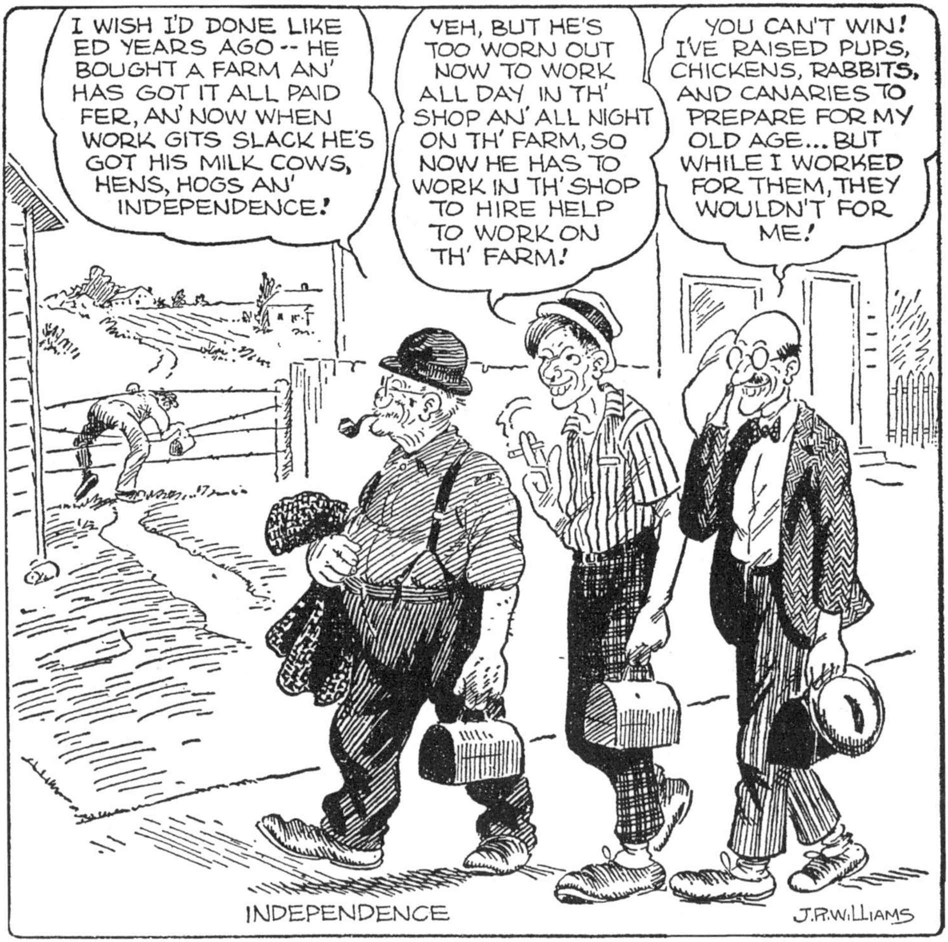
I WISH I'D DONE LIKE ED YEARS AGO -- HE BOUGHT A FARM AN' HAS GOT IT ALL PAID FER, AN' NOW WHEN WORK GITS SLACK HE'S GOT HIS MILK COWS, HENS, HOGS AN' INDEPENDENCE!
YEH, BUT HE'S TOO WORN OUT NOW TO WORK ALL DAY IN TH' SHOP AN' ALL NIGHT ON TH' FARM, SO NOW HE HAS TO WORK IN TH' SHOP TO HIRE HELP TO WORK ON TH' FARM!
YOU CAN'T WIN! I'VE RAISED PUPS, CHICKENS, RABBITS, AND CANARIES TO PREPARE FOR MY OLD AGE... BUT WHILE I WORKED FOR THEM, THEY WOULDN'T FOR ME!
INDEPENDENCE
J.R.WILLIAMS

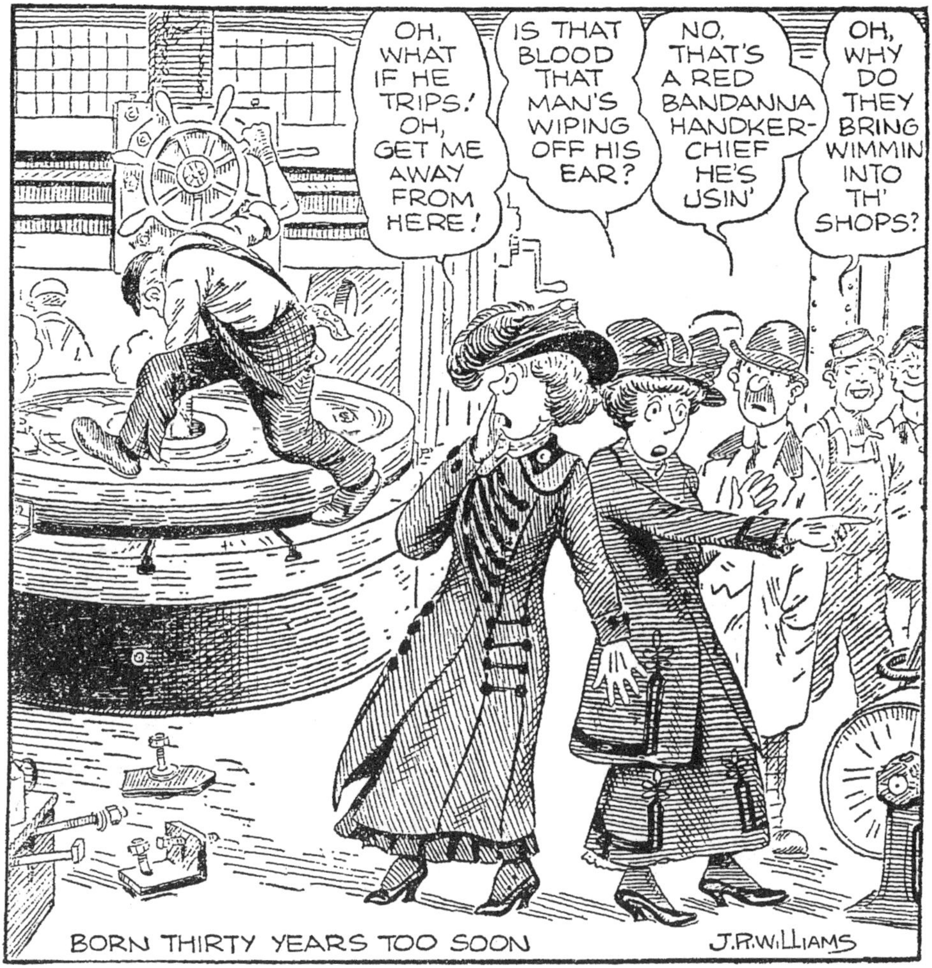
OH, WHAT IF HE TRIPS! OH, GET ME AWAY FROM HERE!
IS THAT BLOOD THAT MAN'S WIPING OFF HIS EAR?
NO, THAT'S A RED BANDANNA HANDKER-CHIEF HE'S USIN'
OH, WHY DO THEY BRING WIMMIN INTO TH' SHOPS?
BORN THIRTY YEARS TOO SOON
J.R. WILLIAMS

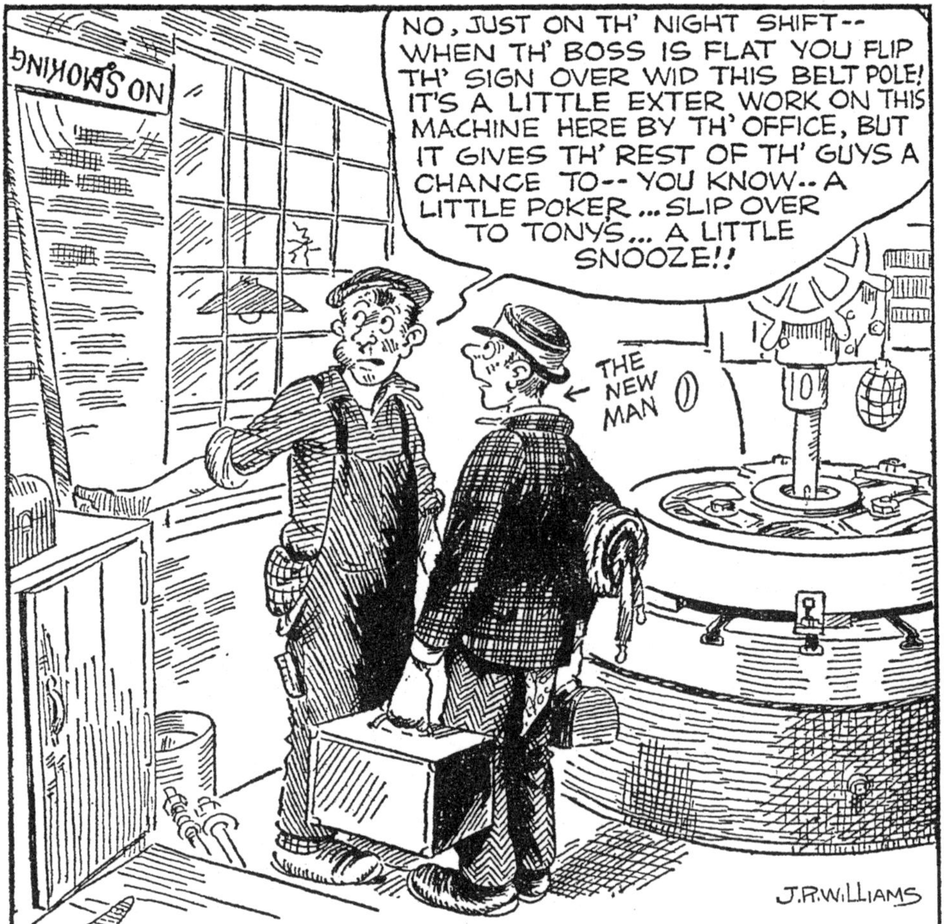
NO SMOKING
NO, JUST ON TH' NIGHT SHIFT-- WHEN TH' BOSS IS FLAT YOU FLIP TH' SIGN OVER WID THIS BELT POLE! IT'S A LITTLE EXTER WORK ON THIS MACHINE HERE BY TH' OFFICE, BUT IT GIVES TH' REST OF TH' GUYS A CHANCE TO-- YOU KNOW-- A LITTLE POKER ... SLIP OVER TO TONYS... A LITTLE SNOOZE!!
THE NEW MAN
J.R.WILLIAMS
BORN THIRTY YEARS TOO SOON

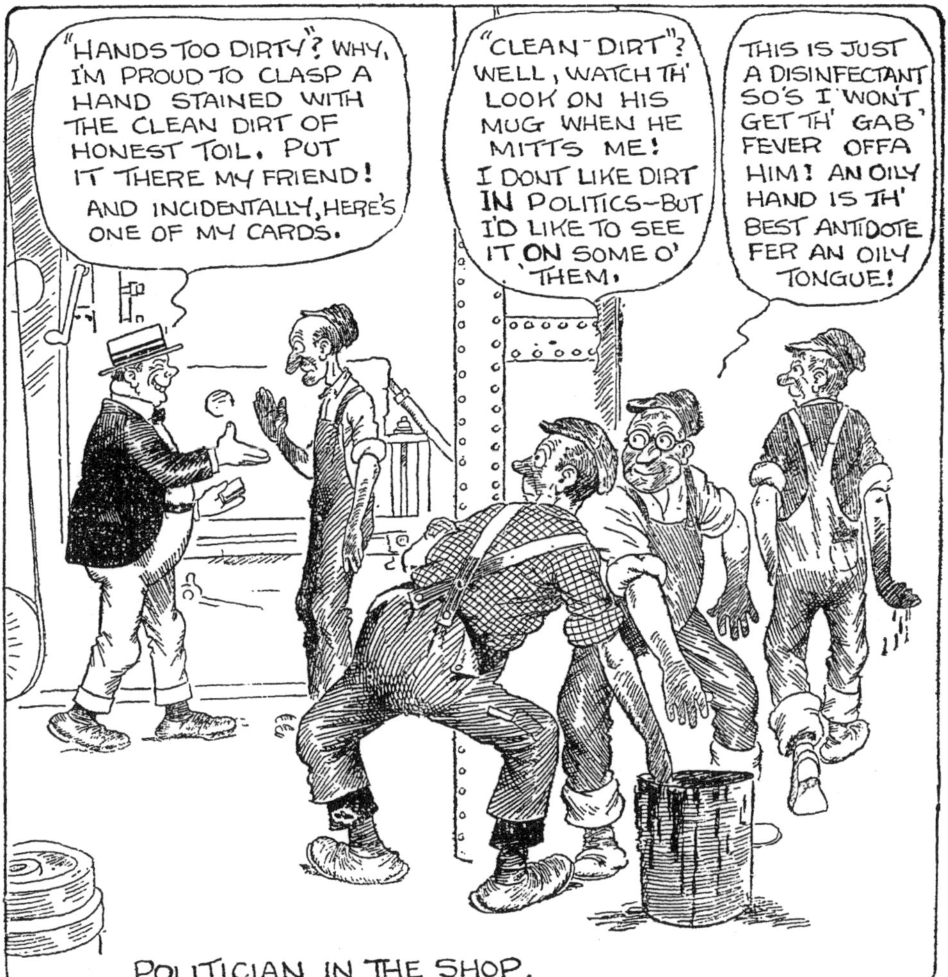
"HANDS TOO DIRTY"? WHY, I'M PROUD TO CLASP A HAND STAINED WITH THE CLEAN DIRT OF HONEST TOIL. PUT IT THERE MY FRIEND! AND INCIDENTALLY, HERE'S ONE OF MY CARDS.
"CLEAN-DIRT"? WELL, WATCH TH' LOOK ON HIS MUG WHEN HE MITTS ME! I DONT LIKE DIRT IN POLITICS—BUT I'D LIKE TO SEE IT ON SOME O' THEM.
THIS IS JUST A DISINFECTANT SO'S I WON'T GET TH' GAB FEVER OFFA HIM! AN OILY HAND IS TH' BEST ANTIDOTE FER AN OILY TONGUE!
POLITICIAN IN THE SHOP.

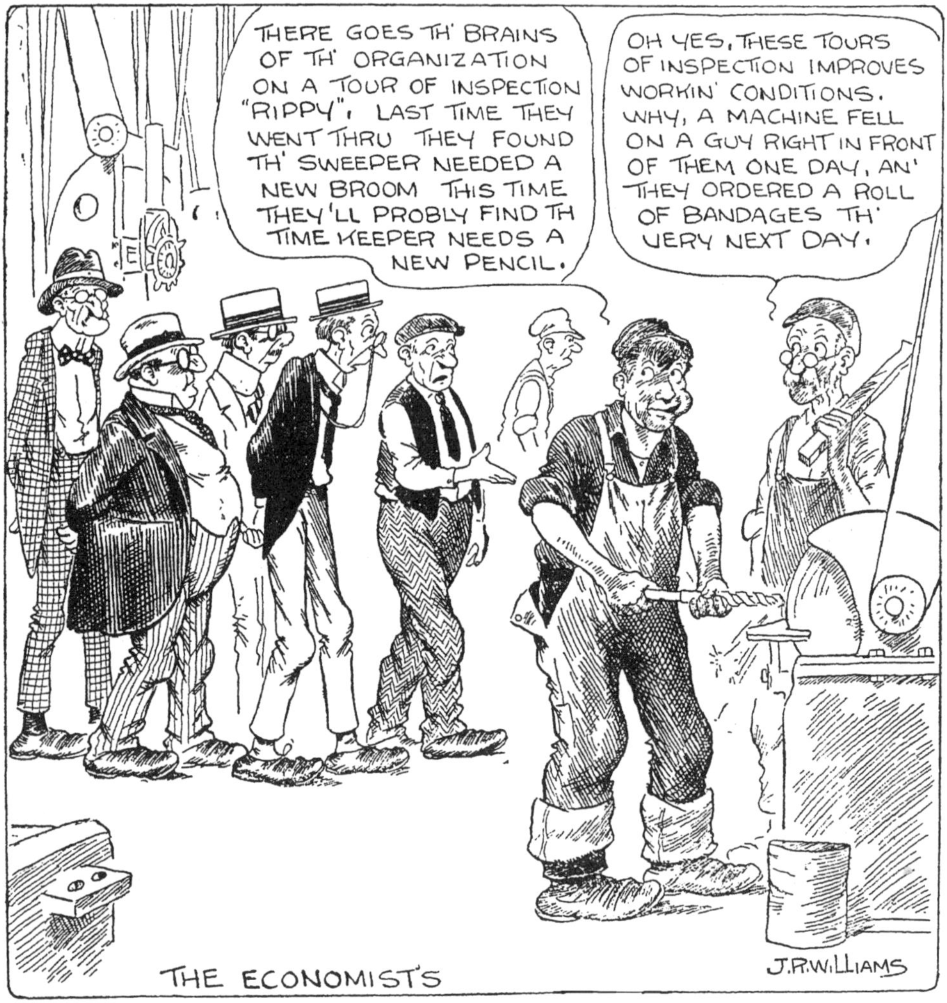
THERE GOES TH' BRAINS OF TH' ORGANIZATION ON A TOUR OF INSPECTION "RIPPY", LAST TIME THEY WENT THRU THEY FOUND TH' SWEEPER NEEDED A NEW BROOM THIS TIME THEY'LL PROBLY FIND TH TIME KEEPER NEEDS A NEW PENCIL.
OH YES, THESE TOURS OF INSPECTION IMPROVES WORKIN' CONDITIONS. WHY, A MACHINE FELL ON A GUY RIGHT IN FRONT OF THEM ONE DAY, AN' THEY ORDERED A ROLL OF BANDAGES TH' VERY NEXT DAY.
THE ECONOMIST'S
J.R.WILLIAMS

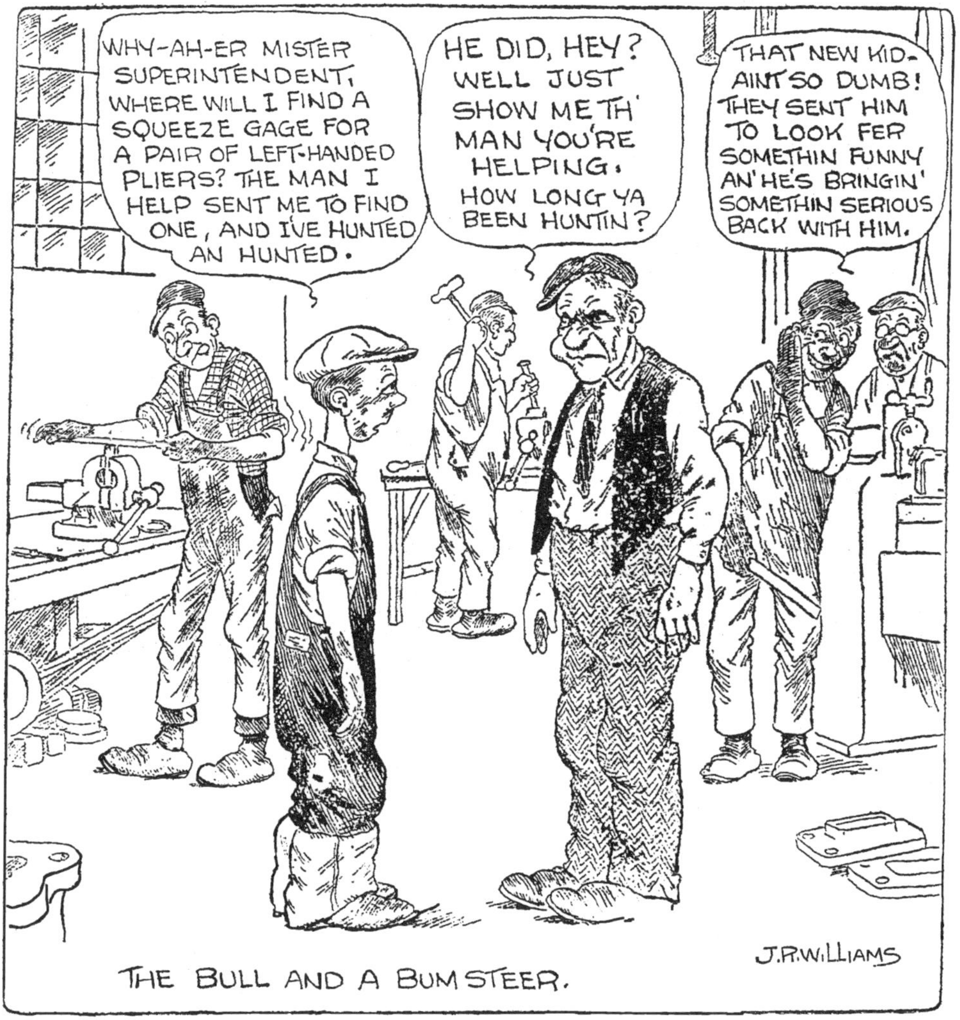
WHY-AH-ER MISTER SUPERINTENDENT, WHERE WILL I FIND A SQUEEZE GAGE FOR A PAIR OF LEFT-HANDED PLIERS? THE MAN I HELP SENT ME TO FIND ONE, AND I'VE HUNTED AN HUNTED.
HE DID, HEY? WELL JUST SHOW ME TH' MAN YOU'RE HELPING. HOW LONG YA BEEN HUNTIN?
THAT NEW KID AINT SO DUMB! THEY SENT HIM TO LOOK FER SOMETHIN FUNNY AN' HE'S BRINGIN' SOMETHIN SERIOUS BACK WITH HIM.
J.R. WILLIAMS
THE BULL AND A BUM STEER.

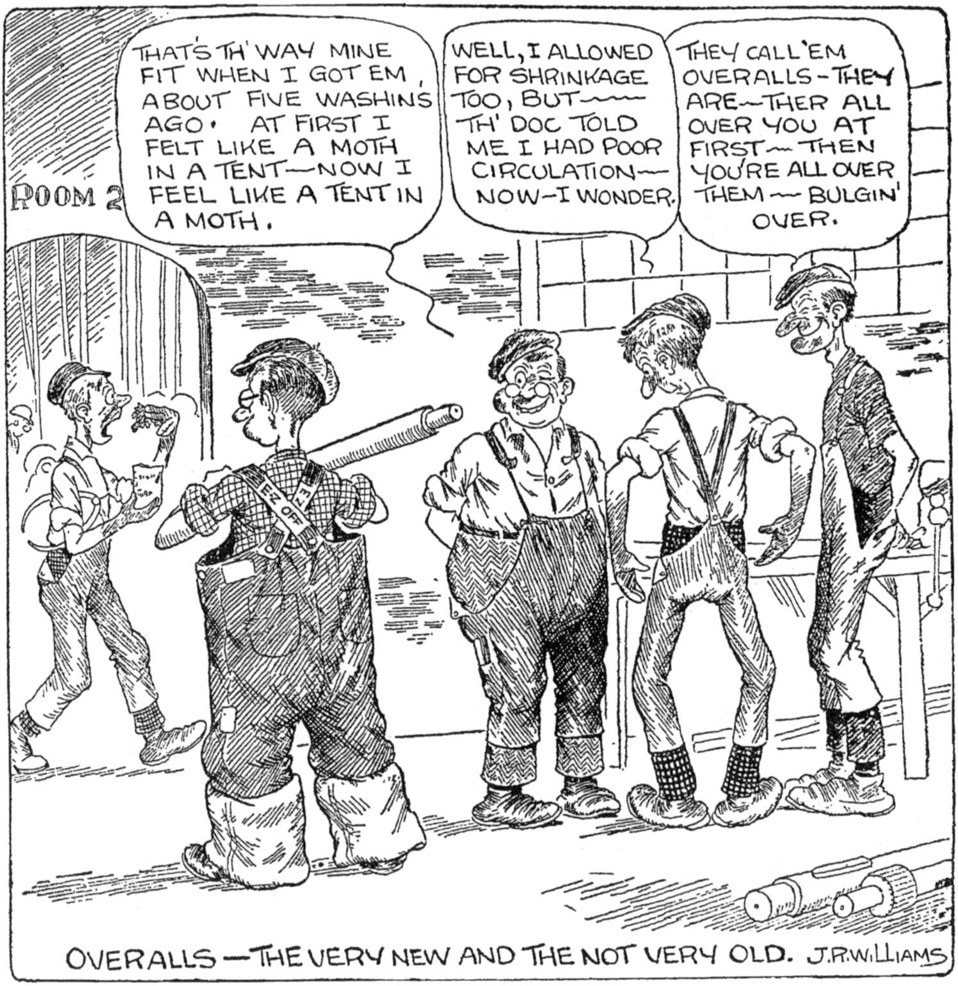
ROOM 2
THAT'S TH' WAY MINE FIT WHEN I GOT EM, ABOUT FIVE WASHIN'S AGO. AT FIRST I FELT LIKE A MOTH IN A TENT—NOW I FEEL LIKE A TENT IN A MOTH.
WELL, I ALLOWED FOR SHRINKAGE TOO, BUT—— TH' DOC TOLD ME I HAD POOR CIRCULATION—— NOW—I WONDER.
THEY CALL 'EM OVERALLS—THEY ARE—THER ALL OVER YOU AT FIRST—THEN YOU'RE ALL OVER THEM—BULGIN' OVER.
EZ OFF
OVERALLS—THE VERY NEW AND THE NOT VERY OLD. J.R.WILLIAMS

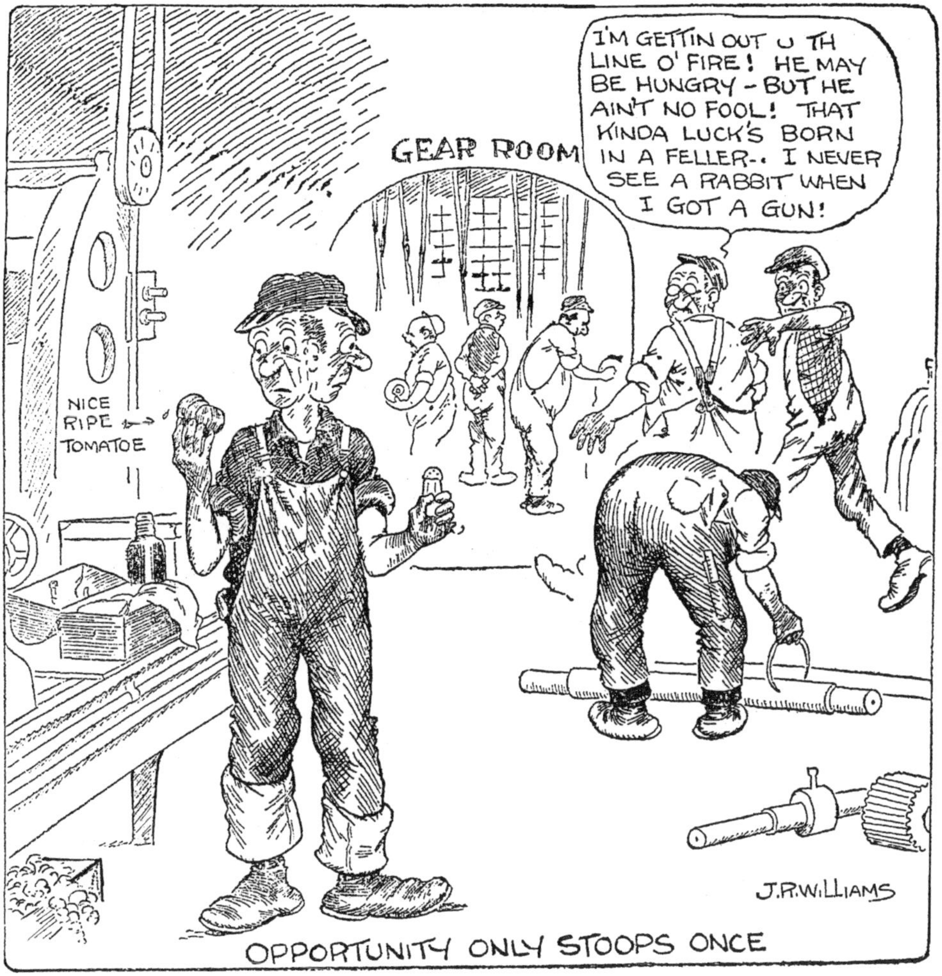
GEAR ROOM
I'M GETTIN OUT u TH LINE O' FIRE! HE MAY BE HUNGRY - BUT HE AIN'T NO FOOL! THAT KINDA LUCK'S BORN IN A FELLER-. I NEVER SEE A RABBIT WHEN I GOT A GUN!
NICE RIPE TOMATOE
J.R.WILLIAMS
OPPORTUNITY ONLY STOOPS ONCE

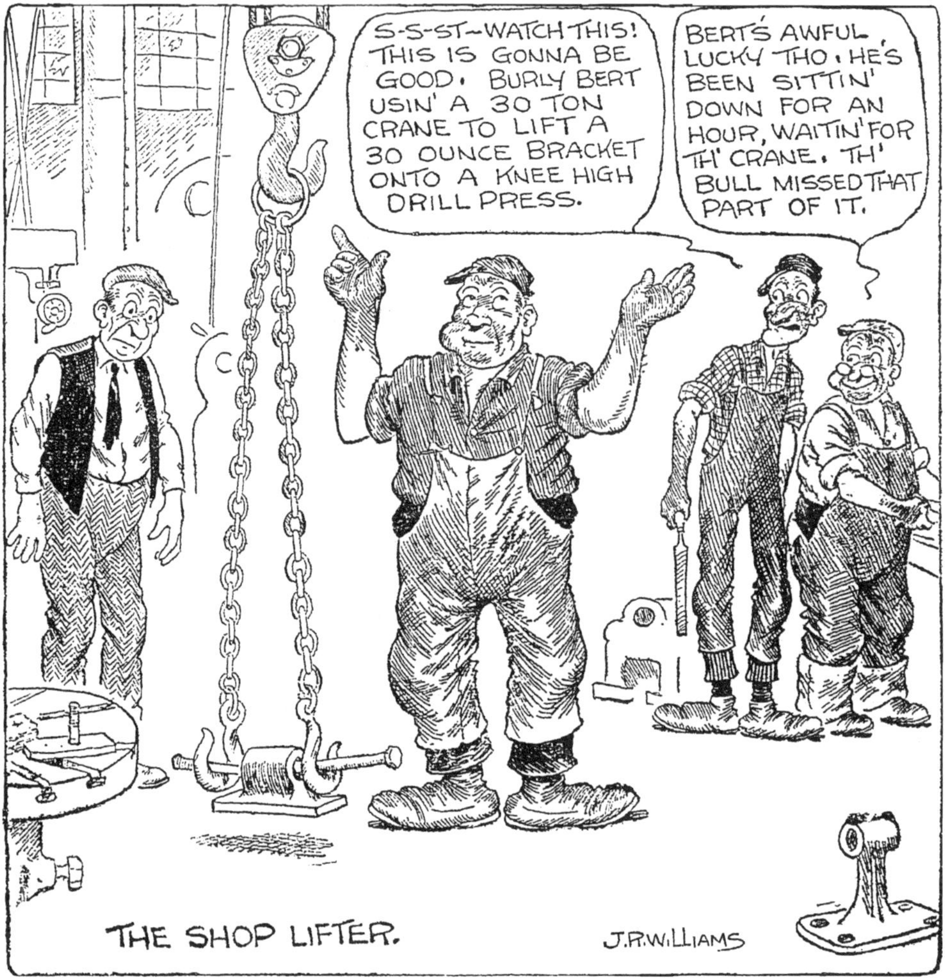
S-S-ST-WATCH THIS! THIS IS GONNA BE GOOD. BURLY BERT USIN' A 30 TON CRANE TO LIFT A 30 OUNCE BRACKET ONTO A KNEE HIGH DRILL PRESS.
BERT'S AWFUL LUCKY THO. HE'S BEEN SITTIN' DOWN FOR AN HOUR, WAITIN' FOR TH' CRANE. TH' BULL MISSED THAT PART OF IT.
THE SHOP LIFTER.
J.R.WILLIAMS

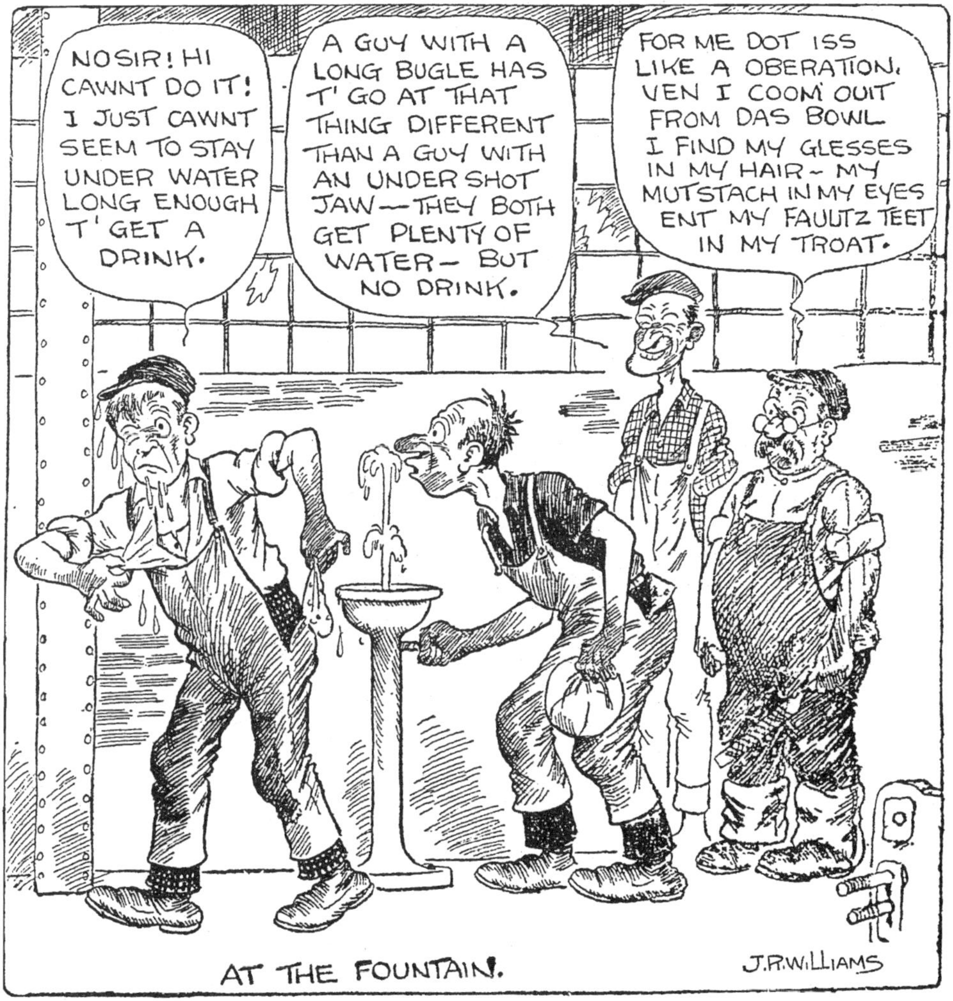
NOSIR! HI CAWNT DO IT! I JUST CAWNT SEEM TO STAY UNDER WATER LONG ENOUGH T' GET A DRINK.
A GUY WITH A LONG BUGLE HAS T' GO AT THAT THING DIFFERENT THAN A GUY WITH AN UNDER SHOT JAW—THEY BOTH GET PLENTY OF WATER—BUT NO DRINK.
FOR ME DOT ISS LIKE A OBERATION. VEN I COOM OUIT FROM DAS BOWL I FIND MY GLESSES IN MY HAIR—MY MUTSTACH IN MY EYES ENT MY FAULTZ TEET IN MY TROAT.
J.R. WILLIAMS
AT THE FOUNTAIN.

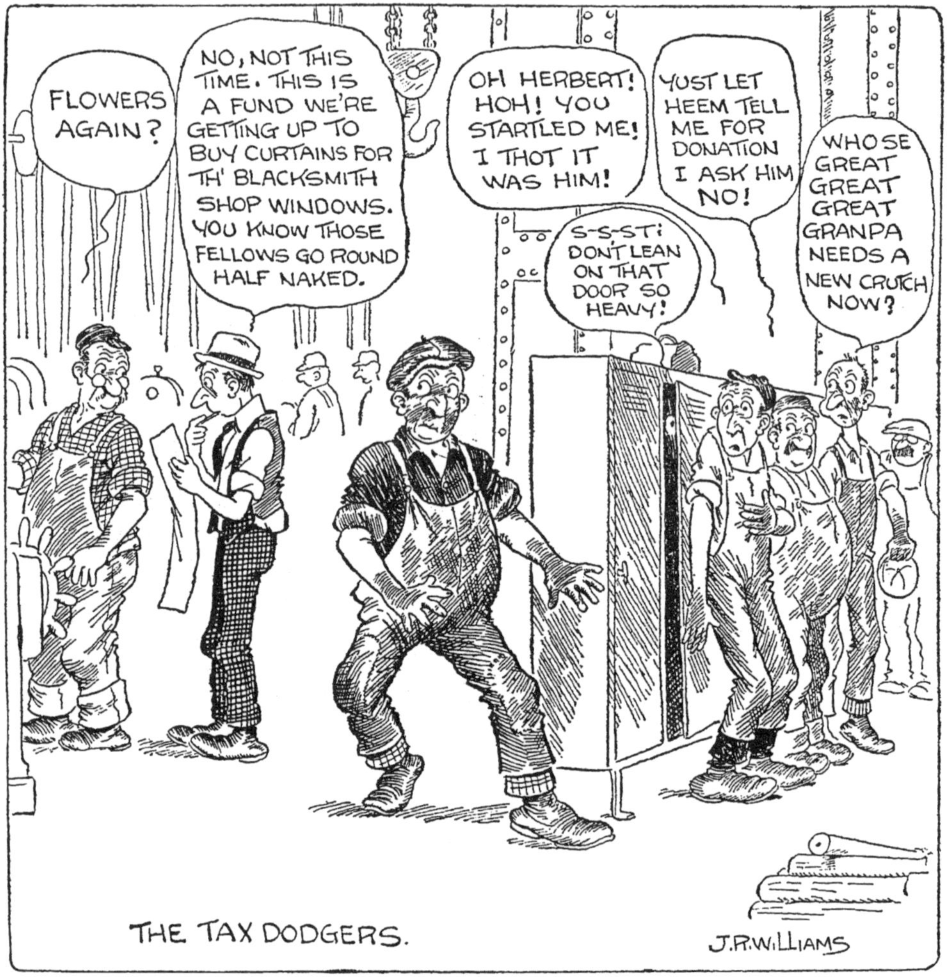
FLOWERS AGAIN?
NO, NOT THIS TIME. THIS IS A FUND WE'RE GETTING UP TO BUY CURTAINS FOR TH' BLACKSMITH SHOP WINDOWS. YOU KNOW THOSE FELLOWS GO ROUND HALF NAKED.
OH HERBERT! HOH! YOU STARTLED ME! I THOT IT WAS HIM!
S-S-ST! DON'T LEAN ON THAT DOOR SO HEAVY!
YUST LET HEEM TELL ME FOR DONATION I ASK HIM NO!
WHOSE GREAT GREAT GREAT GRANPA NEEDS A NEW CRUTCH NOW?
THE TAX DODGERS.
J.R. WILLIAMS

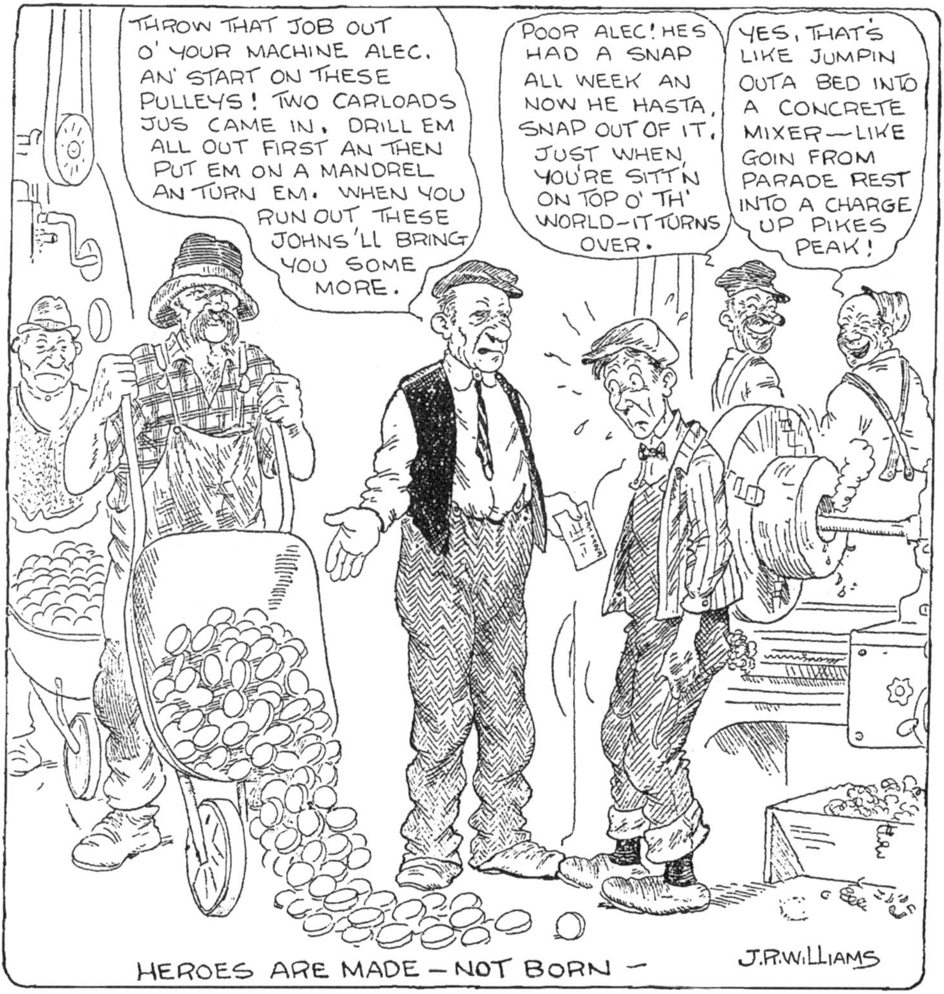
THROW THAT JOB OUT O' YOUR MACHINE ALEC. AN' START ON THESE PULLEYS! TWO CARLOADS JUS CAME IN. DRILL EM ALL OUT FIRST AN THEN PUT EM ON A MANDREL AN TURN EM. WHEN YOU RUN OUT THESE JOHNS'LL BRING YOU SOME MORE.
POOR ALEC! HES HAD A SNAP ALL WEEK AN NOW HE HASTA SNAP OUT OF IT. JUST WHEN YOU'RE SITT'N ON TOP O' TH' WORLD-IT TURNS OVER.
YES, THAT'S LIKE JUMPIN OUTA BED INTO A CONCRETE MIXER—LIKE GOIN FROM PARADE REST INTO A CHARGE UP PIKES PEAK!
HEROES ARE MADE—NOT BORN—
J.R.WILLIAMS

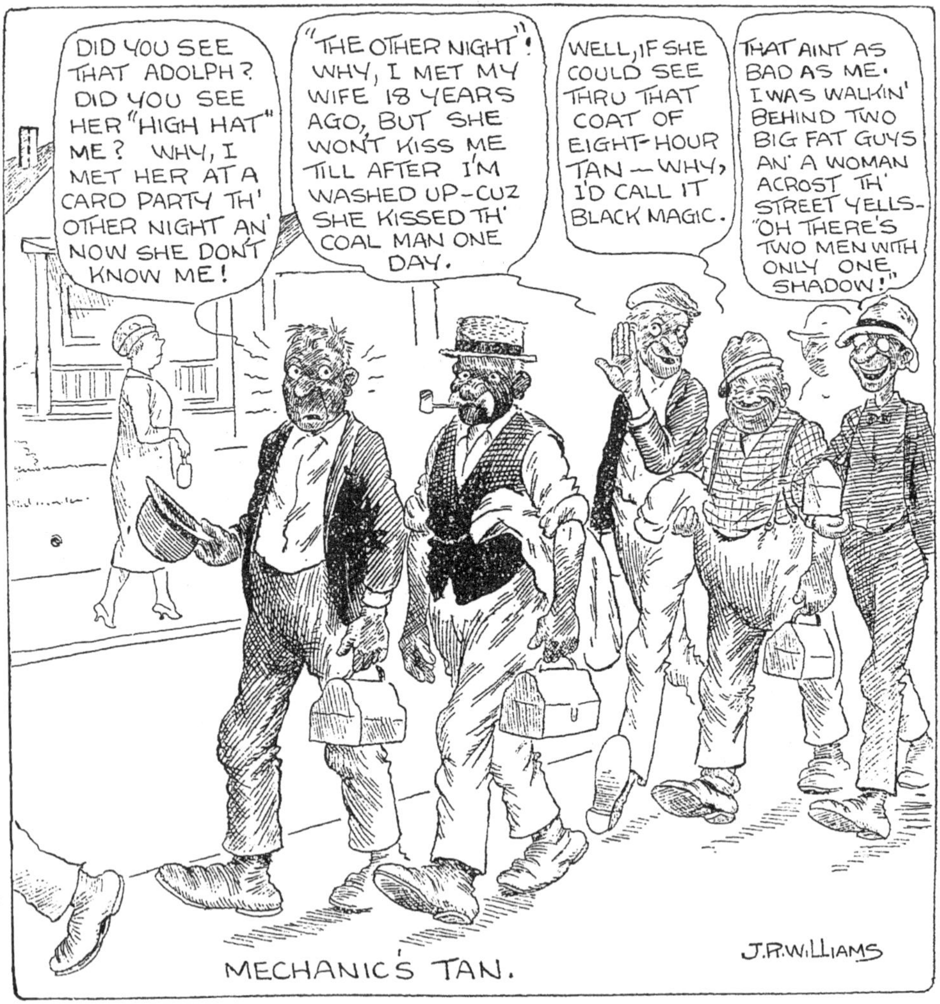
DID YOU SEE THAT ADOLPH? DID YOU SEE HER "HIGH HAT" ME? WHY, I MET HER AT A CARD PARTY TH' OTHER NIGHT AN' NOW SHE DON'T KNOW ME!
"THE OTHER NIGHT"! WHY, I MET MY WIFE 18 YEARS AGO, BUT SHE WON'T KISS ME TILL AFTER I'M WASHED UP-CUZ SHE KISSED TH' COAL MAN ONE DAY.
WELL, IF SHE COULD SEE THRU THAT COAT OF EIGHT-HOUR TAN — WHY, I'D CALL IT BLACK MAGIC.
THAT AINT AS BAD AS ME. I WAS WALKIN' BEHIND TWO BIG FAT GUYS AN' A WOMAN ACROST TH' STREET YELLS- "OH THERE'S TWO MEN WITH ONLY ONE SHADOW!"
MECHANIC'S TAN.
J.R. WILLIAMS

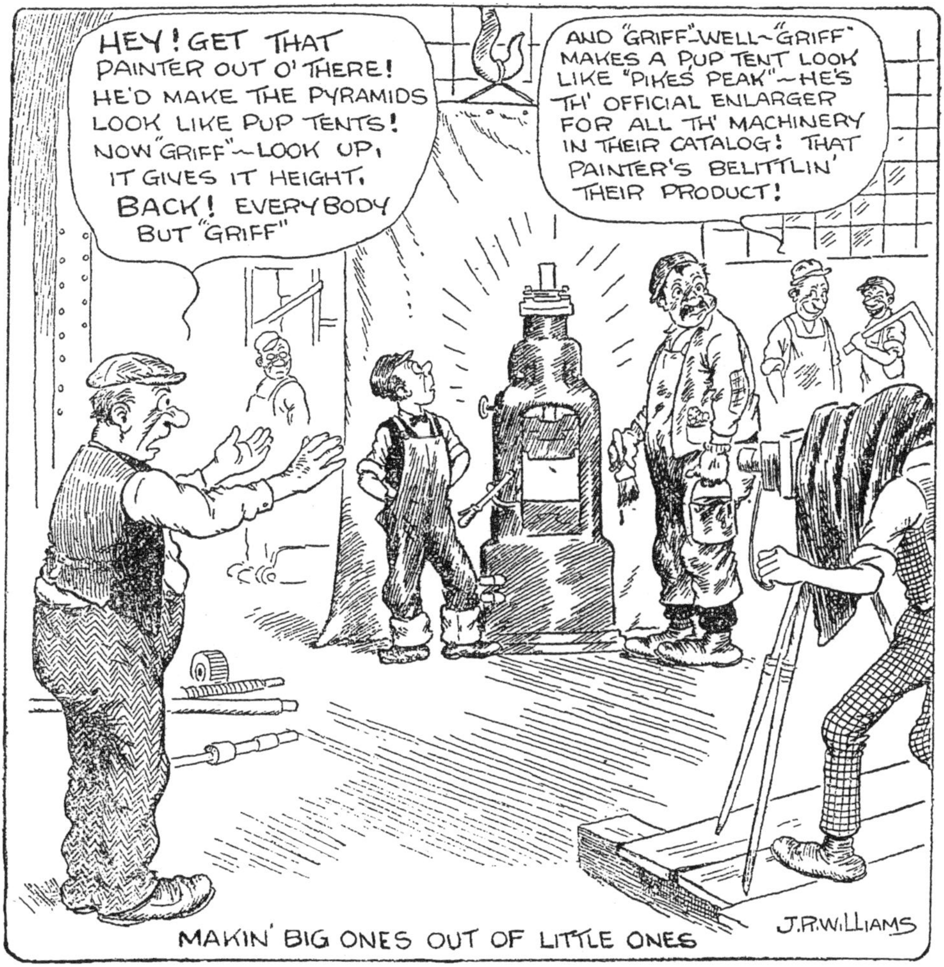
HEY! GET THAT PAINTER OUT O' THERE! HE'D MAKE THE PYRAMIDS LOOK LIKE PUP TENTS! NOW "GRIFF" ~ LOOK UP, IT GIVES IT HEIGHT. BACK! EVERYBODY BUT "GRIFF"
AND "GRIFF" - WELL ~ "GRIFF" MAKES A PUP TENT LOOK LIKE "PIKES PEAK" ~ HE'S TH' OFFICIAL ENLARGER FOR ALL TH' MACHINERY IN THEIR CATALOG! THAT PAINTER'S BELITTLIN' THEIR PRODUCT!
J.R. WILLIAMS
MAKIN' BIG ONES OUT OF LITTLE ONES

If you are a fan of J.R. Williams, you may be interested in our other Williams Classic Reprints.

Classic Cowboy Cartoons

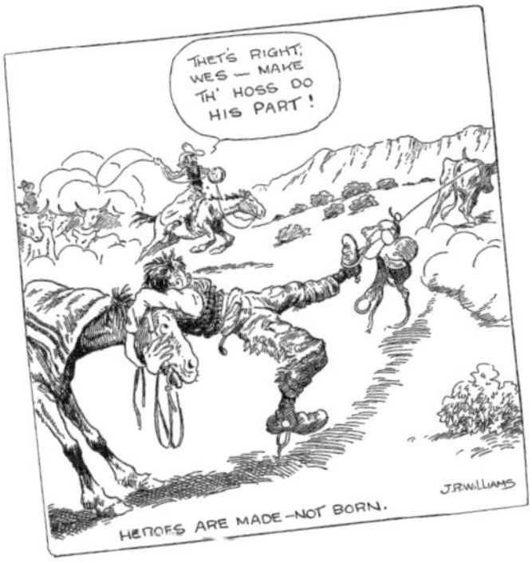
THET'S RIGHT, WES — MAKE TH' HOSS DO HIS PART!
J.R.WILLIAMS
HEROES ARE MADE—NOT BORN.

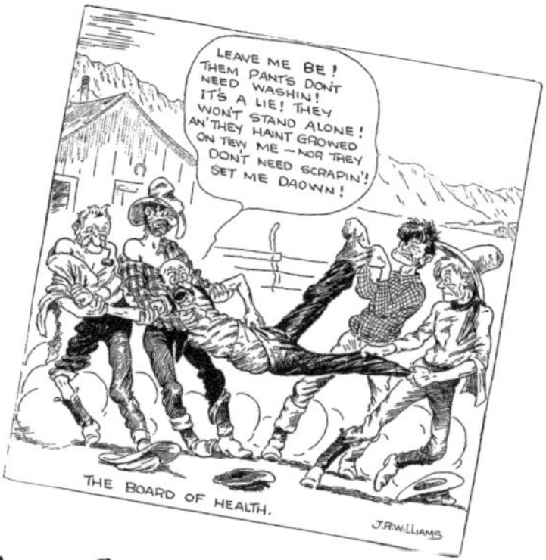
LEAVE ME BE! THEM PANTS DONT NEED WASHIN! IT'S A LIE! THEY WON'T STAND ALONE! AN'THEY HAINT GROWED ON TEW ME — NOR THEY DON'T NEED SCRAPIN'! SET ME DAOWN!
J.R.WILLIAMS
THE BOARD OF HEALTH.

U.S. Cavalry Cartoons

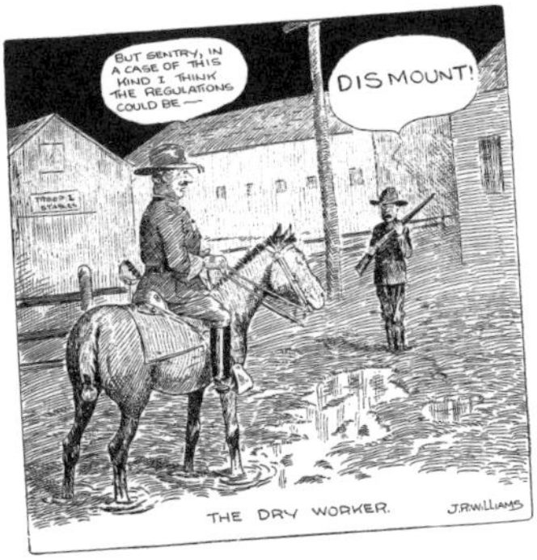
BUT SENTRY, IN A CASE OF THIS KIND I THINK THE REGULATIONS COULD BE —
DIS MOUNT!
J.R.WILLIAMS
THE DRY WORKER.

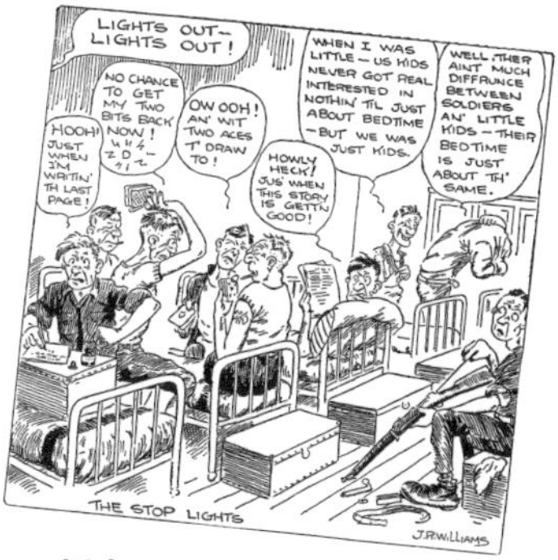
LIGHTS OUT— LIGHTS OUT!
HOOH! JUST WHEN I'M WRITIN' TH LAST PAGE!
NO CHANCE TO GET MY TWO BITS BACK NOW!
OW OOH! AN' WIT TWO ACES T' DRAW TO!
HOWLY HECK! JUS' WHEN THIS STORY IS GETTN GOOD!
WHEN I WAS LITTLE — US KIDS NEVER GOT REAL INTERESTED IN NOTHIN' TIL JUST ABOUT BEDTIME — BUT WE WAS JUST KIDS.
WELL, THER AINT MUCH DIFFRUNCE BETWEEN SOLDIERS AN' LITTLE KIDS — THEIR BEDTIME IS JUST ABOUT TH' SAME.
J.R.WILLIAMS
THE STOP LIGHTS

Out Our Way

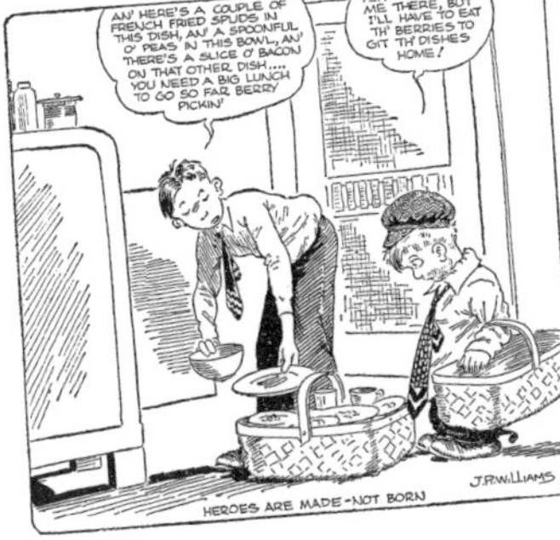
AN' HERE'S A COUPLE OF FRENCH FRIED SPUDS IN THIS DISH, AN' A SPOONFUL O' PEAS IN THIS BOWL, AN' THERE'S A SLICE O' BACON ON THAT OTHER DISH.... YOU NEED A BIG LUNCH TO GO SO FAR BERRY PICKIN'
YEH-- THAT'LL GIT ME THERE, BUT I'LL HAVE TO EAT TH' BERRIES TO GIT TH' DISHES HOME!
J.R.WILLIAMS
HEROES ARE MADE—NOT BORN

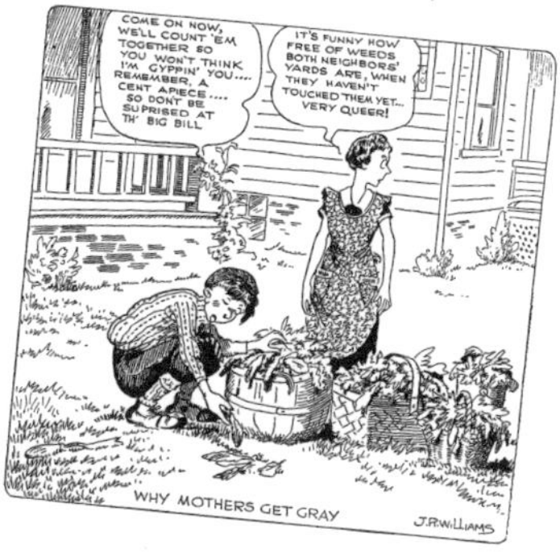
COME ON NOW, WE'LL COUNT 'EM TOGETHER SO YOU WON'T THINK I'M GYPPIN' YOU.... REMEMBER, A CENT APIECE.... SO DON'T BE SUPRISED AT TH' BIG BILL
IT'S FUNNY HOW FREE OF WEEDS BOTH NEIGHBORS' YARDS ARE, WHEN THEY HAVEN'T TOUCHED THEM YET... VERY QUEER!
J.R.WILLIAMS
WHY MOTHERS GET GRAY

Publications by Algrove Publishing Limited

The following is a list of titles from our popular *"Classic Reprint Series"*
as well as other publications by Algrove Publishing Limited.

ARCHITECTURE, BUILDING, AND DESIGN

Item #	Title
49L8038	A BOOK OF ALPHABETS WITH PLAIN, ORNAMENTAL, ANCIENT AND MEDIAEVAL STYLES
49L8096	A GLOSSARY OF TERMS USED IN ENGLISH ARCHITECTURE
49L8016	BARN PLANS & OUTBUILDINGS
49L8046	BEAUTIFYING THE HOME GROUNDS
49L8112	BUILDING WITH LOGS AND LOG CABIN CONSTRUCTION
49L8092	DETAIL, COTTAGE AND CONSTRUCTIVE ARCHITECTURE
49L8015	FENCES, GATES & BRIDGES
49L8706	FROM LOG TO LOG HOUSE
49L0720	HOMES & INTERIORS OF THE 1920'S
49L8111	LOW-COST WOOD HOMES
49L8030	SHELTERS, SHACKS & SHANTIES
49L8050	STRONG'S BOOK OF DESIGNS
49L8064	THE ARCHITECTURE OF COUNTRY HOUSES
49L8021	THE INTERNATIONAL CYCLOPEDIA OF MONOGRAMS
49L8023	THE OPEN TIMBER ROOFS OF THE MIDDLE AGES

CLASSIC CATALOGS

Item #	Title
49L8004	BOULTON & PAUL, LTD. 1898 CATALOGUE
49L8098	CATALOG OF MISSION FURNITURE 1913 – *COME-PACKT FURNITURE*
49L8097	MASSEY-HARRIS CIRCA 1914 CATALOG
49L8089	OVERSHOT WATER WHEELS FOR SMALL STREAMS
49L8079	WILLIAM BULLOCK & CO. – *HARDWARE CATALOG CIRCA 1850*

GARDENING

Item #	Title
49L8082	CANADIAN WILD FLOWERS (C. P. TRAILL)
49L8113	COLLECTING SEEDS OF WILD PLANTS AND SHIPPING LIVE PLANT MATERIAL
49L8029	FARM WEEDS OF CANADA
49L8056	FLORA'S LEXICON
49L8705	REFLECTIONS ON THE FUNGALOIDS
49L8076	THE WILDFLOWERS OF AMERICA
49L8057	THE WILDFLOWERS OF CANADA

HUMOR AND PUZZLES

Item #	Title
49L8074	ARE YOU A GENIUS? WHAT IS YOUR I.Q?
49L8106	CLASSIC COWBOY CARTOONS, VOL. 1
49L8109	CLASSIC COWBOY CARTOONS, VOL. 2
49L8118	CLASSIC COWBOY CARTOONS, VOL. 3
49L8119	CLASSIC COWBOY CARTOONS, VOL. 4
49L8072	CLASSIC PUZZLES AND HOW TO SOLVE THEM
49L8103	GRANDMOTHER'S PUZZLE BOOK
49L8081	MR. PUNCH WITH ROD AND GUN – *THE HUMOUR OF FISHING AND SHOOTING*
49L8073	NAME IT! THE PICTORIAL QUIZ BOOK
49L8126	OUR BOARDING HOUSE 1927
49L8125	OUT OUR WAY – *SAMPLER 20s, 30s, 40s*
49L8044	SAM LOYD'S PICTURE PUZZLES
49L8071	THE BULL OF THE WOODS, VOL. 1
49L8080	THE BULL OF THE WOODS, VOL. 2
49L8104	THE BULL OF THE WOODS, VOL. 3
49L8114	THE BULL OF THE WOODS, VOL. 4
49L8115	THE BULL OF THE WOODS, VOL. 5
49L8116	THE BULL OF THE WOODS, VOL. 6
49L8084	THE ART OF ARTHUR WATTS
49L8107	U.S. CAVALRY CARTOONS

NAVAL AND MARINE

Item #	Title
49L8090	BOAT-BUILDING AND BOATING
49L8707	BUILDING THE NORWEGIAN SAILING PRAM *(MANUAL AND PLANS)*
49L8708	BUILDING THE SEA URCHIN *(MANUAL AND PLANS)*
49L8078	MANUAL OF SEAMANSHIP FOR BOYS AND SEAMEN OF THE ROYAL NAVY, 1904
49L8095	SAILING SHIPS AT A GLANCE
49L8099	THE SAILOR'S WORD-BOOK
49L8058	THE YANKEE WHALER
49L8025	THE YOUNG SEA OFFICER'S SHEET ANCHOR
49L8061	TRADITIONS OF THE NAVY

REFERENCE

Item #	Title
49L8083	AMERICAN MECHANICAL DICTIONARY – KNIGHT VOL. I, VOL. II, VOL. III
49L8093	507 MECHANICAL MOVEMENTS
49L8024	1800 MECHANICAL MOVEMENTS AND DEVICES
49L8055	970 MECHANICAL APPLIANCES AND NOVELTIES OF CONSTRUCTION
49L8602	ALL THE KNOTS YOU NEED
49L8077	CAMP COOKERY
49L8001	LEE'S PRICELESS RECIPES
49L8018	THE BOY'S BOOK OF MECHANICAL MODELS
49L8019	WINDMILLS AND WIND MOTORS

TRADES

Item #	Title
49L8014	BOOK OF TRADES
49L8086	FARM BLACKSMITHING
49L8031	FARM MECHANICS
49L8087	FORGING
49L8027	HANDY FARM DEVICES AND HOW TO MAKE THEM
49L8002	HOW TO PAINT SIGNS & SHO' CARDS
49L8054	HOW TO USE THE STEEL SQUARE
49L8094	THE YOUNG MILL-WRIGHT AND MILLER'S GUIDE
49L8053	THE METALWORKING LATHE

WOODWORKING AND CRAFTS

Item #	Title
49L8101	ARTS-CRAFTS LAMPS & SHADES – *HOW TO MAKE THEM*
49L8012	BOY CRAFT
49L8110	CHAIN SAW AND CROSSCUT SAW TRAINING COURSE
49L8048	CLAY MODELLING AND PLASTER CASTING
49L8005	COLONIAL FURNITURE
49L8065	COPING SAW WORK
49L8032	DECORATIVE CARVING, PYROGRAPHY AND FLEMISH CARVING
49L8091	FURNITURE DESIGNING AND DRAUGHTING
49L8049	HANDBOOK OF TURNING
49L8020	MISSION FURNITURE, HOW TO MAKE IT
49L8033	ORNAMENTAL AND DECORATIVE WOOD CARVINGS
49L8059	PROJECTS FOR WOODWORK TRAINING
49L8003	RUSTIC CARPENTRY
49L8085	SKELETON LEAVES AND PHANTOM FLOWERS
49L8068	SPECIALIZED JOINERY
49L8052	STANLEY COMBINATION PLANES – *THE 45, THE 50 & THE 55*
49L8034	THE ART OF WHITTLING
49L8047	TIMBER – *FROM THE FOREST TO ITS USE IN COMMERCE*
49L8042	TURNING FOR AMATEURS
49L8039	VIOLIN MAKING AS IT WAS, AND IS
49L8013	YOU CAN MAKE IT
49L8035	YOU CAN MAKE IT FOR CAMP & COTTAGE
49L8036	YOU CAN MAKE IT FOR PROFIT
49L8067	WOOD HANDBOOK – *WOOD AS AN ENGINEERING MATERIAL*
49L8060	WOODEN PLANES AND HOW TO MAKE THEM

Algrove Publishing Limited, 36 Mill Street, P.O. Box 1238, Almonte, Ontario, Canada K0A 1A0
Telephone: (613) 256-0350 Fax: (613) 256-0360 Email: sales@algrove.com